Designing and Facilitating Workshops with Intent... who facilitates. With creative, research-backed ideas and practical tools, Tolu equips us for true transformation. This is more than a book—it's a go-to guide you'll return to time and again to enhance your workshop skills and impact.

Bonni Stachowiak, *Producer and Host,* Teaching in Higher Ed *Podcast*

Designing and Facilitating Workshops with Intentionality is impressively-researched, thorough, and thoughtful. Full of easily applicable and concrete techniques, Tolu has written a fresh, comprehensive, and easily readable guide for improving professional development experiences. Give this book to anyone facilitating a workshop!

Jenae Cohn, *Executive Director, Center for Teaching and Learning, University of California, Berkeley, USA*

I've been facilitating workshops for over 20 years and I found valuable ideas and resources in every chapter. This is such a thoughtful, thought-provoking, well-organized, and resource-packed book...all while using a friendly, approachable tone. I know plenty of instructional designers and faculty developers who would love this book!

Kevin Kelly, *Author of* Making College Courses Flexible

Dr. Noah's *Designing and Facilitating Workshops with Intentionality* thoughtfully and methodically addresses every decision a facilitator needs to consider so that you can get down to the heart of the matter and connect with your faculty. You'll be a rock star workshop leader with Dr. Noah's incredible coaching herein!

Lillian Nave, *Faculty and Educational Development Specialist, Appalachian State University, USA*

DESIGNING AND FACILITATING WORKSHOPS WITH INTENTIONALITY

Designing and Facilitating Workshops with Intentionality offers practical guidance, tools, and resources to assist practitioners in creating effective, engaging workshops for adult learners.

Drawing from three key learning frameworks and the author's considerable expertise in facilitating workshops across both educational and corporate settings, this book focuses on ten essential principles to consider when developing professional learning experiences. Whether facilitating on-site or virtually, readers will gain a deeper understanding of how to design and facilitate workshops with an inclusive mindset, thus creating meaningful, active learning opportunities that result in greater involvement among participants and better feedback. Guiding questions, chapter takeaways, and a compendium of additional online resources supply plentiful opportunities to further build and fine-tune these skills.

Within these pages, both new and seasoned facilitators will find inspiration, encouragement, and support, as they craft professional learning experiences that ignite curiosity and spark growth in all learners.

Tolulope Noah, EdD, is an educational developer at California State University, Long Beach, USA, where she designs and facilitates professional learning programs for instructors. She has 16 years of teaching experience, and she enjoys facilitating engaging workshops and keynotes about a variety of teaching, learning, and technology topics. Learn more at www.tolunoah.com.

DESIGNING AND FACILITATING WORKSHOPS WITH INTENTIONALITY

A Guide to Crafting Engaging Professional Learning Experiences in Higher Education

Tolulope Noah

Routledge
Taylor & Francis Group
NEW YORK AND LONDON

Designed cover image: Created by Tolulope Noah (Arrow icon from Veronika Gotovceva)

First published 2025
by Routledge
605 Third Avenue, New York, NY 10158

and by Routledge
4 Park Square, Milton Park, Abingdon, Oxon, OX14 4RN

Routledge is an imprint of the Taylor & Francis Group, an informa business

© 2025 Tolulope Noah

The right of Tolulope Noah to be identified as the author of this work has been asserted in accordance with sections 77 and 78 of the Copyright, Designs and Patents Act of 1988.

All rights reserved. No part of this book may be reprinted or reproduced or utilized in any form or by any electronic, mechanical, or other means, now known or hereafter invented, including photocopying and recording, or in any information storage or retrieval system, without permission in writing from the publishers.

Trademark notice: Product or corporate names may be trademarks or registered trademarks and are used only for identification and explanation without intent to infringe.

Library of Congress Cataloging-in-Publication Data
Names: Noah, Tolulope, author.
Title: Designing and facilitating workshops with intentionality : a guide to crafting engaging professional learning experiences in higher education / Tolulope Noah.
Description: New York, NY : Routledge, 2025. |
Includes bibliographical references and index.
Identifiers: LCCN 2024057061 (print) | LCCN 2024057062 (ebook) |
ISBN 9781032774114 (hardback) | ISBN 9781032758046 (paperback) |
ISBN 9781003482963 (ebook)
Subjects: LCSH: Workshops (Adult education) | Group work in education. |
Education, Higher.
Classification: LCC LC6562 .N63 2025 (print) | LCC LC6562 (ebook) |
DDC 370.71/1–dc23/eng/20250402
LC record available at https://lccn.loc.gov/2024057061
LC ebook record available at https://lccn.loc.gov/2024057062

Icons licensed through the Noun Project

ISBN: 978-1-032-77411-4 (hbk)
ISBN: 978-1-032-75804-6 (pbk)
ISBN: 978-1-003-48296-3 (ebk)

DOI: 10.4324/9781003482963

Typeset in Times New Roman
by Newgen Publishing UK

CONTENTS

Acknowledgments   ix

Introduction   1

1   Begin with Relevance   20

2   Plan with Purpose   36

3   Design a Well-Structured Experience   50

4   Adopt an Inclusive Mindset   76

5   Cultivate Connection   93

6   Use Active Learning Strategies   112

7   Provide Time and Space for Reflection   134

8   Create Ongoing Learning Opportunities   148

9   Be Responsive   162

10   Own Your Distinctive Style   172

11 Optimize Your Workflow	188
12 Continue Growing as a Facilitator	207
Conclusion	220
Appendix: Alphabetical List of All Digital Tools Mentioned in the Book	*223*
About the Author	*226*
Index	*227*

ACKNOWLEDGMENTS

It feels surreal to have this book out in the world. I would not have been able to reach this milestone without the support of others, and I would like to pause and recognize the people who have helped make my dream a reality.

I would like to thank Dyane Smokorowski (Smoke), whose invitation to facilitate a 3-hour workshop about "how to design an awesome synchronous workshop for adult learners" sparked the idea for this book. Smoke, thank you for believing in what I have to offer as a professional learning facilitator and for constantly encouraging me on this journey. Partnering with you and your team over the past few years has truly been a joy, and I have learned just as much from you all as I hope you have from me.

To my friend, Peace Amadi, thank you for always believing that I had a story worth sharing and for providing helpful guidance about the book publishing process. To my friend, Shari Moseley, thank you for your support, encouragement, feedback, and prayers throughout this book writing journey.

I am also grateful for the support of my professional community. Derek Krissoff, thank you for your guidance and feedback during the book proposal process. To my beta readers, Jenae Cohn, Kevin Kelly, Lillian Nave, and Bonni Stachowiak, words cannot express how grateful I am for your time and energy in reading and providing thoughtful feedback on the full draft of my manuscript. Your comments were instrumental in making the book what it is today. Mandy Penney, thank you for your helpful feedback and input about the accessibility considerations in my book. Rudy Leon, Khomotso Leshaba, and Tom Rademacher, thank you for your editing and copy editing assistance. Caitlin Morgan, thank you for your assistance with the index. I would also like to thank the seven fantastic facilitators I interviewed, whose stories added another layer of richness and depth to this book: Karen Costa, Norman Eng, Tasha Souza, Courtney Plotts, Lindsay Masland, Todd Zakrajsek, and Maha Bali.

Finally, I am incredibly grateful for the love, support, and encouragement of my family. To my mother, thank you for being a pillar of strength, faith, and hope. To my sister, Yewande, thank you for being there every step along the way in this book writing journey, offering encouragement, feedback, and funny jokes and memes to keep me going.

INTRODUCTION

In his bestselling book, *Creating Significant Learning Experiences*, Fink (2013) begins by inviting readers (who are primarily college instructors) to dream. He asks instructors to imagine their ideal teaching situation and reflect on these questions:

> In your deepest, fondest dreams, what kind of impact would you most like to have on your students? That is, when the course is over and it is now one or two years later, what would you like to be true about students who have participated in your courses that is not true of others? What is the distinctive educational impact you would like for your teaching and your courses to have on your students?
>
> *(Fink, 2013, p. 10)*

As I read these questions, I could not help but think about their relevance to the context of professional learning. As facilitators, we also seek to create meaningful and impactful learning experiences, whether our learners are instructors, staff, administrators, or students. So inspired by Fink, I also invite you to dream. Think about your ideal professional learning situation and reflect on these questions:

> What unique and lasting impact would you like to have on your learners? What do you hope will be true of learners one to two years after they have participated in your professional learning program?

Take a moment to pause and consider what this ideal professional learning situation would look like for you. What would this experience entail? What do you hope learners will say, feel, and be able to do as a result? How do you envision your role in designing and facilitating such a robust experience?

This book aims to support you in creating engaging, enriching, and effective professional learning experiences with lasting impact. Perhaps you are a new facilitator seeking guidance in how to design and facilitate professional learning experiences for the first time. Maybe you are a seasoned facilitator seeking to glean new ideas to add to your toolkit. Whoever you are, wherever you are in your facilitation journey, this book is for you.

Let's dream together.

Two Short Stories

In May 2019, I was invited to do my first-ever plenary address at the Lilly Conference in Bethesda, Maryland. At the time, I was an associate professor in a teacher education program. While I was excited about the opportunity to share my passion for teaching and learning with such a wide audience, I was also terrified. Introverted me, who struggles with imposter phenomenon? On a stage? In front of over 300 professors and administrators from various disciplines? Who would have thought?

As I planned my plenary address, I made an important decision. Even though I was used to attending keynotes where the speaker primarily spoke to the audience for the entire time, I was going to treat this like a workshop. To be honest, I didn't know any other way to operate. I have never been one to lecture for extensive periods of time, and active learning techniques have always been a cornerstone of my professional learning approach. Thus, facilitating the session like a workshop felt most authentic to who I was and to my facilitation style.

The night before my plenary address, I went into the ballroom and placed small blue paper bags containing playing cards on each of the round tables. I also taped a mini brown envelope containing a card sort activity under each table, and I placed handouts at each seat so that participants would have a place to capture their thoughts and reflections throughout the session.

The next morning, I walked on the stage in a red dress and heels (despite my fear that my legs could give way at any moment), and I facilitated my plenary address entitled "Structuring Your Lectures to Engage Students and Optimize Learning." Within the first few minutes of the session, I had the entire audience of 300+ people using the playing cards to do a suit partner greeting. Not long after that, I had them searching under their tables for the brown envelopes (which was a fun surprise for them) and had them do a card sort activity with their groups. Later in the session, participants did a turn-and-talk activity. Near the end of the session, they completed a digital exit ticket. (You will learn more about these strategies in Chapters 5 and 7.) Although there were times when I talked to the audience, my entire plenary address was punctuated with opportunities for participants to actively engage with the content and each other.

Fast forward to the EDUCAUSE Annual Conference Online Event in November 2023, where I was facilitating a simulive session entitled "Using QR Codes to Design Engaging Student Learning Experiences."[1] As my pre-recorded session was playing and I was monitoring the chat, I saw a comment that immediately brought a smile to my face and tears to my eyes. It said, "I may be Tolu's #1 fan. Saw her first at [the] Lilly Conference in Bethesda, MD pre-COVID, and her creative teaching/learning approaches revolutionized how I instructed and NOW how I train my faculty colleagues to instruct. TY [thank you] TOLU!" Never did I imagine that the plenary address I facilitated years ago would resonate with someone so deeply and result in lasting change in their practice that was now impacting other educators.

On to story #2...

In May 2023, I facilitated a session entitled "Designing Engaging Microlectures" at the online Teaching, Learning, and Technology Conference (TLTCon) for the first time. During the 1-hour session, we explored what microlectures are, their benefits, tools for creating them, and a planning template for designing them. We also discussed recording and accessibility tips, as well as ways in which instructors could share microlectures with their students.

The next year, I had the opportunity to present at TLTCon again, this time about metacognition. On the morning of the first day of the conference, I received a message from another attendee via the conference app. It said, "Good morning, Dr. Noah. I attended your session at TLTCon last year. What I learned from you transformed the way that I approach video creation and online engagement with my students. Your session produced long-term change in my teaching. I wanted to thank you so much for sharing your ideas and demonstrating how you use videos to engage more deeply with students. I am looking forward to your session tomorrow."

I share these stories because my 2019 plenary address at the Lilly Conference and my virtual session at TLTCon in 2023 were only an hour long, and yet each had a meaningful impact on at least one participant. I believe this was because of how the learning experiences were designed.

By designing and facilitating with intentionality, we can create impactful professional learning experiences that help equip, encourage, and empower others in their work.

Who This Book is For

The main goal of this book is to support professional learning facilitators in developing meaningful, impactful, and engaging on-site and synchronous online workshops for adult learners. We will examine both the design and facilitation of workshops. Bell and Goodman's (2023) definitions of design and facilitation are particularly useful here:

> *Design* includes all the planning, assessment, and evaluation activities that facilitators/instructors engage in prior to, during, and after meeting with participants. Design includes establishing goals for learning, setting an agenda for the course or workshop, selecting reading and other course materials, planning activities, and organizing small- and large-group procedures for engaging participants actively. ...*Facilitation* refers to the leadership strategies and skills that we draw upon to actively engage participants in learning, mediate interactions within the group, and guide interpersonal and group dynamics as part of the learning process.
>
> *(p. 58, emphasis in original)*

Whether you facilitate short-term workshops, long-term workshop series, or both, this book will offer helpful principles, practical strategies, and concrete resources that you can apply to the design and facilitation of your sessions. You will also find that many of the principles I share can be applied to other types of professional learning programs.

If you are an educational developer, faculty developer, instructional designer, academic technology specialist, learning designer, educational technologist, teaching consultant, faculty peer mentor, administrator, librarian, trainer, learning and development professional, or other academic leader whose responsibilities involve facilitating professional learning workshops at your college or university, this book is for you. This book will also be useful for consultants who facilitate workshops for multiple educational communities and for individuals who facilitate workshops at conferences. If you facilitate workshops in a different context (such as in a K-12 school/district, nonprofit organization, or corporate setting), you will find helpful principles and resources here that you can adapt to your work.

This book is meant to be a practical guide for facilitators, offering ideas and strategies that you can immediately use. Connections to relevant research and theories are included throughout, with the primary focus being on how you can apply what you've learned to your specific context. As you read the numerous ideas and strategies in this book, you may find that some resonate with you while others do not. That is completely okay (and expected!). A recurring theme you'll find in this book is that there is no one "right" way to design or facilitate a workshop, and you need to choose approaches that align well with who you are and with your unique context. As you read this book, please feel free to use/adapt the strategies (or aspects thereof) that resonate with you and set aside the ones that don't. Or, as Karen Costa often says in her workshops, "Take what you need and leave the rest" (personal communication, May 28, 2024).

A note about language: As an educational developer, I primarily design and facilitate professional learning experiences for instructors in higher education. As such, I will mostly refer to instructors as my participant group throughout this book. However, the principles in this book can be applied to your work with *any* group of adult learners (such as staff, administrators, students, conference participants, and more). Additionally, I may switch between using terms such as *participants* and *learners* throughout this book. Both terms refer to the people who are participating in the workshop.

The Professional Learning Landscape in Higher Education

Professional learning offers an incredible opportunity for people to continuously reflect on their practices, hone their skills, and refine their craft so that they can be even more effective at what they do. For example, Condon et al. (2016) explain that faculty development impacts how faculty teach, which ultimately impacts student learning. They also report that the impact of faculty development programs can extend well beyond the faculty members who participate in the events. Indeed, "a thriving faculty development program reaches faculty who may not attend personally but are themselves affected by their colleagues' experience through conversation, observation, evaluation for tenure and promotion, and other routine interactions within the institution" (Condon et al., 2016, p. 118).

Within the context of higher education, professional learning can incorporate many types of programs and services, including workshops, book clubs, learning communities, classroom observations, orientations, institutes, mentorship, consultations, and more (Ellis & Ortquist-Ahrens, 2010; Zakrajsek, 2016). While each type of program and service differs in its scope, focus, and length, they all contribute to the design of a multifaceted and robust approach to professional learning. For example, book clubs offer the opportunity for sustained discussion around a topic of interest, whereas classroom observations allow instructors to receive important feedback about their teaching practices (Zakrajsek, 2016). Ellis and Ortquist-Ahrens (2010) explain that "no one right mix of programming and activities exists. The needs of your instructors, the institutional culture, and the mandate of your program should help to guide your decisions" (p. 130).

Professional learning in higher education also takes place within both formal and informal spaces (Condon et al., 2016; Steinert, 2010b). For example, Condon et al. (2016) highlight three "sites" in which faculty typically learn about teaching: (a) formal professional learning events (such as workshops, conferences, and book clubs), (b) "intentional, self-directed efforts to examine and improve one's own teaching," and (c) "routine events" (such as performance evaluations [where faculty receive feedback and engage in reflection on their teaching] and committee meetings [where faculty discuss academic initiatives and goals]) (pp. 5–8, 23–24).

Steinert (2010b) offers a helpful model for conceptualizing five different types of professional learning activities (see Figure I.1). The first type, individual and informal, includes learning that occurs in the course of doing one's job. Steinert (2010b) breaks this down into "learning by doing," "learning by observing," and "learning by reflecting on experience" (p. 425). The second type, individual and formal, includes learning from others through more formal activities such as co-teaching, peer observations, collection of student feedback, and online learning. The third type, group and formal, includes learning through formal communal activities such as workshops, fellowships, and courses. The fourth type, group and informal, includes "work-based learning" and "communities of practice" (Steinert, 2010b, p. 427). Work-based learning refers to opportunities to learn from and with colleagues within the context of the actual work setting (such as the classroom). "Communities of practice are groups of people who share a concern or a passion for something they do and learn how to do it better as they interact regularly" (Wenger-Trayner & Wenger-Trayner, 2015, para. 4). The fifth type of professional learning, mentorship, can supplement the previous four types. Steinert (2010b) explains that "any strategy

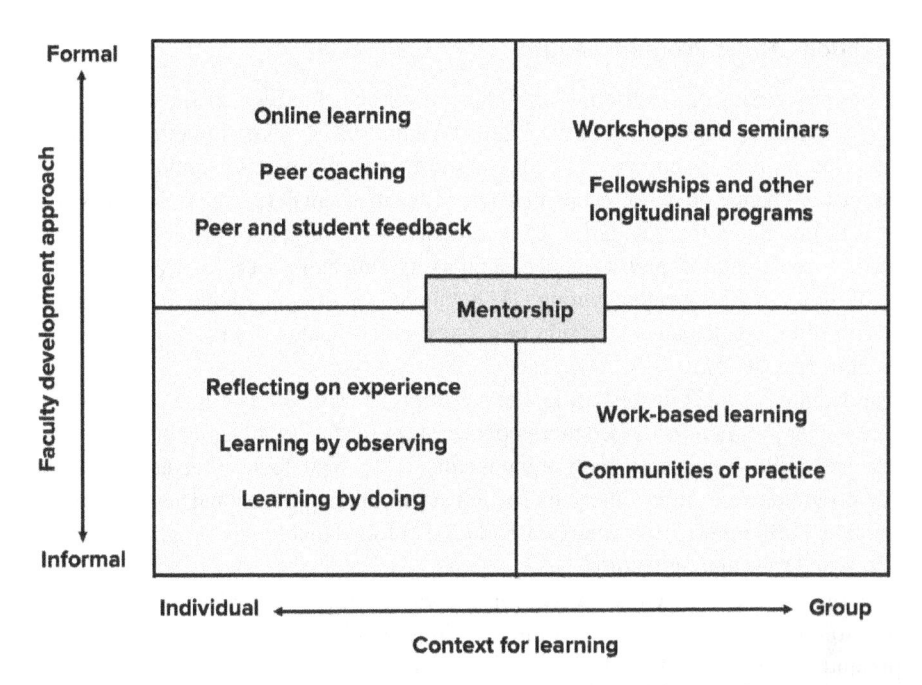

FIGURE I.1 Steinert's (2010b) Faculty Development Matrix (Adapted from Steinert, 2010a; Reprinted with permission of the American College of Physicians.)

for self-improvement can benefit from the support and challenge that an effective mentor can provide" (p. 425).

In this book, we focus on the third type of professional learning—group and formal—with a specific focus on workshops. Workshops are typically designed as singular professional learning experiences where participants gather for a set period of time to explore a topic. Oftentimes, workshops are 1–2 hours in length, although the duration may be shorter or longer depending on the topic, scope, and aims of the session. Since workshops are frequently used at higher education institutions, learning how to design and facilitate them well can help create more meaningful and impactful professional learning experiences.

Historically, workshops were among the first types of programs offered by centers for teaching and learning (CTLs), alongside consultations and classroom observations (Lee, 2010). Studies show that workshops remain a staple at many colleges and universities in the United States. Wright (2023) found that "small-group programs (workshops, series, certificates, and courses)" were the most common types of programs CTLs offered (p. 138). Eynon et al. (2023) found that workshops were the most common professional learning approach used at the higher education institutions surveyed, followed by learning communities and consultations. Pchenitchnaia and Cole (2009), in their study of CTL directors from research-intensive institutions, found that workshops were considered to be "essential" programs, alongside offerings such as consultations and orientations (pp. 302–303). Additionally, Steinert et al. (2016) found that formal group activities (such as workshops and courses) were the most common types of faculty development programs offered to medical educators. Workshops are also common at institutions that do not have a formal CTL.

Considerations About Program Length

Despite the prevalence of workshops in higher education, this type of program is not without critique (Eynon et al., 2023; Cruz et al., 2020; Wright, 2023). A key limitation discussed in the literature is that workshops are typically done as short, one-time events. Condon et al. (2016) assert that sustainable change does not occur through "one-off events" (p. 127). Similarly, Eynon and Iuzzini (2020) maintain that "enduring change comes from ongoing engagement with programs that leverage peer learning and sustained support as educators seek to strengthen their work" (p. 148). Wright (2023) notes that among CTLs, "there is a growing number of efforts to promote change with offerings of longer duration (e.g., series, certificates, courses) or scope (institution-wide events)" (pp. 86–87).

Research indicates other benefits of longer programs as well. For example, Steinert et al. (2016) found that longer programs provided more opportunities for faculty to apply their learning, receive feedback, and build community with other faculty. They also found that faculty who engaged in longer programs were more likely to participate in other professional learning opportunities down the line. Furthermore, Bouwma-Gearhart (2012) found that longer programs fostered deeper connections and trust among faculty.

Long-term programs (such as workshop series, courses, and learning communities) can also tap into the power of spacing and interleaving. Spacing involves breaking up the study of concepts and the practice of skills over time, whereas interleaving involves mixing the types of concepts and skills one practices (Agarwal & Bain, 2019; Brown et al., 2014; Carpenter & Agarwal, 2020). Research shows that spacing and interleaving can result in greater retention and performance (Agarwal & Bain, 2019; Brown et al., 2014; Carpenter & Agarwal, 2020). While it is certainly possible to include elements of interleaving during a singular workshop (such as a half-day or all-day workshop where participants engage in mixed practice of concepts and skills throughout the day), the benefits of spacing and interleaving could be magnified through a long-term program (such as a workshop series or course) where there is time between the different sessions.

While long-term programs can yield many benefits, there are also potential drawbacks to consider. Some participants may not have the time, support, bandwidth, or desire to commit to this type of programming. For example, instructors who manage large teaching loads, heavy service commitments, expectations from their departments to focus more on research, personal responsibilities, or other factors may find it difficult to participate in long-term programs. Another drawback of long-term programs is that if someone misses one or two sessions, they may feel the need to stop attending altogether (even if the program is designed in a flexible, "come when you can" way). Additionally, participants who are just starting to dip their toes into the professional learning water may be hesitant to make a significant commitment upfront. Short-term programs can play an important role in providing professional learning opportunities that meet the diverse scheduling needs and availability of participants. They can also spark participants' curiosity and interest in topics, which may lead to deeper engagement in the future.

Thus, it is helpful to adopt a "both/and" rather than an "either/or" approach in regard to workshops. Short-term workshops can still be valuable in promoting discussion of ideas within the larger campus community, providing opportunities for cross-disciplinary interaction, helping participants develop important knowledge or skills about a topic, and providing timely, targeted support (as many higher education institutions tried to provide during the onset of the COVID-19 pandemic).

However, they should not be the *only* form of professional learning offered. Rather, they should be part of a robust set of offerings that includes both short-term and long-term opportunities for engagement. For example, are there topics that lend themselves to deeper, long-term exploration? Then, perhaps design a workshop series where you offer a set of workshops about the topic that build upon each other and occur throughout the term or year. Or, perhaps design a course, institute, or learning community where participants can meet regularly throughout the term to explore ideas, apply concepts, and discuss their learning. Topics such as Universal Design for Learning, artificial intelligence, community-based learning, and accessibility lend themselves well to these types of approaches.

Additionally, when designing workshops of any duration, it can be helpful to remember that "learning is a journey, not an event" (Boller & Fletcher, 2020, p. 18). When creating short-term workshops, we can be intentional about designing them with scaffolding, depth, and longevity in mind. For example, you could ask participants to complete a brief task prior to the workshop to prepare for the learning experience or after the workshop to apply their learning. When creating longer programs (such as workshop series, institutes, or courses), you can also leverage a blended learning approach, which Howles (2022) defines as "the combination of synchronous and asynchronous elements that together comprise a project or course" (p. 302). For instance, participants can do pre-work, followed by a synchronous session, followed by independent work, followed by another synchronous session, followed by post-work (Howles, 2022). In short, just because the live workshop or series is limited to a certain period of time doesn't mean that the learning opportunities have to be, too.

Ultimately, the quality of a professional learning experience is driven less by its duration and more by its design. So yes, be sure to offer sustained, long-term programs that allow learners to dive deeper into the content, apply their learning, and build a sense of community over time. And yes, offer short-term opportunities to meet the diverse needs, interests, and availability of learners. And whatever type of program you choose, and however long it runs, make sure it is designed and facilitated with intentionality.

Every professional learning experience is an opportunity to make an impact.

Workshop Modalities

As a result of the COVID-19 pandemic, colleges and universities have made major shifts in the modalities used for professional learning programs. In their 2022 study of 95 CTL directors and other campus leaders, Eynon et al. (2023) found that 86.6% of their institutions offered on-site professional learning opportunities, 85.4% offered synchronous online opportunities, 85.4% offered asynchronous online opportunities, and 57.3% offered HyFlex opportunities.[2]

As previously mentioned, this book focuses specifically on two modalities of professional learning workshops: on-site workshops (where everyone gathers at the same time in the same physical location) and synchronous online workshops (where everyone gathers at the same time in the same virtual room, such as Zoom). On-site workshops are often referred to as "in-person," "face-to-face," or "on-campus" workshops, whereas synchronous online workshops are often referred to as "virtual workshops" or "virtual trainings." While workshops can be conducted in other modalities (such as hybrid and HyFlex), those formats are beyond the scope of this book.

Benefits and Limitations of On-Site Workshops

One reason often cited for the value of on-site workshops is the communal aspect. Some participants feel that they are better able to connect with others and strike up conversations when they are gathered in the same physical location. Virant-Young et al. (2021) note how networking opportunities "can happen more organically both in sessions and breaks" (p. 306). Likewise, some facilitators find it easier, preferable, or more energizing to facilitate in on-site settings where they can feed off the energy in the room.

Another benefit of on-site workshops that facilitators often mention is that it's easier for them to observe dynamics in the room and pick up on nonverbal cues that offer insight into how participants are doing. Facilitators may notice shifts in participants' facial expressions, tone, and body language that may indicate that participants are excited, confused, tired, or more. They may use this information to adjust in the moment (e.g., checking in with participants, providing a break, revisiting a concept that people appear to be stuck on, or providing more time for people to discuss an invigorating topic). It is important to note, however, that the assumptions facilitators make based on nonverbal cues may not always be accurate (Cohn & Greer, 2023), an idea we will discuss further in Chapter 4.

On-site workshops also offer familiarity. Because they have been the main format of professional learning programs for so long, facilitators and participants know what to expect. As such, people may feel more comfortable facilitating and participating in this modality. Additionally, on-site workshops often include "travel perks" (such as meals). Facilitators may also find benefit in modeling certain skills when in the same room with participants (Virant-Young et al., 2021, p. 306).

On-site workshops also present challenges. One key limitation is access; Bali and Caines (2018) note that on-site "conferences and workshops continue to reproduce inequality in access to those whose time and mobility are more limited" (p. 3). For example, on-site workshops may structurally exclude part-time instructors who may only visit campus on the days they teach, unlike full-time instructors, who often spend time on campus beyond their teaching times. On-site workshops and conferences are also more costly because of meals, room reservations, and travel expenses (Virant-Young et al., 2021). Additionally, on-site factors such as room capacity may limit how many people are able to participate (Virant-Young et al., 2021). Moreover, for facilitators, on-site workshops can be more physically demanding in terms of setting up and tearing down the room.

Benefits and Limitations of Synchronous Online Workshops

Synchronous online workshops have many benefits. First, they allow greater access to professional learning experiences. People who would normally face barriers to participation due to a disability, transportation challenges, distance, caretaking responsibilities, injuries, or other factors can still participate in virtual events. Additionally, virtual workshops provide an avenue for people who are immunocompromised and/or COVID-conscious to participate in a way that feels safe. Overall, more people can participate in virtual events, allowing more diverse voices to contribute to the conversation (Kuntz et al., 2022; Meyer et al., 2021; Minor et al., 2022; Virant-Young et al. 2021; Zakrajsek, 2021).

Virtual workshops can also be easier for participants to fit into their schedules since travel time is not a concern. For example, adjunct instructors who are often teaching multiple courses at multiple campuses may find it easier to participate in virtual workshops where they can join from anywhere. Virtual offerings can also make it easier for clinical faculty who work at various sites to participate in professional learning programs (Minor et al., 2022).

Well-designed virtual events can also create a more accessible professional learning experience. For example, events with live captioning allow deaf/hard of hearing participants, multilingual participants, and those who simply prefer to use captions to easily follow the workshop. Participants in virtual workshops also have greater control over their physical environment. They can adjust the lighting in the room, the volume of the event, and other factors, unlike when attending on-site workshops where conditions are not under their control.

Another benefit of virtual workshops is that they are easy to record (Virant-Young et al., 2021), and the recording quality tends to be better than that of on-site recordings (Virant-Young et al., 2021; Zakrajsek, 2021). Recorded workshops can also increase "the reach of FD [faculty development] programming" (Minor et al., 2022, p. 513). Additionally, recorded sessions benefit participants who need to miss part or all of a session, allowing access to the recorded program at a more convenient time. Participants can also watch recordings as often as necessary, which may help build their confidence and competence with the knowledge and skills addressed in the session (Minor et al., 2022).

Virtual workshops also provide additional avenues for participation and engagement through the built-in features of the platform, such as the polling tools, chat box, and breakout rooms (Virant-Young et al., 2021; Zakrajsek, 2021). For example, the chat box encourages participation of more quiet and introverted participants (Minor et al., 2022; Zakrajsek, 2021). It also gives facilitators access to information that they would not normally have in on-site sessions. Howles (2022) explains:

> One of the affordances of chat's real-time interaction is that virtual facilitators can observe the stream of consciousness from their learners. This provides a window into how learners are thinking about the conversation at any moment, which is something you were not privy to as a traditional in-person trainer.
>
> *(p. 179)*

Virtual workshops and conferences are also a climate-conscious, time-saving, and cost-effective approach to professional learning. They reduce the impact on the environment that would normally occur when everyone commutes to campus or flies to a conference. This, in turn, helps participants save money on gas, flights, and other transportation-related costs. Additionally, online events allow participants and facilitators alike to save valuable time that would otherwise be spent traveling (Minor et al., 2022; Virant-Young et al., 2021; Zakrajsek, 2021). Furthermore, online conferences are typically more cost-friendly than on-site conferences, allowing those with limited funding to be able to participate. Online conferences also allow people from around the world to join without the limitations typically imposed by heavy travel expenses and visa requirements (Meyer et al., 2021).

Opportunities for collaboration can be enhanced through virtual events, too. For example, participants can easily engage "with outside experts" (Eynon et al., 2023, p. 23). Having experts join virtually is not only easier scheduling-wise (Zakrajsek, 2021) but also more cost-effective for the institution (Minor et al., 2022). Additionally, virtual events can allow for more "cross-institutional collaboration," where multiple institutions can pool their collective resources and expertise to develop programs for participants (Minor et al., 2022, p. 512). On a larger scale, virtual conferences can provide greater opportunities for global learning and collaboration.

While there are many benefits of virtual workshops, there are also some important challenges. First, virtual workshops require both facilitators and participants to be comfortable using technology. This includes being able to easily navigate the virtual platform, along with any other digital tools that will be used during the session. Participants may not "have access to the same technology and internet capabilities" (Virant-Young et al., 2021, p. 306). Additionally, facilitators must be adept at managing the technology and the flow of the session simultaneously.

Another challenge of virtual workshops is fatigue, particularly for long workshops and conferences (Meyer et al., 2021). To address this, Meyer et al. (2021) suggest incorporating frequent breaks and minimizing the length of virtual programs. Furthermore, some participants may find it more challenging to connect with others in virtual spaces. Intentionally incorporating well-designed community-building activities (such as virtual scavenger hunts, discussion platforms, and breakout rooms) can help (Meyer et al., 2021).

Finally, since virtual facilitation is a newer format of professional learning for many facilitators, it takes time to learn how to do it well. Virant-Young et al. (2021) note that it may take more planning time to determine how to foster interaction in virtual settings. While it is certainly possible to design virtual learning experiences that are just as engaging and effective as on-site experiences (if not more so), facilitators must be willing to invest time, energy, and creativity to develop their craft in this modality. As with anything new, it can feel uncomfortable and disorientating at first, and facilitators may feel tempted to just stick with what they know in the on-site realm. As Ozenc and Fajardo (2021) explain, "We can have a tendency to romanticize the comfortably familiar and demonize the uncomfortably unfamiliar" (p. 42). However, by leaning into the discomfort and taking it on as a learning opportunity, facilitators can greatly expand the scope of their facilitation skills, provide more equitable learning opportunities for participants, and perhaps even discover the beauty and joy of virtual facilitation. Ozenc and Fajardo (2021) note:

> The key is to **avoid a deficiency mindset**. Don't get stuck on what you don't have available in virtual that you do have available in person. Instead, **flip it to a generative mindset**. …Get curious about what you do have available in virtual that you might not have available in person.
> *(p. 50, emphasis in original)*

A Way Forward

The combined benefits and limitations of on-site and synchronous online workshops make it clear that the path forward lies not in abolishing virtual professional learning for the sake of on-site professional learning (as some universities and conference organizations have unfortunately chosen to do in recent years) but in developing approaches that leverage the benefits of both formats and provide access to the greatest number of people. For example, many universities continue to offer both on-site and virtual programs (Kuntz et al., 2022). Still others have incorporated more innovative approaches, such as HyFlex workshops, where participants can choose to engage on-site, synchronously online, or asynchronously online via recordings. Hybrid events offer yet another approach (Meyer et al., 2021), and they may take different forms. For example, a facilitator may facilitate the workshop virtually to a group that is meeting together on-site. Alternatively, in the case of a workshop series or conference, certain sessions or days may be held on-site and others may be held online. Regardless of the modalities chosen, it is important to adopt an inclusive mindset, considering how to offer professional learning programs that provide access and accessibility for participants rather than excluding them.

Key Frameworks

To design meaningful workshops, we must consider what is known about the nature of learning along with what is known about the nature of professional learning. Three guiding frameworks will be used throughout this book: the five themes from the book, *How Humans Learn*; Universal

TABLE I.1 Key Frameworks

The five themes from How Humans Learn (Eyler, 2018)	Universal Design for Learning (CAST, 2024b)	The New Learning Compact (Bass et al., 2019)
Curiosity Sociality Emotion Authenticity Failure	Design multiple means of engagement Design multiple means of representation Design multiple means of action & expression	Individual Community Institutional Ecosystem

Design for Learning; and the New Learning Compact (see Table I.1). Next, I will provide a brief overview of each framework.

How Humans Learn

Eyler's (2018) book, *How Humans Learn*, synthesizes the research on learning and highlights five key themes that capture how people of all ages learn: curiosity, sociality, emotion, authenticity, and failure. Each theme and its instructional implications is briefly summarized below.

- **Curiosity**: "In order to learn something, we must first wonder about it" (Eyler, 2018, p. 18). Eyler encourages the use of instructional strategies that promote inquiry, discussion, and questioning.
- **Sociality**: "Sure, we can learn things on our own, but we rarely learn them as deeply, because so much of our learning derives from our social nature and our visceral need to communicate with other people" (Eyler, 2018, pp. 66–67). Eyler encourages the use of instructional strategies that promote a sense of belonging, collaboration, and play.
- **Emotion**: Eyler (2018) describes the interconnected nature of emotions and cognition, noting that "each needs the other, as dance partners do, in order to follow the choreography that leads to deep learning" (p. 115). Eyler encourages the use of instructional strategies that allow learners to make an emotional connection to the content, promote positive emotions (such as happiness), recognize the impact of negative emotions (such as fear and anxiety), and demonstrate care for learners.
- **Authenticity**: "The human brain is pretty adept at detecting the degree to which an activity, assignment, or exercise is authentic or artificial. The greater the authenticity, the deeper the learning" (Eyler, 2018, p. 153). Eyler encourages the use of instructional strategies that situate tasks within realistic contexts, incorporate experiential learning, and provide learners with opportunities to engage in authentic tasks.
- **Failure**: "Our brains are designed to find and to construct knowledge from errors" (Eyler, 2018, p. 196). Eyler suggests using instructional strategies that help learners embrace failure (e.g., helping learners develop a growth mindset). He also discusses the importance of creating low-stakes opportunities where learners can learn from failure and fostering a learning climate where mistakes are valued.

While Eyler's work focuses on applying research about curiosity, sociality, emotion, authenticity, and failure to college-level teaching, the five themes are applicable to learners of all ages, thus offering valuable insight for professional learning settings, too. In this book, we will explore how you can apply the five themes to your design and facilitation of workshops. (Hat tip to Jessamyn Neuhaus for inspiring the use of Eyler's work as a guide for shaping educational development programming.)

Universal Design for Learning

Universal Design for Learning (UDL) is a research-based framework that values learner variability and seeks to proactively minimize barriers to learning that exist within the learning environment (CAST, n.d.-a; CAST, n.d.-b; CAST, n.d.-c). The three main principles of CAST's (2024b) UDL framework are as follows:

- "Design multiple means of engagement" (which includes options for learners to engage)
- "Design multiple means of representation" (which includes options for learners to access and process information)
- "Design multiple means of action and expression" (which includes options for learners to navigate tasks and demonstrate learning)

The current iteration of the UDL guidelines (version 3.0) consists of nine guidelines and 36 considerations that are aligned with the three principles (see Figure I.2). The guidelines are geared toward "learners" and "practitioners" alike (CAST, 2024a), and they aim to promote learner agency (CAST, n.d.-c). Overall, the guidelines offer a valuable tool for creating more inclusive learning spaces. In this book, we will explore how to incorporate UDL guidelines into the design and facilitation of workshops. While a detailed explanation of the UDL framework is beyond the scope of this book, you can learn more about it and its supporting research via CAST's website (https://udlguidelines.cast.org/).

The New Learning Compact

The New Learning Compact (NLC) is a research-based framework that focuses on "high-impact professional learning" in higher education (Eynon et al., 2022, p. 41). This framework highlights important professional learning principles at four levels: individual (which focuses on engaging individual educators), community (which focuses on engaging communities of educators, such as departments and faculty learning communities), institutional (which focuses on the larger university context, including campus priorities, policies, and culture), and ecosystem (which focuses on engaging broader educational partners) (Bass et al., 2019; Eynon, 2020; Eynon et al., 2022, 2023). The NLC framework includes 16 professional learning principles that are organized according to the four levels. You can learn more about the framework via the Every Learner Everywhere website (https://www.everylearnereverywhere.org/resources/the-new-learning-compact/).

The principles in the first two levels of the NLC framework (individual and community) offer valuable insight into how to design effective professional learning programs (Eynon & Iuzzini, 2020; Eynon et al., 2022). The four principles at the individual level are:

- Respect educators' knowledge
- Connect with practice
- Engage inquiry and reflection
- Protect participant time (Bass et al., 2019, p. 30)

The Universal Design for Learning Guidelines

The goal of UDL is **learner agency** that is purposeful & reflective, resourceful & authentic, strategic & action-oriented.

Design Multiple Means of Engagement

Design Options for Welcoming Interests & Identities (7)
- Optimize choice and autonomy (7.1)
- Optimize relevance, value, and authenticity (7.2)
- Nurture joy and play (7.3)
- Address biases, threats, and distractions (7.4)

Access

Design Options for Sustaining Effort & Persistence (8)
- Clarify the meaning and purpose of goals (8.1)
- Optimize challenge and support (8.2)
- Foster collaboration, interdependence, and collective learning (8.3)
- Foster belonging and community (8.4)
- Offer action-oriented feedback (8.5)

Support

Design Options for Emotional Capacity (9)
- Recognize expectations, beliefs, and motivations (9.1)
- Develop awareness of self and others (9.2)
- Promote individual and collective reflection (9.3)
- Cultivate empathy and restorative practices (9.4)

Executive Function

Design Multiple Means of Representation

Design Options for Perception (1)
- Support opportunities to customize the display of information (1.1)
- Support multiple ways to perceive information (1.2)
- Represent a diversity of perspectives and identities in authentic ways (1.3)

Design Options for Language & Symbols (2)
- Clarify vocabulary, symbols, and language structures (2.1)
- Support decoding of text, mathematical notation, and symbols (2.2)
- Cultivate understanding and respect across languages and dialects (2.3)
- Address biases in the use of language and symbols (2.4)
- Illustrate through multiple media (2.5)

Design Options for Building Knowledge (3)
- Connect prior knowledge to new learning (3.1)
- Highlight and explore patterns, critical features, big ideas, and relationships (3.2)
- Cultivate multiple ways of knowing and making meaning (3.3)
- Maximize transfer and generalization (3.4)

Design Multiple Means of Action & Expression

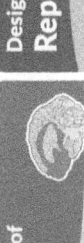

Design Options for Interaction (4)
- Vary and honor the methods for response, navigation, and movement (4.1)
- Optimize access to accessible materials and assistive and accessible technologies and tools (4.2)

Design Options for Expression & Communication (5)
- Use multiple media for communication (5.1)
- Use multiple tools for construction, composition, and creativity (5.2)
- Build fluencies with graduated support for practice and performance (5.3)
- Address biases related to modes of expression and communication (5.4)

Design Options for Strategy Development (6)
- Set meaningful goals (6.1)
- Anticipate and plan for challenges (6.2)
- Organize information and resources (6.3)
- Enhance capacity for monitoring progress (6.4)
- Challenge exclusionary practices (6.5)

CAST | Until learning has no limits®

udlguidelines.cast.org © CAST, Inc. 2024

Suggested Citation: CAST (2024). Universal Design for Learning Guidelines version 3.0 [graphic organizer]. Lynnfield, MA: Author.

FIGURE I.2 CAST's (2024c) UDL Guidelines Version 3.0 Graphic Organizer (Reprinted with permission of CAST)

14 Designing and Facilitating Workshops with Intentionality

The four principles at the community level are:

- Create supportive professional communities
- Learn from and with students
- Involve all sectors of the professoriate
- Break boundaries (Bass et al., 2019, p. 30)

In this book, we will explore how you can apply these principles to your design and facilitation of workshops.

How This Book Is Structured

This book highlights ten essential principles that are important to consider when designing and facilitating professional learning workshops. These principles are presented as a model that I call the Workshop Wheel, which offers an intentional approach to workshop design and facilitation (see Figure I.3). The ten essential principles are:

- Relevant
- Purposeful
- Structured
- Inclusive
- Connective
- Active
- Reflective
- Ongoing
- Responsive
- Distinctive

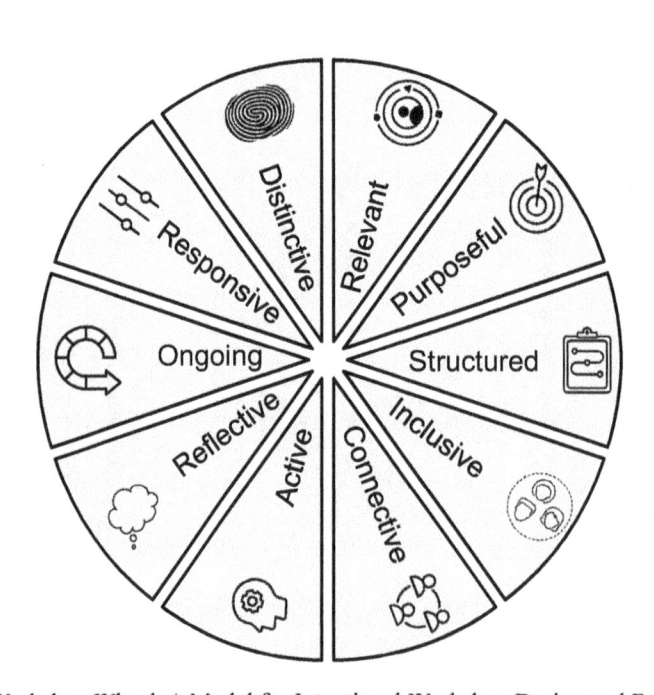

FIGURE I.3 The Workshop Wheel: A Model for Intentional Workshop Design and Facilitation

By intentionally designing and facilitating workshops with these ten principles in mind, you can create more well-rounded (pun intended!) and worthwhile professional learning experiences.

The first ten chapters of this book each focus on a different principle of the Workshop Wheel.

- Chapter 1 sets the stage by discussing the importance of learning about your learners and their context so that you can create more **relevant** professional learning experiences.
- Chapter 2 describes how to design a high-level and **purposeful** workshop plan.
- Chapter 3 dives deeper into the planning process, describing how to turn the big-picture workshop plan into a well-**structured** professional learning experience.
- Chapter 4 explains the importance of creating an **inclusive**, welcoming, and equitable learning experience.
- Chapter 5 shares strategies for cultivating a **connective** learning experience that fosters a sense of belonging and rapport.
- Chapter 6 provides a plethora of **active** learning techniques that can help participants engage in learning.
- Chapter 7 discusses **reflective** activities that can help participants process their learning and determine next steps.
- Chapter 8 suggests strategies for creating **ongoing** learning opportunities that extend beyond the scope of the workshop.
- Chapter 9 outlines ways to be **responsive** to learners before, during, and after the workshop.
- Chapter 10 examines how our identity, values, beliefs, and prior experiences as facilitators shape our **distinctive** approaches to workshop design and facilitation. Here, I share insights from interviews I conducted with seven fantastic facilitators.

The final two chapters of this book focus on ways to enhance your workshop design and facilitation skills.

- Chapter 11 offers practical tips for optimizing your workshop workflow, along with a dedicated set of tips about virtual facilitation.
- Chapter 12 recommends strategies for continuing to hone your craft as a facilitator.

This book also includes several special features, which you will find at the end of each chapter. First, there is a Recap, which briefly summarizes the key points and themes from the chapter. Second, since sticky notes are a facilitator's best friend, there is a Sticky Note Reflection at the end of each chapter where you will be prompted to pause, reflect on what you read, and jot down your thoughts. Third, you will find a Workshop Toolkit that you can access via a QR code or link. The toolkit includes a curated collection of websites, readings, videos, sample materials, and/or other helpful resources related to the chapter so that you can go further with your learning. Fourth, there is a Design Time activity, where you will have the chance to apply what you learned in the chapter.

This book is also designed to be a social reading experience where you can engage with other readers. Each chapter ends with a Facilitators' Lounge QR code and link which take you to a dedicated online discussion page for the chapter. Here, you can post comments, questions, takeaways, next steps, and share helpful resources and ideas with others. As we will discuss throughout this book, communal and multidirectional learning opportunities are essential aspects of any professional learning experience, and I wanted to ensure that those aspects were built into the design of this book as well. Whether you are reading this book on your couch, in your office, at the beach, or anywhere else, know that you can join the lounge at any time to share with and learn from other readers.

My hope is that this book will serve as a helpful guide that you can return to time and time again as you design and facilitate workshops. As you read, please feel free to share your

16 Designing and Facilitating Workshops with Intentionality

takeaways on social media via the hashtag, **#TheWorkshopWheel**. I also invite you to connect with me! You can find me on LinkedIn by searching for my name, Tolulope (Tolu) Noah, or connect with me on Bluesky (@drtolunoah.bsky.social). You can also reach me via my website, www.tolunoah.com.

Thank you for joining me on this exciting journey, as we explore how we can turn our professional learning dreams into reality and create more engaging and impactful learning experiences.

Recap

- Professional learning can occur through a variety of avenues, both formal and informal.
- Consider offering a mix of professional learning programs in different modalities and durations to meet more learners where they are.
- Leverage the Workshop Wheel as a tool to design and facilitate workshops with intentionality.

Sticky Note Reflection

Goal Setting: What are 1–2 goals you have for reading this book?

Workshop Toolkit

Scan the QR code or visit the URL to access additional resources related to this chapter.

www.tolunoah.com/workshop-toolkits

Design Time

Review Figure I.3 (the Workshop Wheel) as you reflect on your workshop design and facilitation practices. Next to each principle, jot down either something you are *currently* doing in relation to the principle or something you *hope* to learn about or do in relation to the principle.

Facilitators' Lounge

Join the Facilitators' Lounge to connect with other readers and share your takeaways, strategies, and next steps!

www.tolunoah.com/facilitators-lounge/

Notes

1 A simulive session is a pre-recorded session played at a designated time, with the presenter attending live and engaging with attendees in the chat.
2 HyFlex (or hybrid flexible) programs give participants the option to choose their mode of participation (e.g., on-site, synchronous online, or asynchronous online via program recordings).

References

Agarwal, P.K., & Bain, P.M. (2019). *Powerful teaching: Unleash the science of learning.* Jossey-Bass.

Bali, M., & Caines, A. (2018). A call for promoting ownership, equity, and agency in faculty development via connected learning. *International Journal of Educational Technology in Higher Education, 15*, Article 46. https://doi.org/10.1186/s41239-018-0128-8

Bass, R., Eynon, B., & Gambino, L.M. (2019). *The New Learning Compact: A framework for professional learning and educational change.* Every Learner Everywhere. www.everylearnereverywhere.org/resources/the-new-learning-compact/

Bell, L.A., & Goodman, D.J. (2023). Design and facilitation. In M. Adams, L.A. Bell, D.J. Goodman, & D. Shlasko (with R.R. Briggs & R. Pacheco) (Eds.), *Teaching for diversity and social justice* (4th ed., pp. 57–96). Routledge.

Boller, S., & Fletcher, L. (2020). *Design thinking for training and development: Creating learning journeys that get results.* ATD Press.

Bouwma-Gearhart, J. (2012). Research university STEM faculty members' motivation to engage in teaching professional development: Building the choir through an appeal to extrinsic motivation and ego. *Journal of Science Education and Technology, 21*, 558–570. https://doi.org/10.1007/s10956-011-9346-8

Brown, P.C., Roediger, H.L., & McDaniel, M.A. (2014). *Make it stick: The science of successful learning.* The Belknap Press of Harvard University Press.

Carpenter, S.K., & Agarwal, P.K. (2020). *How to use spaced retrieval practice to boost learning.* https://pdf.retrievalpractice.org/SpacingGuide.pdf

CAST. (n.d.-a). *About Universal Design for Learning.* www.cast.org/impact/universal-design-for-learning-udl

CAST. (n.d.-b). *Frequently asked questions.* https://udlguidelines.cast.org/more/frequently-asked-questions/

CAST. (n.d.-c). *The goal of UDL: Learner agency.* https://udlguidelines.cast.org/more/udl-goal/

CAST. (2024a, July 30). *UDL guidelines 3.0: Rationale for updates.* https://docs.google.com/document/d/1U4kvxFht8g8t4Ye6Gu97fByGuNI65yWE-7n0yL__BzU/edit?usp=sharing

CAST. (2024b). *Universal Design for Learning guidelines version 3.0.* https://udlguidelines.cast.org/

CAST. (2024c). *Universal Design for Learning guidelines version 3.0* [graphic organizer]. Author. https://udlguidelines.cast.org/more/downloads/

Cohn, J., & Greer, M. (2023). *Design for learning: User experience in online teaching and learning.* Rosenfeld Media.

Condon, W., Iverson, E.R., Manduca, C.A., Rutz, C., & Willett, G. (2016). *Faculty development and student learning: Assessing the connections.* Indiana University Press.

Cruz, L., Parker, M.A., Smentkowski, B., & Smitherman, M. (2020). *Taking flight: Making your center for teaching and learning soar.* Routledge.

Ellis, D.E., & Ortquist-Ahrens, L. (2010). Practical suggestions for programs and activities. In K.J. Gillespie, D.L. Robertson, & Associates (Eds.), *A guide to faculty development* (2nd ed., pp. 117–132). Jossey-Bass.

Eyler, J.R. (2018). *How humans learn: The science and stories behind effective college teaching.* West Virginia University Press.

Eynon, B., Bass, R., Iuzzini, J., & Gambino, L.M. (2022). The New Learning Compact: A systemic approach to a systemic problem. *Change: The Magazine of Higher Learning, 54*(2), 38–46. https://doi.org/10.1080/00091383.2022.2030162

Eynon, B., & Iuzzini, J. (2020). *ATD teaching and learning toolkit: A research-based guide to building a culture of teaching & learning excellence.* Achieving the Dream. https://achievingthedream.org/teaching-learning-toolkit/

Eynon, B., Iuzzini, J., Keith, H.R., Loepp, E., & Weber, N. (2023, January 17). *Teaching, learning, equity and change: Realizing the promise of professional learning.* Every Learner Everywhere. www.everylearnereverywhere.org/resources/teaching-learning-equity-and-change-realizing-the-promise-of-professional-learning/

Fink, L.D. (2013). *Creating significant learning experiences: An integrated approach to designing college courses* (2nd ed.). Jossey-Bass.

Howles, D.L. (2022). *Next level virtual training: Advance your facilitation.* ATD Press.

Kuntz, A., Davis, S., & Fleming, E. (2022, May 3). *7 ways the pandemic changed faculty development.* EDUCAUSE Review. https://er.educause.edu/articles/2022/5/7-ways-the-pandemic-changed-faculty-development

Lee, V.S. (2010). Program types and prototypes. In K.J. Gillespie, D.L. Robertson, & Associates (Eds.), *A guide to faculty development* (2nd ed., pp. 21–33). Jossey-Bass.

Meyer, M.F., Ladwig, R., Dugan, H.A., Anderson, A., Bah, A.R., Boehrer, B., Borre, L., Chapina, R.J., Doyle, C., Favot, E.J., Flaim, G., Forsberg, P., Hanson, P.C., Ibelings, B.W., Isles, P., Lin, F.-P., Lofton, D., Moore, T.N., Peel, S., …Weathers, K.C. (2021, February 18). Virtual growing pains: Initial lessons learned from organizing virtual workshops, summits, conferences, and networking events during a global pandemic. *Limnology and Oceanography Bulletin, 30*(1), 1–11. https://doi.org/10.1002/lob.10431

Minor, S., Berry, A., Luhanga, U., Chen, W., Drowos, J., Rudd, M., Kaprielian, V.S., Bailey, J.M., & Gupta, S. (2022). Faculty development advancements – Lessons learned in a time of change. *Medical Science Educator, 32*, 511–515. https://doi.org/10.1007/s40670-022-01523-y

Ozenc, K., & Fajardo, G. (2021). *Rituals for virtual meetings: Creative ways to engage people and strengthen relationships.* Wiley.

Pchenitchnaia, L., & Cole, B.R. (2009). Essential faculty development programs for teaching and learning centers in research-extensive universities. *To Improve the Academy, 27*, 287–308. http://dx.doi.org/10.3998/tia.17063888.0027.019

Steinert, Y. (2010a). Becoming a better teacher: From intuition to intent. In J. Ende (Ed.), *Theory and practice of teaching medicine* (pp. 73–94). American College of Physicians.

Steinert, Y. (2010b). Faculty development: From workshops to communities of practice. *Medical Teacher, 32*(5), 425–428. https://doi.org/10.3109/01421591003677897

Steinert, Y., Mann, K., Anderson, B., Barnett, B.M., Centeno, A., Naismith, L., Prideaux, D., Spencer, J., Tullo, E., Viggiano, T., Ward, H., & Dolmans, D. (2016). A systematic review of faculty development initiatives designed to enhance teaching effectiveness: A 10-year update: BEME guide no. 40. *Medical Teacher, 38*(8), 769–786. http://dx.doi.org/10.1080/0142159X.2016.1181851

Virant-Young, D.L., Purcell, J., Moutsios, S., & Iobst, W.F. (2021). Practice makes better: Effective faculty educator skill development in the virtual space. *Journal of Graduate Medical Education, 13*(2), 303–308. https://doi.org/10.4300%2FJGME-D-21-00212.1

Wenger-Trayner, E., & Wenger-Trayner, B. (2015, June). *Introduction to communities of practice: A brief overview of the concept and its uses.* www.wenger-trayner.com/introduction-to-communities-of-practice.

Wright, M.C. (2023). *Centers for teaching and learning: The new landscape in higher education.* Johns Hopkins University Press.

Zakrajsek, T. (2016, December 20). Oh, the places your center can go: Possible programs to offer. *Journal on Centers for Teaching and Learning, 8*, 93–109. https://openjournal.lib.miamioh.edu/index.php/jctl/article/view/160

Zakrajsek, T. D. (2021). The COVID-19 pandemic impact: Current changes in faculty development that have the potential to persist. *Journal on Centers for Teaching and Learning, 13*, 92–110. https://openjournal.lib.miamioh.edu/index.php/jctl/article/view/225

1
BEGIN WITH RELEVANCE

Guiding Question:
How can you use a learner-centered approach to design relevant workshops?

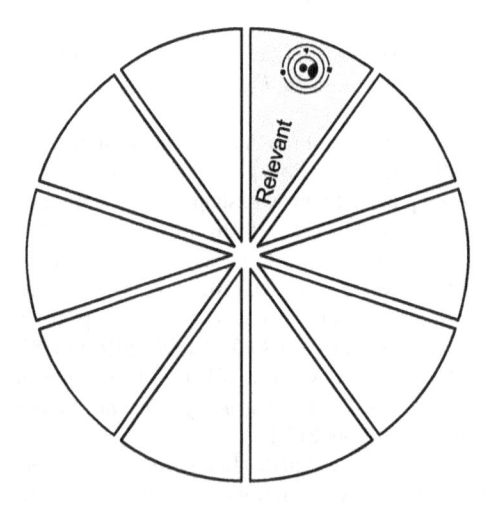

Before we design a workshop or workshop series, we must first listen. It is only through active listening that we can determine if a workshop is even needed, and if so, how to design it in a way that will truly meet learners' interests, goals, and needs. In other words, active listening is an important precursor to intentional workshop design.

In one of my previous roles, I was a senior professional learning specialist at Apple. This role entailed facilitating professional learning programs at more than 20 universities, schools, and districts nationwide. When working with an educational partner for the first time, I would schedule an introductory virtual meeting so that I could learn more about who they were, what their context was like, and what their goals were for professional learning.

As you can imagine, each university, school, and district was very different. Most were higher education institutions, while others were K-12 schools and districts. Some had instructors and staff who were transitioning to using Apple devices for the first time, whereas others had instructors and staff who were experienced with the tools and ready to dive deeper. Some institutions wanted me to work with specific groups of instructors and staff (such as nursing instructors or educational technology coaches), while others wanted me to facilitate more general professional learning sessions that were open to all instructors and staff.

The information I gleaned from the introductory conversations was instrumental in developing a deeper understanding of who I would be working with and important factors to keep in mind. This information also helped me to design more relevant programs. For example, when working with nursing instructors at universities, I was intentional about using examples that directly

DOI: 10.4324/9781003482963-2

pertained to their discipline and incorporating authentic tasks. We explored how they could create interactive case studies and clinical logs with Numbers (spreadsheet software), design multimodal digital textbooks and workbooks about nursing concepts with Pages (word processing software), and produce instructional videos about nursing content with Keynote and Clips (presentation and video software) (Baker et al., 2020; Manacek & Pitcher, 2020). I also spoke with my mother and one of my younger sisters (both of whom are nurses) to ensure that the topics and activities I was planning to use were conceptually accurate and representative of the topics, tasks, and processes that are common within the nursing field. Because I invested time in learning about the people I was partnering with and their unique context, interests, and goals, I was able to develop more meaningful and applicable learning activities.

This experience reinforced the importance of relevance and authenticity when designing professional learning programs. The importance of these factors is also reflected in the Universal Design for Learning (UDL) guidelines, Eyler's themes from *How Humans Learn*, and the New Learning Compact (NLC) principles. UDL guideline 7, "Design options for welcoming interests & identities," prompts practitioners to "optimize relevance, value, and authenticity (7.2)" (CAST, 2024b). This can occur through linking content and tasks to learners' personal goals, demonstrating the usefulness of the information, and using authentic tasks (CAST, 2024a). Eyler (2018) explains that authenticity is a driver of deep learning. Furthermore, the NLC principle, "Connect with practice," highlights that "educational development is most productive when it relates to, draws on, and informs teaching-learning practice as it unfolds in diverse settings" (Bass et al., 2019, p. 30). Additionally, the "Center for Teaching and Learning Matrix," developed by the American Council on Education and the POD Network, notes that "accomplished/exemplary" centers for teaching and learning have a "strong reputation for programs highly responsive to identified needs" (Collins-Brown et al., 2018, p. 6).

In this chapter, we will explore the important role of relevance in designing effective professional learning programs. To do so, we'll use a simple tool I developed called the Relevance Map (Figure 1.1). This tool encourages facilitators to consider five key questions:

- Who are your learners?
- Where are they situated?

Learners	Context	Focus	Format	Fulfillment
Who are your learners?	Where are they situated?	What is the focal point?	What would be an appropriate way to address this?	What conditions might learners find fulfilling?

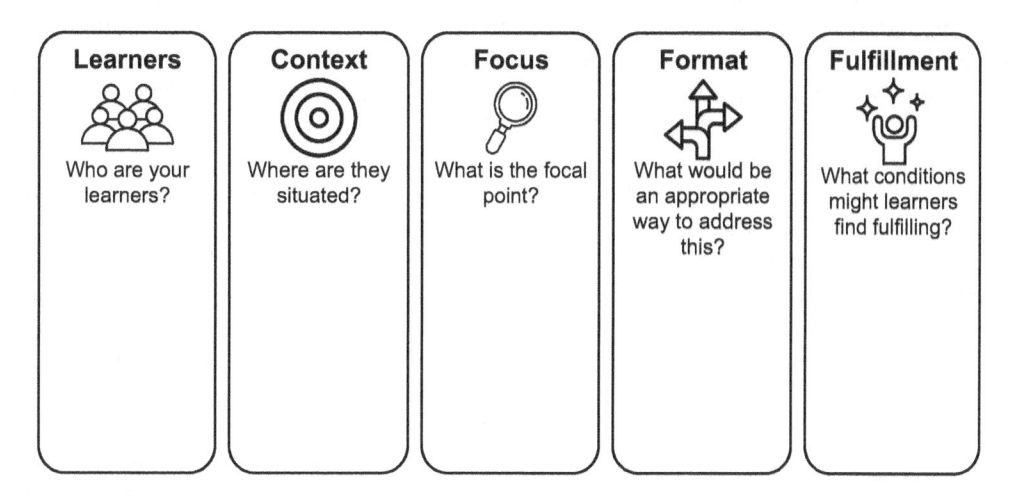

FIGURE 1.1 The Relevance Map

- What is the focal point?
- What would be an appropriate way to address this?
- What conditions might learners find fulfilling?

If you have been working in your educational community for some time, you may already have helpful insight into some of these questions. However, regardless of how long you have been working there, it's important to frequently revisit these questions with a listening posture to ensure that the programs you're designing are truly meeting learners' ever-evolving goals, interests, and needs.

Next, we'll unpack what each question entails and explore options for how you might seek answers.

Who Are Your Learners?

Professional learning is ultimately about people. As such, when designing professional learning programs, we should begin by asking ourselves, "Who are our learners?" Designing programs through this lens helps us to ensure that the programs will be more relevant, useful, applicable, and meaningful to them.

In my current educational development role, I facilitate programs about teaching and technology for instructors. Your role may be different; perhaps you facilitate programs for graduate students, administrators, staff, undergraduate students, or other groups. Regardless of who your learners are, investing time in learning about them can make all the difference in creating a meaningful experience.

It's also important to bear in mind that whichever group you're working with is not a monolith. For example, the needs and interests of early career faculty often differ from those of mid- or late-career faculty (Austin, 2010; Seldin, 2006), and there is incredible diversity within each of these subgroups. The NLC principle, "Involve all sectors of the professoriate," encourages educational developers to design professional learning opportunities that engage instructors in different career stages, along with adjunct and full-time instructors (Bass et al., 2019, p. 38). Offering a mix of general and specialized programs can be a helpful way to support the diverse needs and interests of the people you partner with.

Start by identifying who your learners are—whether that is a general group or a specific subgroup. Then, invest time in learning more about them and their perspectives. One helpful framework that I draw from is design thinking, which prioritizes "human-centered" design (Boller & Fletcher, 2020, p. 5; Lee, 2018, pp. 34—35). The design thinking approach includes five phases (Boller & Fletcher, 2020; d.school, n.d.-b; Lee, 2018):

- **Empathize**: Learn about the people for whom you are designing, including their needs, desires, feelings, and challenges.
- **Define**: Determine the specific problem that you are trying to help them address.
- **Ideate**: Brainstorm as many solutions as you can.
- **Prototype**: Create a physical or digital model of a solution.
- **Test**: Have them try out the prototype, and use their feedback to revise it accordingly.

The first phase of design thinking—empathize—is relevant to the question of "Who are your learners?" Common techniques for empathizing with others include interviews, focus groups, observations, research, and learner personas[1] (Boller & Fletcher, 2020; Cohn & Greer, 2023; Lee,

2018). Another popular technique is administering surveys (Cohn & Greer, 2023; Cruz et al., 2020; Sheffield & Moore, 2023), and you might consider including optional demographic questions where participants can provide insight into their backgrounds and social identities if they wish. Within the educational development field, this process of collecting information in order to learn more about people's needs and desires is commonly referred to as "needs assessment."[2] To learn more about these different techniques and explore sample tools, please visit the resources linked in the Workshop Toolkit at the end of this chapter.

In my personal work, I have used surveys and pedagogical consultations with instructors to learn more about who they are, what they teach, what is important to them, which goals they are working toward, and what they need/desire. For example, each term, I send out a short survey to instructors to ask about topics they want to explore, their scheduling preferences, and more. Additionally, my consultations with instructors provide valuable insight into their backgrounds, experiences, successes, challenges, and goals. Through these consultations, I not only learn more about the individual instructors I am speaking with, but I am also able to note trends across conversations that are helpful in identifying specific areas of support. (We will discuss pedagogical consultations further in Chapter 8.) Routine tools (such as email) have also been useful sources of data for me. The questions that instructors email me and the requests they make help me to understand their priorities and identify current gaps in my program offerings that can support them in their goals.

The educational development literature also highlights the important role of conversations in learning about learners. Neal and Peed-Neal (2009) explain that "you should talk to faculty members—as many as you can, as often as you can, individually and in groups. Find out what's on their minds, their hopes, their fears, their challenges" (p. 20). Zakrajsek (2016) recommends conducting focus groups with faculty and asking them about "areas of challenge rather than areas of need," as understanding the challenges faculty are facing can help surface their needs and inform your program offerings (p. 96). In "The Four Rs: Guiding CTLs with Responsiveness, Relationships, Resources, and Research," the authors share how a new director of a center for teaching and learning conducted informational interviews with faculty, staff, students, and administrators across campus to "discern patterns of need and interest" (Wright et al., 2018, Relationships section). For example, during conversations with faculty, the new director asked questions such as, "What teaching topics or pedagogies do you wish you knew more about, had a better handle on, could explore, [or] had opportunities to discuss with colleagues?" and "If you had one wish for something I might accomplish, introduce, or facilitate in the next years related to teaching and learning, what would it be?" (Wright et al., 2018, Relationships section). A link to this article, which includes additional helpful interview questions, is provided in the Workshop Toolkit at the end of this chapter.

The educational development literature also recommends anticipating areas of support. Neal and Peed-Neal (2009) explain, "As a professional developer, you should also try to ascertain needs that are *not expressed* and create programs that address these as well" (p. 26, emphasis in original). This requires keeping up with the latest research, staying current on emerging trends and shifts in higher education, and asking yourself what is not currently on your radar that should be. Neal and Peed-Neal (2009) suggest practices such as reading the school newspaper and reviewing academic senate documentation to identify "hidden needs" at the institution (p. 27).

As you invest time in listening to and empathizing with learners, be sure to take notes about what you are learning. This may include notes about any key needs, desires, priorities, challenges, feelings, or other factors that learners share. You will revisit this information later on in the Relevance Map process.

Where Are They Situated?

While developing a deep understanding of your learners is an essential first step, it is not the final destination. You also need to consider where they are situated. You and your learners are working within a larger context that impacts your work.

Most readers of this book are likely working within a college or university setting, and every educational community is unique. Whether you are working at a small liberal arts college, a large public university, a faith-based university, a community college, a research university, a specialized college (such as an arts school), or anywhere else, "organizational history, culture, and politics create unique environmental conditions at each institution" (Neal & Peed-Neal, 2009, p. 15). Each community has distinct priorities, goals, and demographics that are important to understand. Moreover, each community has a distinct culture of teaching and learning (Condon et al., 2016, pp. 89–91), which extends to professional learning as well. Eynon et al. (2023) explain:

> If a college fails to consistently encourage engagement with professional learning and 'consistently encourage a focus on teaching improvement,' faculty and staff educators will focus elsewhere. Conversely, a clear message about the value of teaching improvement, reinforced at every level of faculty life, supports a pervasive focus on student learning and creates opportunities for innovation, collaboration and transformation.
>
> *(p. 35)*

In short, context matters.

Thus, an important next step is to develop a deep understanding of the context. This includes getting to know your university's mission, policies, structure, and the people in your educational community (such as instructors, students, and administrators) (Neal & Peed-Neal, 2009; Zakrajsek, 2016). It also includes learning about the culture of professional learning on campus, and the degree to which it is valued, encouraged, and supported. Felten et al. (2013) note:

> Being context sensitive means that the work we do is shaped by the setting in which we are working and the circumstances of audience, politics, timing, or external pressures that inform it. Our work needs to take into consideration the environment, relationships, and power dynamics at each level in which we operate.
>
> *(p. 188)*

The authors explain that the levels of operation include individual (which refers to "individual faculty members"), departmental (which includes departments and programs), and institutional (which includes the broader university as a whole) (Felten et al., 2013, pp. 189–190).

Cohen (2010) recommends using institutional documents and conversations to learn more about the context. This includes reading the university's mission statement, strategic plan, and program review documentation. It also includes conducting interviews with people from across the university (e.g., administrators, department chairs, instructors, etc.) to learn more about their views, goals, needs, and recent initiatives.

As you learn more about the context of your educational community, it can be helpful to reflect on how these factors might influence your program offerings. Cruz et al. (2020) offer helpful questions to consider, such as:

- Are there aspects of your institutional mission that indicate specific programming should be a priority?

- Are there timely issues or challenges on campus that you could address with your programming?
- Are there specific programs that reflect who you are as an institution and what is important to your faculty, staff, and students? (p. 78)

Cruz et al. (2020) also recommend reflecting on potential programs related to issues under consideration by faculty senate, along with programs related to pertinent "national, regional, or statewide initiatives" (p. 79).

Finally, it's important to remember that because each institution's context is unique, there is no one "right" or "perfect" approach to designing and facilitating professional learning programs. What works well in one context may or may not work well in another. While this book offers principles and strategies that will hopefully be helpful to you, you will ultimately need to consider what would work best for you and the people you work with based on your unique context.

What is the Focal Point?

Once we have a good understanding of who our learners are and the contextual factors that influence their work, we should pause and reflect on what we have learned thus far. Here, we can draw upon the second phase of design thinking: define. In the traditional design thinking process, this phase entails reflecting on your findings by synthesizing the needs of the people you are designing for, identifying the unique insights you have gained, and developing a problem statement that outlines the particular need you are trying to address (d.school, n.d.-b; Lee, 2018).

What might this process look like within the context of professional learning? First, synthesize your key findings about your learners by identifying their specific goals, interests, needs, priorities, or challenges. Then, reflect on the unique insights you gained about your learners and their context. Next, select a specific area of focus. It's important to note that in reviewing the information you've gathered about learners and their context, you may find that there are *multiple* areas of challenge or possibility. Furthermore, some of these areas may be things that cannot or should not be addressed through professional learning programs but rather by addressing a larger policy, practice, or other systemic issue impacting the situation. Thus, when selecting a focus area, be sure to choose something that can be appropriately addressed within the scope of your professional learning programs.

Once you have identified a focus area, develop a focus statement. (I use the term "focus statement" rather than "problem statement" because professional learning is not just about addressing problems or challenges; it is also about exploring new ideas, approaches, and possibilities.) You can use the following sentence starter (adapted from d.school, n.d.-a & Lee, 2018) to craft your focus statement.

> _____ (general or specific group of learners) in my educational community want/seek/need/are interested in _____ (learners' common or priority goal) so that/because/in order to _____ (specific insight gained about learners and/or their context).

Examples:

> *Graduate student instructors in my educational community seek support with how to plan their lessons in order to improve student learning and engagement.*

Instructors in my educational community want to learn more about how to facilitate discussions about challenging topics so that they can lay the foundation for productive dialogue and better manage "hot moments" in the classroom.

What Would be an Appropriate Way to Address This? (AKA Should This be a Workshop?)

At this point, we know who our learners are, the contextual factors that impact them, and the focal point that will guide our work. Our next step is to pause and consider how we should address the focal point. This step in the process has some overlap with the third phase of design thinking (ideate), which involves brainstorming possible solutions. However, within the context of professional learning, our "solutions" are often in the form of some type of program. Thus, a secondary question I encourage you to think about is, "Should this be a workshop?"

Often, the default answer to this question is, "Yes!" In other words, it is often assumed that a workshop is the best (or only) way to address a specific topic. However, there are *numerous* types of professional learning programs and resources that facilitators can develop. Some topics may lend themselves to short-term programs (such as workshops), whereas others may lend themselves to longer programs (such as workshop series, book clubs, courses, institutes, or learning communities). Additionally, some topics can be addressed through the creation and dissemination of a resource, such as a website, newsletter, blog, video, podcast, or document that learners can revisit anytime. You could even leverage email as an asynchronous professional learning tool! For example, Katopodis (2024) created a 10-day syllabus challenge, where each day, she emailed participants a short video and a task that they could complete to design a more welcoming and inclusive syllabus.

You may also decide to use a combination of short- and long-term programs to address a particular topic; it all depends on your goals. For a new topic for learners on your campus, your goal might be to introduce key ideas to as many people as possible, spark their interest, and encourage them to learn more. In this case, an interactive workshop could be a good place to start. From there, you might decide to follow up with additional opportunities to dive deeper (such as facilitating a book club or learning community about the topic or offering a workshop series, institute, or course).

While there are no hard and fast rules about what should or should not be a workshop, I think reflecting on a working definition of workshops can be a helpful place to start. In this book, I define workshops as follows:

> A workshop is a formal learning experience where a group of people engage in active, multidirectional learning opportunities in order to develop a deeper understanding of a specific topic.

Let's break this definition down further:

- **Formal**: A workshop is a structured learning experience designed by a facilitator for a specific purpose. Workshops typically aim to support participants in developing knowledge, skills, and/ or attitudes about a topic.
- **Active**: Workshops involve *work* on the part of participants. They are distinct from presentations, where a speaker spends all (or the majority) of the time talking to participants while participants primarily sit and listen. Instead, workshops involve a facilitator operating

as a *guide* and providing participants with ample opportunities to process, practice, discuss, reflect, interact, and share in ways that promote deeper learning and transfer of the knowledge and skills gained.
- **Multidirectional**: Workshops include opportunities for communal learning, where participants can learn from the facilitator, the facilitator can learn from participants, and participants can learn from each other.

Workshops are versatile and can be used for a wide variety of purposes. For example, a workshop can be designed to do the following:

- Introduce key concepts in an interactive way (e.g., exploring the Transparency in Learning and Teaching [TILT] framework)
- Teach pedagogical skills (e.g., how to use active learning techniques, such as jigsaws)
- Teach technical skills (e.g., how to use an edtech tool such as Mentimeter for formative assessments)
- Facilitate dialogue about a topic (e.g., discussing the implications of artificial intelligence for teaching and learning)
- Brainstorm ideas (e.g., generating strategies for building classroom community)
- Analyze data (e.g., analyzing student writing samples)
- Provide an avenue for people to obtain feedback (e.g., gaining input on a teaching challenge or the design of a class assignment)
- Help people learn about wellness and workload management practices (e.g., how to set appropriate boundaries)
- Teach other work-related policies, processes, and procedures in an interactive way (e.g., how to craft a teaching statement)

If you plan to primarily present information to learners, it may be that the topic is best suited to another format. For example, you could record a video that can be viewed asynchronously, record a podcast episode that can be listened to, or create a self-paced course instead. Workshops are best suited for learning experiences where participants will have the opportunity to actively engage with the content and with each other. As Howles (2022) explains, "We want to leverage the activities in our [synchronous] time together that make the most of our shared community" (p. 307). Howles (2022, pp. 307–308) offers the following list of activities that are best suited to synchronous gatherings:

- Presenting and receiving corrective feedback
- Delivering a teach-back and receiving feedback
- Doing a skill practice and receiving feedback
- Practicing a role-play exercise
- Large-group discussion
- Small-group breakout discussions
- Critiquing good examples and non-examples as a group
- Analysis
- Brainstorming
- Live question and answer periods
- Applying what learners will do back on the job
- Collaboration activities
- Problem solving in small groups

Additional factors that may impact your decision about whether to do a workshop include the time and resources you have available, the scope of the program (e.g., introductory versus deeper dive), and the desired reach of the program.

What Conditions Might Learners Find Fulfilling?

Let's assume that a workshop or a workshop series would be an appropriate way to address the focal point. (That is the focus of this book, after all!) The final step in the Relevance Map process is to consider the professional learning conditions that learners may find fulfilling. One theory that can be helpful in this regard is self-determination theory (SDT). While a detailed examination of SDT is beyond the scope of this book, central to SDT is the idea that humans have "basic psychological needs" that drive behavior (Ryan & Deci, 2000b, pp. 68–69, 74–76). Meeting these needs is the foundation for an individual's level of motivation. These needs are (Niemiec & Ryan, 2009; Ryan & Deci, 2000a; Ryan & Deci, 2000b):

- **Autonomy**: The need to feel in control of one's actions (such as the ability to make decisions about what one does)
- **Relatedness**: "The need to feel belongingness and connectedness with others" (Ryan & Deci, 2000b, p. 73)
- **Competence**: The need to feel that you can do something successfully

Bouwma-Gearhart (2012) conducted a study about STEM faculty members' motivation to participate in professional learning events, using SDT as a guiding framework. She found that faculty members' desire to strengthen their teaching skills (competence), connect with other faculty around teaching (relatedness), and "become more comfortable with the locus of control granted via the nature of their position" (autonomy) were key drivers in their motivation to participate in professional learning events (Bouwma-Gearhart, 2012, pp. 563–565). Additionally, the author found that faculty who previously attended professional learning events that met their teaching needs were more likely to continue participating in professional learning events thereafter.

Other studies have examined additional factors that influence instructors' participation in and satisfaction with professional learning events. In one study, Burdick et al. (2015) surveyed 238 faculty in the United States to determine which factors had the greatest influence on their decision to attend professional learning events. They found that some of the most significant factors were related to the topic of the session, the value of the session, who was attending it, who was facilitating it, and when it was scheduled. With respect to the first three factors, the authors noted the following:

> Faculty members showed interest in attending if the event resonates with personal interest, personal practices, or with their discipline. More encouragingly, they indicated they would also attend if the topic either advanced the common good on campus or if it addressed a problem the campus has faced for several years. Finally, they would attend if a friend or someone they respect is attending.
>
> *(Burdick et al., 2015, Discussion section)*

With respect to the remaining two factors, the authors found that faculty were most likely to attend if someone they knew or respected was facilitating and if the event fit their schedule (Burdick et al., 2015).

In another study, Muammar and Alkathiri (2022) examined the factors that were most important to faculty in terms of their satisfaction with professional learning programs. They surveyed 2,330 instructors in Saudi Arabia, focusing on three broad areas of satisfaction: "objectives and content," "facilitator and delivery," and "logistics and supporting facilities" (Muammar & Alkathiri, 2022, p. 225). The authors found that the area that had the greatest impact on faculty satisfaction was the "objectives and content" of the program, followed by the "facilitator and delivery" and "logistics and supporting facilities." Broken down further, seven key factors had the greatest impact on faculty satisfaction (Muammar & Alkathiri, 2022, p. 221, 228–230):

- Area 1: Objectives and Content
  - Achievement of the program objectives
  - Appropriateness of the program topics
  - Appropriateness of the program activities
  - Appropriateness of the program objectives
- Area 2: Facilitator and Delivery
  - Academic developers' teaching skills
  - Academic developers' skills in discussion management
- Area 3: Logistics and Supporting Facilities
  - Duration of the program

Overall, Muammar and Alkathiri (2022) found that in terms of program content, faculty wanted to learn about topics, do activities, and focus on goals that were relevant to them. They also wanted to achieve the goals of the program. In terms of facilitation, faculty cared about the facilitator having strong pedagogical and discussion facilitation skills. Finally, in terms of the general logistics of the program, faculty cared that the length fit the purpose of the session.

The core needs of SDT, along with the additional factors identified in these studies, offer valuable insight into the conditions that learners may find fulfilling in a professional learning experience. Below are some practical suggestions for how you can design workshops with these conditions in mind. This is by no means an exhaustive checklist of everything you must do; rather, it is meant to spark ideas and offer multiple options. I have organized these suggestions into four broad categories: workshop topic and content, workshop activities and tasks, facilitation practices, and workshop duration and scheduling.

Workshop Topic and Content

- Select workshop topics that address the work, needs, and goals of learners.
  - Steinert et al. (2016) note that "relevant content" is a key component of effective faculty development programs (p. 777). Furthermore, Cilliers and Tekian (2016) explain that connecting programs to instructors' job duties can support the transfer of learning.
- Be intentional about the naming of the workshop.
  - A former colleague taught me about the importance of naming workshops in a way that clearly conveys their pedagogical value (Noah, 2023). For example, instead of naming a pedagogical workshop, "Introduction to QR Codes," I might call it, "Creating Engaging Student Learning Experiences with QR Codes," as this better conveys the relevance and value of the session. The importance of naming is also reflected in Priya Parker's bestselling book, *The Art of Gathering*. Parker (2018) explains that "to name a gathering affects the way people perceive it. The name signals what the purpose of the event is, and it also prepares people for their role and level of expected participation" (p. 159).

- Design clear, achievable objectives for the workshop. (We will explore this further in Chapter 2.)
- Use examples during the workshop that relate to learners' work (such as the disciplines instructors teach and/or the common situations/scenarios they encounter in their work).
    - One way to learn more about the disciplines of instructors is to request this information when they register for the session. For example, the workshop registration form at my university automatically captures information about the department from which each registrant is coming. As such, I can easily review the registration form so that I can see the specific departments of the instructors and include examples and/or activities in my workshop that pertain to them.
- Reference research and evidence-based practices that are related to the topic of the workshop.
    - This not only grounds the workshop in evidence but also provides participants with resources they can use to deepen their learning after the session. The NLC principle, "Connect with practice," also highlights the importance of "[linking] exploration of theory to practical possibilities" (Bass et al., 2019, p. 33), and Steinert et al. (2016) note that the use of "evidence-informed educational design" is a key feature of effective faculty development offerings (p. 777).
- Relate the topic of the workshop to larger campus issues or goals (as appropriate).
    - When I started my current role, my supervisor encouraged me to review the university's strategic plan so that I could gain a better sense of the institutional priorities and highlight how the programs I was offering supported them. This practice is also in line with the NLC principle, "Connect professional development with strategic priorities," which encourages educational developers to use "strategic models" of professional learning that are "aligned with institutional goals" (Bass et al., 2019, p. 41).

Workshop Activities and Tasks

- Design workshops in ways that offer opportunities for learners to meet their needs for competence, autonomy, and relatedness.
    - Examples of ways to help learners meet these needs include incorporating scaffolded practice activities with feedback to help participants build their sense of competence, providing choices that support autonomy, and incorporating social learning opportunities that foster relatedness. (We will explore additional strategies throughout this book.)
- Create authentic tasks that clearly relate to the work and goals of participants.
    - Have participants do activities during the session that are applicable to and useful in their work (Noah, 2023). For example, during my technology workshops, I have instructors practice using whichever tool we are focusing on to do authentic tasks, such as using Scribe to create a how-to guide for their students or using Clips to record a welcome video for their class (Noah, 2023). This way, instructors are not just learning about the tool for the sake of learning about the tool (and using random practice activities to do so); rather, they are using the tool during the workshop, in authentic ways, to accomplish a larger, relevant teaching goal. (We will explore workshop tasks and activities further in Chapter 6).
- Include opportunities for participants to help shape what occurs during the session.
    - Aguilar and Cohen (2022) note that inviting participants' input is an important way in which facilitators can share power with participants in professional learning settings.
- Provide time for participants to reflect on how they have grown as a result of the professional learning experience and how they will apply what they have learned. (We will explore reflection strategies further in Chapter 7.)

Facilitation Practices

- Use and model effective facilitation strategies as you facilitate the session (Noah, 2023). (We will explore specific techniques further in Chapters 4–9).
- Get "meta" about the strategies you're using by naming what you're doing and why.
  - Encourage participants to consider how they could adopt similar strategies in their own work.
- Invite others to co-facilitate workshops with you.
  - When facilitating a teaching-related workshop, consider partnering with an instructor to co-facilitate the session. By doing so, you can offer multiple perspectives and create a workshop experience that is more aligned with instructors' needs, interests, and priorities because they can *directly* shape the topics and activities for the session. Additionally, other instructors may be more interested in attending if someone they know on a personal level is facilitating. Co-facilitation also taps into the NLC principle, "Respect educators' knowledge," which notes that "effective educational development recognizes the deep expertise of faculty, student affairs educators, and staff" (Bass et al., 2019, p. 32). You might also consider co-facilitating workshops with leaders from other campus offices and programs. This supports the NLC principle, "Break boundaries" (Bass et al., 2019, p. 39).
- Craft a well-designed experience that will add value to learners' work and (hopefully) keep them coming back for more.
  - As Bouwma-Gearhart (2012) notes, it "may be that the best way to secure TPD [teaching professional development] involvement is to get people to one meaningful TPD activity. Once there, the potential to recognize the value of TPD with respect to pedagogical needs is strong" (p. 568).
- Encourage learners to share their feedback about the workshop, and use it to make improvements. (We will explore strategies for being responsive to learners in Chapter 9.)

Workshop Duration and Scheduling

- Schedule workshop topics in alignment with what learners typically need at different times of the academic year.
  - For example, prior to the start of a new semester, instructors typically focus on designing syllabi for their courses and considering how to build connections with their students. Offering workshops that align with topics that are top of mind for instructors during specific times of year is a helpful way to make the workshops feel more relevant.
- Be mindful about how much you are trying to accomplish in any given workshop.
  - Avoid packing too much content or too many activities into a single workshop than can reasonably be achieved (Noah, 2023).
- Offer workshops of various lengths and at different times of day to better meet learners' scheduling needs.
  - This practice ties into the NLC principle, "Protect participant time," which encourages educational developers to consider how they can "equitably and effectively address diverse professional schedules and availabilities" (Bass et al., 2019, p. 35). In my personal work, I typically offer 1-hour workshops. However, I also offer shorter, 30-minute workshops as part of my "Teaching Tips in 30" program, and I offer longer 75-minute, 90-minute, 2-hour, and 3-hour workshops on occasion. Furthermore, whenever I am facilitating virtual workshops, I offer the workshop twice during the day: once in the morning and again in the afternoon. (I often reserve on-site workshops for long sessions or sessions where campus facilities are needed and thus typically facilitate them once per

day.) Offering virtual workshops multiple times during the day provides a convenient way for instructors to join sessions that fit into their dynamic schedules and boosts instructor participation.

Recap

- Invest time in learning about your learners and their context. Using a learner-centered approach will help you to identify potential areas of focus that are relevant to their goals, interests, and/or needs.
- Consider what type of program would best address the selected area of focus. Ask yourself, "Should this be a workshop?"
- Consider how to create conditions in your workshop that learners may find fulfilling.

Sticky Note Reflection

Self-Assessment: List the five relevance topics (learners, context, focus, format, and fulfillment). Draw a checkmark next to the topics you frequently think about when designing professional learning experiences and a star next to the topics you would like to be more intentional about considering in the future.

Workshop Toolkit

Scan the QR code or visit the URL to access additional resources related to this chapter.

www.tolunoah.com/workshop-toolkits

Design Time

Create a Relevance Map. You can access a blank template in the Workshop Toolkit.

Facilitators' Lounge

Join the Facilitators' Lounge to connect with other readers and share your takeaways, strategies, and next steps!

www.tolunoah.com/facilitators-lounge/

Notes

1 A learner persona is "a fictionalized biography of an imagined person with a mix of demographic details… and their anticipated needs, frustrations, or motivations" (Cohn & Greer, 2023, p. 21).
2 According to Cruz et al. (2020), "conducting a needs assessment, which can be formal or informal, is a systematic means of gathering helpful information" to learn about the needs of people in your educational community (p. 27). The authors explain that the process typically entails (a) planning the method(s) that will be used for the needs assessment (e.g., surveys, interviews, focus groups) and determining whose needs will be assessed, (b) implementing the needs assessment and gathering data, (c) analyzing the data, and (d) using the results to determine next steps.

References

Aguilar, E., & Cohen, L. (2022). *The PD book: 7 habits that transform professional development.* Jossey-Bass.

Austin, A.E. (2010). Supporting faculty members across their careers. In K.J. Gillespie, D.L. Robertson, & Associates (Eds.), *A guide to faculty development* (2nd ed., pp. 363–378). Jossey-Bass.

Baker, M.J., Clark, A.T., Garritano, N., Grover, L., Findletar Hines, H., Groller, K.D., Manacek, S., Stec, M., & Zemmer, J. (2020). *Active learning: Near and far.* ADE Community. https://books.apple.com/us/book/active-learning-near-and-far/id1520884249

Bass, R., Eynon, B., & Gambino, L.M. (2019). *The New Learning Compact: A framework for professional learning and educational change.* Every Learner Everywhere. www.everylearnereverywhere.org/resources/the-new-learning-compact/

Boller, S., & Fletcher, L. (2020). *Design thinking for training and development: Creating learning journeys that get results.* ATD Press.

Bouwma-Gearhart, J. (2012). Research university STEM faculty members' motivation to engage in teaching professional development: Building the choir through an appeal to extrinsic motivation and ego. *Journal of Science Education and Technology, 21,* 558–570. https://doi.org/10.1007/s10956-011-9346-8

Burdick, D., Doherty, T., & Schoenfeld, N. (2015). Encouraging faculty attendance at professional development events. *To Improve the Academy, 34*(1–2). http://dx.doi.org/10.3998/tia.17063888.0034.103

CAST. (2024a). *Optimize relevance, value, and authenticity.* https://udlguidelines.cast.org/engagement/interests-identities/relevance-value-authenticity/

CAST. (2024b). *Universal Design for Learning guidelines version 3.0.* https://udlguidelines.cast.org/

Cilliers, F.J., & Tekian, A. (2016). Effective faculty development in an institutional context: Designing for transfer. *Journal of Graduate Medical Education, 8*(2), 145–149. https://doi.org/10.4300%2FJGME-D-15-00117.1

Cohen, M.W. (2010). Listen, learn, lead: Getting started in faculty development. In K.J. Gillespie, D.L. Robertson, & Associates (Eds.), *A guide to faculty development* (2nd ed., pp. 67–81). Jossey-Bass.

Cohn, J., & Greer, M. (2023). *Design for learning: User experience in online teaching and learning.* Rosenfeld Media.

Collins-Brown, E., Haras, C., Hurney, C., Iuzzini, J., Magruder, E., Sorcinelli, M.D., Taylor, S.C., & Wright, M. (2018). *A center for teaching and learning matrix.* American Council on Education & POD Network. https://podnetwork.org/resources/center-for-teaching-and-learning-matrix/

Condon, W., Iverson, E.R., Manduca, C.A., Rutz, C., & Willett, G. (2016). *Faculty development and student learning: Assessing the connections.* Indiana University Press.

Cruz, L., Parker, M.A., Smentkowski, B., & Smitherman, M. (2020). *Taking flight: Making your center for teaching and learning soar.* Routledge.

d.school. (n.d.-a). *An introduction to design thinking: Facilitator's guide.* https://static1.squarespace.com/static/57c6b79629687fde090a0fdd/t/5ccb6a7bec212d9f4f544355/1556834942164/1TheGiftGivingProjectFacilitatorsGuide-English.pdf

d.school. (n.d.-b). *An introduction to design thinking: Process guide.* https://web.stanford.edu/~mshanks/MichaelShanks/files/509554.pdf

Eyler, J.R. (2018). *How humans learn: The science and stories behind effective college teaching.* West Virginia University Press.

Eynon, B., Iuzzini, J., Keith, H.R., Loepp, E., & Weber, N. (2023, January 17). *Teaching, learning, equity and change: Realizing the promise of professional learning.* Every Learner Everywhere. www.everylearnereverywhere.org/resources/teaching-learning-equity-and-change-realizing-the-promise-of-professional-learning/

Felten, P., Little, D., Ortquist-Ahrens, L., & Reder, M. (2013). Program planning, prioritizing, and improvement: A simple heuristic. *To Improve the Academy, 32,* 183–198. http://dx.doi.org/10.3998/tia.17063888.0032.015

Howles, D.L. (2022). *Next level virtual training: Advance your facilitation.* ATD Press.

Katopodis, C. (2024). *10-day syllabus challenge.* https://christinakatopodis.com/syllabus-challenge/

Lee, D. (2018). *Design thinking in the classroom: Easy-to-use teaching tools to foster creativity, encourage innovation, and unleash potential in every student.* Ulysses Press.

Manacek, S., & Pitcher, L. (2020). *Innovations in the simulation lab: Innovative ideas for the healthcare simulation setting using iPads*. Sarah Manacek. https://books.apple.com/us/book/innovations-in-the-simulation-lab/id1493866410

Muammar, O.M., & Alkathiri, M.S. (2022). What really matters to faculty members attending professional development programs in higher education. *International Journal for Academic Development, 27*(3), 221–233. https://doi.org/10.1080/1360144X.2021.1897987

Neal, E., & Peed-Neal, I. (2009). Experiential lessons in the practice of faculty development. *To Improve the Academy, 27*, 14–31. http://dx.doi.org/10.3998/tia.17063888.0027.006

Niemiec, C.P., & Ryan, R.M. (2009). Autonomy, competence, and relatedness in the classroom: Applying self-determination theory to educational practice. *Theory and Research in Education, 7*(2), 133–144. https://doi.org/10.1177/1477878509104318

Noah, T. (2023, March 14). *Designing virtual edtech faculty develop workshops that stick: 10 guiding principles*. EDUCAUSE Review. https://er.educause.edu/articles/2023/3/designing-virtual-edtech-faculty-development-workshops-that-stick-10-guiding-principles

Parker, P. (2018). *The art of gathering: How we meet and why it matters*. Riverhead Books.

Ryan, R.M., & Deci, E.L. (2000a). Intrinsic and extrinsic motivations: Classic definitions and new directions. *Contemporary Educational Psychology, 25*(1), 54–67. https://doi.org/10.1006/ceps.1999.1020

Ryan, R.M., & Deci, E.L. (2000b). Self-determination theory and the facilitation of intrinsic motivation, social development, and well-being. *American Psychologist, 55*(1), 68–78. https://doi.org/10.1037/0003-066X.55.1.68

Seldin, P. (2006). Tailoring faculty development programs to faculty career stages. *To Improve the Academy, 24*, 137–146. http://dx.doi.org/10.3998/tia.17063888.0024.013

Sheffield, J.P., & Moore, D. (2023). Facing wicked problems during a pandemic and beyond: A case study in using design thinking for CTL development and growth. *To Improve the Academy, 42*(1), 166–195. https://journals.publishing.umich.edu/tia/article/id/675/#R5

Steinert, Y., Mann, K., Anderson, B., Barnett, B.M., Centeno, A., Naismith, L., Prideaux, D., Spencer, J., Tullo, E., Viggiano, T., Ward, H., & Dolmans, D. (2016). A systematic review of faculty development initiatives designed to enhance teaching effectiveness: A 10-year update: BEME guide no. 40. *Medical Teacher, 38*(8), 769–786. http://dx.doi.org/10.1080/0142159X.2016.1181851

Wright, M.C., Lohe, D.R., Pinder-Grover, T., & Ortquist-Ahrens, L. (2018). The four Rs: Guiding CTLs with responsiveness, relationships, resources, and research. *To Improve the Academy, 37*(2). http://dx.doi.org/10.3998/tia.17063888.0037.206

Zakrajsek, T. (2016, December 20). Oh, the places your center can go: Possible programs to offer. *Journal on Centers for Teaching and Learning, 8*, 93–109. https://openjournal.lib.miamioh.edu/index.php/jctl/article/view/160

2
PLAN WITH PURPOSE

Guiding Question:
How can you design a purposeful workshop plan?

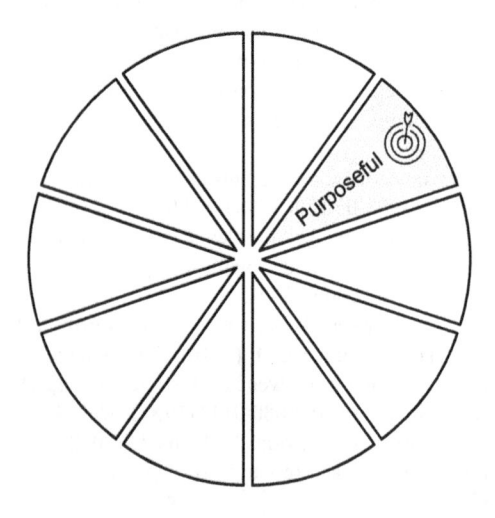

One of the most important questions we should ask when designing any workshop is, "Why?" By starting with "Why?," we maintain our focus on the ultimate purpose of the professional learning experience—our reason for bringing people together in the first place. The importance of purpose is also reflected in the New Learning Compact (NLC) framework, which explains that "all educational development should be framed by a clear sense of purpose that clarifies 'to what end' it is designed and executed" (Bass et al., 2019, p. 28).

In *The Art of Gathering,* Parker (2018) highlights the important role that purpose plays in gatherings. She explains:

> The purpose of your gathering is more than an inspiring concept. It is a tool, a filter that helps you determine all the details, grand and trivial. …Make purpose your bouncer. Let it decide what goes into your gathering and what stays out. When in doubt about any element, even the smallest detail, hark back to that purpose and decide in accordance with it.
>
> *(Parker, 2018, pp. 31–32)*

This quote is of particular importance to the realm of professional learning, where there is a common temptation to include too much or try to do too many different things in our workshops. By becoming clear on our purpose, we can avoid this trap and ensure that everything we include in our workshops is truly aligned with it.

I find it helpful to distinguish between two types of purposes in regard to workshops. The lowercase p purpose focuses on the specific goals or objectives of a particular workshop. The capital P Purpose focuses on the larger, deeper, lasting aims for professional learning. It is the reason behind the reason.

Think of it like an iceberg. On the surface, a workshop may have the lowercase p purpose of helping learners become adept at using a specific pedagogical strategy or tech tool. Below the surface, this may be driven by a capital P Purpose that is shaped by a larger vision, mission, or "dream" (like the one we discussed in the Introduction). For example, the capital P Purpose may be to empower instructors to create more engaging and inclusive learning environments for their students; to foster a sense of community among instructors where they can explore pedagogical possibilities together; or to spark curiosity and promote lifelong learning.

In this chapter, we will focus on the lowercase p purpose for your workshop, exploring how to design a purposeful workshop plan with clear, meaningful goals. We'll begin by reviewing a few educational design frameworks, and then we'll unpack how you can apply those frameworks to your design of a high-level macro plan for your workshop.

Educational Design Frameworks

The frameworks I have found most useful in creating purposeful workshop plans are Wiggins and McTighe's (2005) backward design process and Fink's (2013) taxonomy of significant learning and integrated course design model. Below, I provide a brief overview of each framework. You can visit the resources linked in the Workshop Toolkit at the end of this chapter for more comprehensive information about each framework.

Backward Design

Backward design is a planning approach where you "plan with the end in mind" (McTighe & Wiggins, 2012, p. 7). Instead of starting by thinking about the content you will teach and the activities learners will do, you start by thinking about what you want your learners to know or be able to do by the end of the learning experience and then plan backward from there.

The backward design approach includes three main stages (Wiggins & McTighe, 2005). First, you identify the learning goals (i.e., what learners should know or be able to do). Second, you determine the assessments (i.e., how learners will demonstrate their achievement of or progress toward the learning goals). Last, you plan the activities (i.e., the tasks learners will do, the content they will learn, and the resources they will use to accomplish the learning goals). Planning in this order can help you design learning experiences that are ultimately geared toward learners' understanding (McTighe & Wiggins, 2012). It can also help you to ensure that the learning goals, assessments, and instructional activities are all in alignment with each other (Fink, 2013).

Taxonomy of Significant Learning and Integrated Course Design Model

In his book, *Creating Significant Learning Experiences*, Fink (2013) shares a taxonomy for significant learning that includes six different categories: foundational knowledge, application, integration, human dimension, caring, and learning how to learn (see Figure 2.1). The first category, foundational knowledge, focuses on understanding important facts, concepts, and viewpoints. The second category, application, focuses on developing key skills, including thinking skills such as

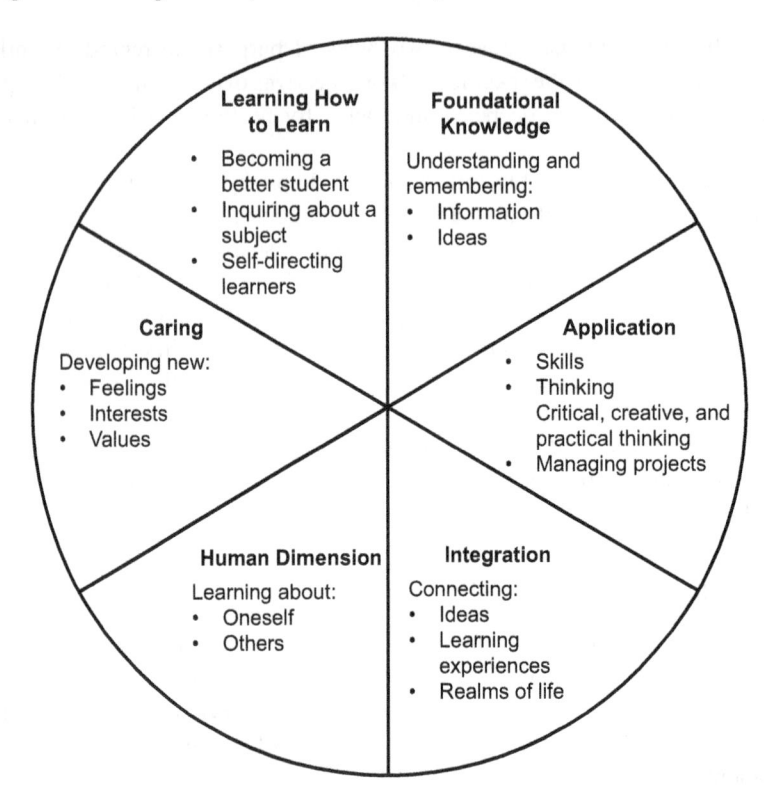

FIGURE 2.1 Fink's Taxonomy of Significant Learning (Used with permission of John Wiley & Sons Books, from *Creating Significant Learning Experiences* by L. Dee Fink., 2nd edition, 2013; Permission conveyed through Copyright Clearance Center, Inc.)

critical and creative thinking. The third category, integration, focuses on connecting what one is learning to other content or areas of life. The fourth category, human dimension, focuses on developing a greater understanding of oneself and others. The fifth category, caring, focuses on developing "new feelings, interests, or values" about the topic (Fink, 2013, p. 36). The final category, learning how to learn, involves strengthening one's awareness of the learning process, such as "how to become a self-directing learner" (Fink, 2013, pp. 36–37). Fink's taxonomy offers a useful framework for developing meaningful course learning goals. When developing these goals, Fink encourages educators to begin by thinking about the long-term impact they want their course to have on students, as this will shape their decisions about the learning goals for each category of the taxonomy (Fink, n.d., 2013).

Along with the taxonomy, Fink (2013) shares a 12-step process for designing courses called "integrated course design" (p. 74). Of particular relevance to this book are the first five steps of the process: "1. Identify important situational factors, 2. Identify important learning goals, 3. Formulate appropriate feedback and assessment procedures, 4. Select effective teaching and learning activities, [and] 5. Make sure the primary components are integrated" (Fink, 2013, p. 74). The first step of this process entails developing a deep understanding of the learners in the course, the context of the course, and other important factors. The next three steps mirror the backward design process, where educators determine the learning goals, assessments, and activities for the course. Finally, the fifth step entails confirming that all of these elements are aligned.

Macro Workshop Plan

Although these frameworks were initially developed to assist educators with unit planning and course design, I have also found them to be invaluable in my design of professional learning experiences. The backward design model has been useful for ensuring that my workshops are designed around a clear purpose. As facilitators, it can be tempting to start the workshop design process by thinking about the content we plan to address or the activities we plan to have participants do. However, starting with the goals of the workshop keeps the focus on the new understandings that learners will hopefully develop as a result of the experience, and it helps ensure that all other aspects of the workshop are intentionally designed with these goals in mind. Likewise, Fink's taxonomy has been helpful for crafting workshop learning goals that extend beyond a focus on knowledge and skills to other important goals (like caring). Additionally, the first five steps of his integrated course design model are useful for ensuring that workshop goals, assessments, and activities are aligned.

We will now turn our attention to how you can use these frameworks to develop a Macro Workshop Plan. Think of this as a high-level outline that captures the big picture of the workshop. The macro plan process begins by revisiting your Relevance Map from Chapter 1. From there, you will outline the circumstances, goals, assessments, and activities of the workshop, ending with an outline of how you will evaluate the impact of the workshop. Figure 2.2 shows the Macro Workshop Plan template, which includes guiding prompts to consider during each step. (There is an editable copy of this template in the Workshop Toolkit at the end of this chapter.)

Next, we will unpack each part of the macro plan process step-by-step. I will also provide examples of how this process can be used to map out a sample workshop.

Relevance

In Chapter 1, we discussed the importance of beginning the planning process with relevance by taking the time to think about five topics: learners, context, focus, format, and fulfillment. When developing the macro plan for your workshop, start by revisiting your Relevance Map, as this will shape your decisions about how to design the workshop in a relevant and meaningful way.

Let's imagine that instructors at your university have expressed interest in learning more about inclusive teaching practices. Based on these findings, you've determined that one program that would be helpful is a workshop about how to design inclusive syllabi. In the Relevance section of the Macro Workshop Plan template, you would jot down any important information from the Relevance Map that would be helpful to keep in mind as you plan the workshop.

In Table 2.1, I provide an example of what this might look like. For simplicity's sake, I have jotted down the focus statement from the Relevance Map, although you may wish to add other key information.

Circumstances

The second step in the macro plan process is to note other factors that will impact the design of the workshop. This includes the number of anticipated learners, the duration of the workshop, the modality of the workshop (e.g., on-site, virtual, other), the experience level the workshop is geared toward (e.g., beginner, intermediate, advanced, all), and where the workshop fits in the larger sequence of professional learning programs offered. This step (along with the previous step of revisiting the Relevance Map) is similar to the first step in Fink's integrated course design

Macro Workshop Plan

Relevance

Revisit your Relevance Map. Note any important factors to keep in mind during the workshop planning process.

Circumstances

- How many learners are you inviting to the workshop?
- What is the duration of the workshop?
- What is the modality of the workshop (on-site, virtual, other)?
- What experience level is the workshop geared toward (beginner, intermediate, advanced, all)?
- Where does this workshop fit in the sequence of other professional learning programs offered? Will this workshop be part of a series?
- What other factors are important to take into consideration?

Goals	Assessments	Activities
What do you hope learners will know or be able to do by the end of the workshop? Consider which types(s) of learning from Fink's taxonomy the learning goals will address. (Select all that apply.) □ Foundational Knowledge □ Application □ Integration □ Human Dimension □ Caring □ Learning How to Learn	How will you assess learners' progress toward the learning goals? In other words, what will learners do to demonstrate their accomplishment of the goals?	• What activities will learners do in order to make progress toward the learning goals? • What content will they need to learn? • Which resources will be useful?

Impact

How will you evaluate the impact of the workshop? Consider which types of evaluation data you will collect and how you will gather that data. (Select all that apply.)

□ Participation Data
□ Satisfaction Data
□ Learning Data
□ Implementation Data
□ Impact Data

FIGURE 2.2 Macro Workshop Plan Template

TABLE 2.1 Relevance Section of Macro Workshop Plan

Relevance
Focus Statement: Instructors at my university are interested in learning more about inclusive teaching practices so that they can help their students feel welcome, supported, and capable of success.

TABLE 2.2 Circumstances Section of the Macro Workshop Plan

Circumstances
• Number of learners: Open • Duration of workshop: 2 hours • Modality: Virtual (Zoom) • Experience level workshop is geared toward: Beginner & Intermediate • Sequence of workshop: This is a singular workshop that will be offered in the weeks prior to the start of the new academic year, when instructors are typically in syllabus-prep mode. A more comprehensive course design institute will be offered the following summer for instructors who are interested in diving deeper into inclusive and equitable course design principles and practices.

process, where educators examine the "situational factors" that will influence their design. See Table 2.2 for an example of what this section might look like for the "Designing Inclusive Syllabi" workshop.

Goals

The third step in the macro plan process is to determine the specific learning goals for the workshop. In other words, what do you hope learners will know or be able to do by the end of the workshop? Fink's taxonomy offers a valuable framework for developing meaningful workshop learning goals that address different kinds of learning. As you craft your workshop goals, remember to use verbs that specify the objectives you hope learners will achieve (Fink, 2013). Arend (2021b) provides a list of verbs for each category of Fink's taxonomy that can be helpful in crafting workshop goals. (A link to this list is available in the Workshop Toolkit for this chapter.)

In Table 2.3, I provide sample learning goals for each category of Fink's taxonomy based on two sample workshops: the "Designing Inclusive Syllabi" workshop and a technology workshop entitled, "Personalizing Learning with iPad Accessibility Tools." These goals merely serve as examples; I'm certain that you could generate additional goals that align with each category of learning.

While I provide examples of goals for all six categories of Fink's taxonomy, in reality, you may not address all categories of learning during a single workshop. For example, a workshop may focus primarily on helping learners build foundational knowledge about a topic. Alternatively, it might address a combination of categories geared toward helping learners care about the topic and unpack the "human dimension" implications of it. Additionally, there may be some goals that you want learners to focus on prior to the workshop, others that you want them to focus on during the workshop, and still others that you want them to work on after the workshop. For example, you might leverage a flipped approach where learners engage with content prior to the workshop in order to build their foundational knowledge so that workshop time can focus on application of the content. The workshop may also be part of a larger series, where each workshop within the series will focus on a specific category of learning goals (or different combinations thereof).

TABLE 2.3 Sample Workshop Goals Based on Fink's Taxonomy

Fink's Taxonomy Category	Sample Pedagogical Workshop Goals: "Designing Inclusive Syllabi"	Sample Technology Workshop Goals: "Personalizing Learning with iPad Accessibility Tools"
Foundational Knowledge	Describe the characteristics of an inclusive syllabus.	Describe the functions of five iPad accessibility tools (Magnifier, AssistiveTouch, Safari Reader, Spoken Content, & Dictation).
Application	Revise your syllabus so that it incorporates more inclusive practices.	Use each accessibility tool to perform relevant tasks.
Integration	Relate inclusive syllabus design to the larger context of equitable course design and teaching practices.	Draw connections between the iPad accessibility tools and the Universal Design for Learning guidelines they support.
Human Dimension	Reflect upon how your personal beliefs, values, assumptions, positionality, goals, and other factors shape the design of your syllabus. Examine how the language, policies, materials, and practices in a syllabus may impact students.	Describe how the accessibility tools support equitable learning experiences for students with disabilities, chronic conditions, and neurodivergence. Identify ways in which the accessibility tools may also be beneficial to others.
Caring	Demonstrate a commitment to using inclusive practices that promote equity, belonging, accessibility, and student success.	Value accessibility as essential to teaching and learning.
Learning How to Learn	Identify resources that can help you continue learning about inclusive syllabus and course design.	Reflect upon the areas in which you need to further develop your knowledge and/or skills related to accessibility tools and practices.

Furthermore, it is important to consider what can reasonably be accomplished within the time available. The duration of your workshop (whether it is 30 minutes, 1 hour, half a day, or a longer series) will impact how much you can do, and you should avoid the temptation to pack as much as possible into the session just for the sake of "coverage." This approach typically results in learners feeling frustrated and overwhelmed rather than confident and equipped (Noah, 2023). Less is more. Focus on depth rather than breadth, giving learners the opportunity to explore concepts, practice skills, connect with others, and explore the implications of the topic at hand in a way that will actually stick. Hershock et al. (2022) explain that they focus on two to three goals in a 90-minute workshop to provide learners with adequate time to engage in active and authentic learning opportunities where they can practice important skills.

Finally, we should recognize the potential limitations of pre-defined learning goals and consider how to create space for learners' goals in the process. Adams et al. (2023) explain:

> Although concrete objectives are helpful in planning…, they can also be limiting. Sometimes the ideal outcomes depend on who the participants are and what they need, which we cannot entirely predict in advance. …we should be open to unexpected learnings emerging from the group.

(p. 45)

TABLE 2.4 Goals Section of the Macro Workshop Plan

Goals	Assessments	Activities
Examine how the language, policies, materials, and practices in a syllabus may impact students.		
Revise your syllabus so that it incorporates more inclusive practices.		

The Universal Design for Learning (UDL) guidelines also highlight the importance of learner-created goals. Guideline 6, "Design options for strategy development," prompts learners to "set meaningful goals (6.1)," and guideline 9, "Design options for emotional capacity," encourages learners to "recognize expectations, beliefs, and motivations (9.1)" (CAST, 2024). Creating space for learners' goals can be a simple yet powerful way to help them make a more personal connection to the workshop topic, which may enhance their overall learning experience.

One way to create space for learners' goals and "unexpected learnings" is by inviting participants to share their own personal goals for participating in the workshop at the start of the session. You can also invite participants to share their goals prior to the workshop via a brief pre-workshop survey so that you can design the session with their goals in mind. Additionally, designing the session in a flexible way (which we will discuss further in Chapter 3) can help you adjust in the moment based on learners' expressed interests and needs.

Let's revisit the Macro Workshop Plan for the "Designing Inclusive Syllabi" workshop. Table 2.4 lists two examples of goals that the workshop will address.

Assessments

The fourth step in the macro plan process is to determine possible assessments that align with the learning goals. Ask yourself, "What will learners do to demonstrate their accomplishment of or progress toward the goals?"

Formative assessments are of particular relevance to the workshop model of professional learning. These types of assessments are "process-oriented and developmental in nature" and aim "to provide feedback that encourages adjustments and corrections" (Barkley, 2010, p. 29). There are many different types of formative assessments you can use, including questions, observations, discussions, knowledge checks, "open-ended" prompts, and authentic tasks (Wiggins & McTighe, 2005, pp. 152–153). Wiggins and McTighe (2005) encourage practitioners to use a variety of assessment methods, with a particular focus on authentic tasks that prompt learners to apply what they have learned in realistic contexts.

Arend (2021a) acknowledges that while people often feel comfortable developing assessments based on the first three categories of Fink's taxonomy, the latter three categories (such as caring) can feel trickier. In her piece, "The Caring Category in Fink's Taxonomy: How Do We Support and Assess Caring?," Arend offers helpful advice, such as using reflection activities that can help learners reflect on shifts in their beliefs and attitudes. (There is a link to her article in this chapter's Workshop Toolkit.)

Let's return to the Macro Workshop Plan for the "Designing Inclusive Syllabi" workshop. Table 2.5 lists sample assessments that align with each goal.

TABLE 2.5 Assessments Section of the Macro Workshop Plan

Goals	Assessments	Activities
Examine how the language, policies, materials, and practices in a syllabus may impact students.	Participants will read and annotate a mock syllabus called "The Worst Syllabus Ever."[a] They will also explain how the content of the syllabus may create barriers for students.	
Revise your syllabus so that it incorporates more inclusive practices.	Participants will self-assess their syllabi and revise it based on the inclusive practices they learned in the workshop. Afterward, participants will share a specific example of a change they made to their syllabus via a Padlet board.	

[a] Syllabus developed by Masland (2020).

Activities

The fifth step in the macro plan process entails brainstorming possible activities. Ask yourself, "What activities, content, and resources will help learners meet the learning goals?"

As you can imagine, there is no shortage of activities you can use in a workshop, and in Chapters 5–7, we will take a deep dive into practical activities that can foster collaboration, promote active learning, and encourage reflection. For now, consider what participants would need to learn and practice doing to make progress toward the learning goals. Additionally, consider which activities would be most relevant, applicable, and valuable to your learners.

Table 2.6 lists possible learning activities based on the "Designing Inclusive Syllabi" workshop.

Impact

The final step in the macro plan process is to consider how you will evaluate the impact of the workshop. Evaluation is important not only for demonstrating the value of a program but also for collecting information that can inform future programming decisions (Collins-Brown et al., 2018; Kirkpatrick & Kirkpatrick, 2016; Zakrajsek, 2018). While workshop surveys are a common evaluation tool, the professional learning literature encourages the use of robust evaluation strategies that capture more than attendance and participant satisfaction data (Collins-Brown et al., 2018; Eynon & Iuzzini, 2020; Eynon et al., 2023; Plank & Kalish, 2010).

One of the most popular evaluation models in the training world is the New World Kirkpatrick Model, which includes four levels of evaluation (Kirkpatrick & Kirkpatrick, 2016). Level one focuses on reactions, evaluating how engaged learners feel, how relevant the program is to their work, and how satisfied they are with the program. Level two focuses on learning, evaluating how well learners achieve the goals of the program. This level focuses on evaluating learners' "knowledge, skills, attitude, confidence, and commitment" (Kirkpatrick & Kirkpatrick, 2016, pp. 15–16). Level three focuses on behavior, evaluating how much or how often learners apply what they have learned to their work. This level of evaluation often includes observing learners' performance and providing ongoing support to help them be successful. Finally, level four focuses on results, evaluating how well the program impacts the achievement of larger organizational goals.

TABLE 2.6 Activities Section of the Macro Workshop Plan

Goals	Assessments	Activities
Examine how the language, policies, materials, and practices in a syllabus may impact students.	Participants will read and annotate a mock syllabus called "The Worst Syllabus Ever."[a] They will also explain how the content of the syllabus may create barriers for students.	**Activity**: In this case, "The Worst Syllabus Ever" will serve as both the assessment and the activity. Through this exercise, participants will learn about noninclusive syllabus practices that can create barriers for students. **Content**: Following "The Worst Syllabus Ever" exercise, participants will listen to personal stories of instructors who realized they needed to be more inclusive in their syllabi. Participants will also learn about how their conceptions of "rigor" may impact their syllabi, and ultimately, students. **Resources**: 1. "The Worst Syllabus Ever" Google Doc 2. Podcast clip 3. Articles about rigor in higher education
Revise your syllabus so that it incorporates more inclusive practices.	Participants will self-assess their syllabi and revise it based on the inclusive practices they learned in the workshop. Afterward, participants will share a specific example of a change they made to their syllabus via a Padlet board.	**Content**: Participants will explore recommendations from the literature about inclusive syllabus practices. **Activities**: Participants will engage in discussions about the inclusive syllabus practices. **Resources**: 1. Sample syllabus snippets that demonstrate the inclusive syllabus practices 2. A handout of inclusive syllabus recommendations

[a] Syllabus developed by Masland (2020).

In his article, "Documenting and Assessing the Work of the CTL," Zakrajsek (2018) offers practical tips for how educational developers can evaluate their work. He shares six different types of data that educational developers can collect, many of which reflect the four levels of the New World Kirkpatrick Model.

- First, educational developers can collect **participation data**, which can include not only how many people registered for and attended an event but also background information about participants, such as their departments and roles (e.g., adjunct professor, associate professor, etc.).
- Second, educational developers can collect **satisfaction data** through surveys that invite learners to share what was helpful about the learning experience, what could be improved, and how they would rate the experience overall. This type of data aligns with level one (reaction) in the New World Kirkpatrick Model.
- Third, educational developers can collect **learning data** by having learners respond to a question such as, "What did you learn in this workshop that you did not know previously?" (Zakrajsek, 2018, p. 65). This type of data aligns with level two (learning) in the New World Kirkpatrick Model. Level two data sources can also include tasks that learners completed during the learning experience (such as knowledge checks, authentic tasks, and other formative assessment activities), along with interviews and focus groups conducted after the experience

(Kirkpatrick & Kirkpatrick, 2016). Additionally, pre- and post-assessments can be sources of learning data (Hershock et al., 2022; Kirkpatrick & Kirkpatrick, 2016).
- Fourth, educational developers can collect **implementation data** by observing instructors teaching after the learning experience or by sending a delayed survey several weeks after the experience that asks about their implementation of what they learned. This type of data aligns with level three (behavior) of the New World Kirkpatrick Model. William Horton suggests that portfolio tasks (where learners submit evidence of how they have applied their learning, accompanied by a reflection) can also serve as another source of level three data (Kirkpatrick & Kirkpatrick, 2016).
- Fifth, educational developers can collect **impact data** that provides insight into how the learning experience has impacted student learning. This may include soliciting student feedback, reviewing course evaluation data, and more. These approaches align with level four (impact) of the New World Kirkpatrick Model. Additional sources for level four data may include the examination of other organizational data and metrics (Kirkpatrick & Kirkpatrick, 2016).
- Finally, Zakrajsek (2018) explains that educational developers can collect **logistical information**, such as instructors' open rates for emails and their interactions with social media posts. (This type of information is most useful for informing the general operations and marketing approach of a center for teaching and learning. As such, we will primarily focus on the first five types of data, which are geared toward program evaluation.)

Kirkpatrick and Kirkpatrick (2016) stress the importance of determining how you will evaluate a program while you are in the initial planning stages rather than waiting until after the program is over. The authors also explain that it is not necessary to evaluate every level for every program, and they recommend focusing full evaluation efforts on "mission critical" programs that align with larger organizational goals (Kirkpatrick & Kirkpatrick, 2016, pp. 21, 149).

As you develop the macro plan for your workshop, consider which type(s) of evaluation data you want to collect and how you will gather that data. Also, don't forget to remain open to unexpected impacts that may happen as a result of the workshop (such as participants developing new relationships with colleagues). Not everything that is impactful and meaningful in a professional learning experience may be captured by evaluation data.

Let's revisit the Macro Workshop Plan for the "Designing Inclusive Syllabi" workshop one more time. Table 2.7 lists possible tools that can be used to evaluate the impact of the workshop.

TABLE 2.7 Impact Section of the Macro Workshop Plan

Impact

- **Participation Data**: I will collect attendance data for the workshop using Zoom's meeting attendance report.
- **Satisfaction Data**: Participants will complete a feedback form at the end of the workshop.
- **Learning Data**: The activities participants complete during the workshop will provide insight into their learning. This includes:
  - The annotations participants add to "The Worst Syllabus Ever" collaborative document and the examples they share about how the syllabus may create barriers for students
  - The comments participants make during the discussions about inclusive syllabus practices
  - The Padlet posts where participants share changes they made to their syllabi

Next Steps

Once you have completed your Macro Workshop Plan, be sure to check for alignment between all of the different elements. Are the workshop goals, assessments, and activities aligned? Do they reflect what you learned during the Relevance Map process? Do they take into account the unique circumstances in which the workshop will be held? Have you determined how you will evaluate the impact of the experience? Additionally, remember that the planning process is often iterative. You may return to your Macro Workshop Plan a few times, tweaking different elements as needed. In the next chapter, we will turn our attention to how you can use your macro plan to develop a micro plan that details the specifics of what will occur during the workshop.

Recap

Plan with purpose by developing a Macro Workshop Plan. Start by revisiting what you learned during the Relevance Map process, and then outline the circumstances, goals, assessments, and activities for the workshop. Finally, determine how you will evaluate the workshop's impact.

Sticky Note Reflection

Compare and Contrast: How does your personal workshop planning process compare and contrast with the macro plan process outlined in this chapter?

Workshop Toolkit

Scan the QR code or visit the URL to access additional resources related to this chapter.

www.tolunoah.com/workshop-toolkits

Design Time

Create a Macro Workshop Plan for an upcoming workshop. You can access a blank template in the Workshop Toolkit.

Facilitators' Lounge

Join the Facilitators' Lounge to connect with other readers and share your takeaways, strategies, and next steps!

www.tolunoah.com/facilitators-lounge/

References

Adams, M., Briggs, R.R., & Shlasko, D. (2023). Pedagogical foundations for social justice education. In M. Adams, L.A. Bell, D.J. Goodman, & D. Shlasko (with R.R. Briggs, & R. Pacheco) (Eds.), *Teaching for diversity and social justice* (4th ed., pp. 27–55). Routledge.

Arend, B. (2021a, March 2). *The caring category in Fink's taxonomy: How do we support and assess caring?* Intentional College Teaching. https://intentionalcollegeteaching.org/2021/03/02/the-caring-category-in-finks-taxonomy-how-do-we-support-and-assess-caring/

Arend, B. (2021b, May 13). *Learning outcome verb list for Fink's taxonomy of significant learning.* Intentional College Teaching. https://intentionalcollegeteaching.org/2021/05/13/learning-outcome-verb-list-for-fink-taxonomy-of-significant-learning/

Barkley, E.F. (2010). *Student engagement techniques: A handbook for college faculty.* Jossey-Bass.

Bass, R., Eynon, B., & Gambino, L.M. (2019). *The New Learning Compact: A framework for professional learning & educational change.* Every Learner Everywhere. www.everylearnereverywhere.org/resources/the-new-learning-compact/

CAST. (2024). *Universal Design for Learning guidelines version 3.0.* https://udlguidelines.cast.org/

Collins-Brown, E., Haras, C., Hurney, C., Iuzzini, J., Magruder, E., Sorcinelli, M.D., Taylor, S.C., & Wright, M. (2018). *A center for teaching and learning matrix.* American Council on Education & POD Network. https://podnetwork.org/resources/center-for-teaching-and-learning-matrix/

Eynon, B., & Iuzzini, J. (2020). *ATD teaching & learning toolkit: A research-based guide to building a culture of teaching & learning excellence.* Achieving the Dream. https://achievingthedream.org/teaching-learning-toolkit/

Eynon, B., Iuzzini, J., Keith, H.R., Loepp, E., & Weber, N. (2023, January 17). *Teaching, learning, equity, and change: Realizing the promise of professional learning.* Every Learner Everywhere. www.everylearnereverywhere.org/resources/teaching-learning-equity-and-change-realizing-the-promise-of-professional-learning/

Fink, L.D. (n.d.). *A self-directed guide to designing courses for significant learning.* https://intentionalcollegeteaching.org/wp-content/uploads/2022/07/GuidetoCourseDesignAug05.pdf

Fink, L.D. (2013). *Creating significant learning experiences: An integrated approach to designing college courses* (2nd ed.). Jossey-Bass.

Hershock, C., Stimson, J., Pottmeyer, L.O., Melville, M.C., Harrell, J., Weiss, E.D., Rodriguez, M., le Blanc, S., & Adams, A. (2022). Thin-sliced embedded direct assessment (T-SEDA): Measuring impacts of development workshops on participants' learning gains. *Journal on Centers for Teaching and Learning, 14,* 58–89. https://openjournal.lib.miamioh.edu/index.php/jctl/article/view/246

Kirkpatrick, J.D., & Kirkpatrick, W.K. (2016). *Kirkpatrick's four levels of training evaluation.* ATD Press.

Masland, L. (2020). *Worst syllabus ever workshop – Syllabus.* https://docs.google.com/document/d/1B0XLubyZ3qI0GVsUQDJY0k1ct4yH5hlR29hGdGKuxjk/edit

McTighe, J., & Wiggins, G. (2012). *Understanding by design framework.* ASCD. https://files.ascd.org/staticfiles/ascd/pdf/siteASCD/publications/UbD_WhitePaper0312.pdf

Noah, T. (2023, March 14). *Designing virtual edtech faculty develop workshops that stick: 10 guiding principles.* EDUCAUSE Review. https://er.educause.edu/articles/2023/3/designing-virtual-edtech-faculty-development-workshops-that-stick-10-guiding-principles

Parker, P. (2018). *The art of gathering: How we meet and why it matters.* Riverhead Books.

Plank, K.M., & Kalish, A. (2010). Program assessment for faculty development. In K.J. Gillespie, D.L. Robertson, & Associates (Eds.), *A guide to faculty development* (2nd ed., pp. 135–149). Jossey-Bass.

Wiggins, G., & McTighe, J. (2005). *Understanding by design* (2nd ed.). ASCD.

Zakrajsek, T. (2018). Documenting and assessing the work of the CTL. *Journal on Centers for Teaching and Learning, 10,* 59–71. https://openjournal.lib.miamioh.edu/index.php/jctl/article/view/198

3
DESIGN A WELL-STRUCTURED EXPERIENCE

Guiding Question:
How can you structure the workshop to support participants' learning?

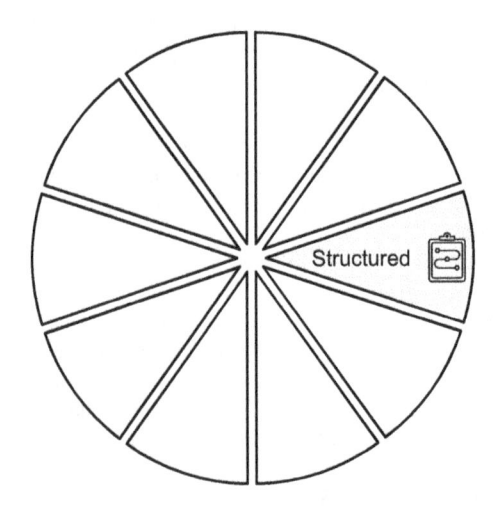

In Chapter 2, we discussed the importance of workshops having a clear purpose, and we explored how to use Wiggins and McTighe's (2005) backward design process along with Fink's (2013) taxonomy of significant learning and integrated course design model to craft a high-level macro plan for a workshop. In this chapter, we will turn that macro plan into a micro plan that fleshes out the details of what will occur during the workshop.

Structure is core to the development of an effective micro plan. That is, we want to intentionally design the workshop to help learners make progress toward the learning goals and ensure that the valuable time we have with them is well spent. In fact, the New Learning Compact (NLC) principle, "Protect participant time," echoes this same sentiment, noting that "educational development activities should be well-structured and designed, making efficient use of participant time" (Bass et al., 2019, p. 35).

In this chapter, we will explore different ways to design a well-structured workshop. We'll begin by examining my personal workshop structure, followed by additional structures that can be useful. Finally, we'll examine the important roles that timing, materials, and technology play in designing a well-structured learning experience.

Tolu's Typical Workshop Structure

Over the years, I have developed a structure for my professional learning workshops, whether I'm facilitating on-site or virtually (see Table 3.1). A Micro Workshop Plan template based on this

TABLE 3.1 Tolu's Typical Workshop Structure

Beginning of Workshop	*Middle of Workshop* (Based on Marzano's, 2009, "Five Avenues to Understanding")	*End of Workshop*
Unofficial start	Chunked & scaffolded content	Recap
Welcome	Opportunities for participants to interact with the content & each other throughout	Reflection
Opening activity	Well-paced activities	Resources
Roadmap	Frequent check-ins (monitoring)	Reminders
		Reactions
		Recognition

structure is shown in Figure 3.1, and an editable copy of this template is in this chapter's Workshop Toolkit.

My personal workshop structure is organized into three parts: beginning, middle, and end. Next, I will provide an example of each part of the workshop planning template based on the "Designing Inclusive Syllabi" workshop we developed a macro plan for in Chapter 2.

Beginning of Workshop

The beginning of the workshop is where I focus on setting a warm and welcoming tone, engaging learners from the start, and clarifying the aims of the session. This part of the workshop typically incorporates four main components: an unofficial start, a welcome, an opening activity, and a roadmap.

Unofficial Start

One facilitation technique that I use prior to the official start of the workshop is having an activity for participants to do as they wait for the session to begin (Douglas & McKenzie, 2016; Hughes, 2023). Mark Collard refers to this as an "unofficial start" (Littlefield & Wise, 2021; Playmeo, n.d., 2024). An unofficial start is "any strategy that facilitates early engagement & interaction and amplifies the purpose & productivity of your group and/or program" (Playmeo, n.d., 2024). It makes the most of the wait time prior to a gathering, engaging participants from the moment they enter the learning space.

Unofficial starts work well in both on-site and virtual workshops. In an on-site workshop, for example, you might invite participants to create a name tent, write a response to a prompt or question that is hung on a sheet of chart paper in the room, or select a photo or quote card to reflect on or discuss with a neighbor (Douglas & McKenzie, 2016; Hughes, 2023). In virtual workshops, I typically invite participants to respond to a workshop-related prompt in the chat. I have also attended virtual sessions where the facilitator invited us to use the Zoom annotation tools to complete a workshop-related word search or word scramble on the screen. Simple, low-stakes activities like these can help participants "transition" to the workshop space (Hughes, 2023, p. 101). (You can learn more about the unofficial start technique and explore sample activities via the links in this chapter's Workshop Toolkit.)

Welcome

Once it's the official start time, I formally welcome all participants to the workshop and express gratitude for their presence.

Micro Workshop Plan

Background Information	
Workshop Title	
Date	
Time	
Location	
Learning Goals/Objectives	

Beginning of Workshop		
Plan	Duration	Materials & Technology Needed
☐ Unofficial start ☐ Welcome ☐ Opening activity ☐ Roadmap		

Middle of Workshop		
Plan	Duration	Materials & Technology Needed
☐ Content & activity chunks designed with Marzano's "Five Avenues" in mind (chunking, scaffolding, interacting, pacing & monitoring) ☐ Break(s)		

End of Workshop		
Plan	Duration	Materials & Technology Needed
☐ Closing activities designed with the 6Rs in mind (recap, reflection, resources, reminders, reactions, & recognition)		

FIGURE 3.1 Micro Workshop Plan Template

Opening Activity

After welcoming learners, I facilitate an opening activity that relates to the topic of the workshop. Oftentimes, this is an activity that activates participants' prior knowledge of the workshop topic or invites them to share their feelings and attitudes about the topic. For example, participants might complete a poll, brainstorm, turn-and-talk, chat discussion, Padlet post, or other activity. My goal is to convey that this will be a participatory session where participants' thoughts and experiences are welcomed and valued.

Starting workshops in an engaging way is key. Parker (2018) explains that "attention is at its highest at the outset" of a gathering (p. 173). Additionally, people tend to remember how an experience began and ended most (Bowman, 2009; Parker, 2018). Thus, instead of starting an experience with logistics (such as the agenda, goals, norms, and announcements), it's ideal to open the session in an interesting way, and save the logistics for afterward (Bowman, 2009; Hughes, 2023; Parker, 2018).

Roadmap

After the opening activity, I share a roadmap that outlines the agenda and learning goals for the workshop (Noah, 2023a). This way, participants know why we are gathering and what to expect. Within the realm of teaching, conveying learning goals can help students understand the aims of the learning experience and assess their progress (Lovett et al., 2023). The same is true in the context of professional learning workshops.

The Universal Design for Learning (UDL) guidelines also support the sharing of the agenda and goals. Guideline 8, "Design options for sustaining effort & persistence," prompts practitioners to "clarify the meaning and purpose of goals (8.1)" (CAST, 2024b). Furthermore, guideline 7, "Design options for welcoming interests & identities," prompts practitioners to "address biases, threats, and distractions (7.4)," and one suggested strategy for doing so is sharing the schedule so that learners know what to expect (CAST, 2024a). By explicitly sharing the agenda and goals during the beginning of the workshop, we can ensure that the session has a clear, communicated purpose and that learners can anticipate what will occur during the session.

Micro Workshop Plan Update

Let's begin completing the Micro Workshop Plan template for the "Designing Inclusive Syllabi" workshop. Tables 3.2 and 3.3 show the background information and beginning of workshop sections of the template.

Middle of Workshop

The middle of the workshop is where we dive deeper into the topic of the session. A key framework that shapes this part of the workshop is Marzano's (2009) "Five Avenues to Understanding." The first avenue, chunking, is about teaching content in small portions with pausing points throughout. The second avenue, scaffolding, is about organizing content so that each chunk builds upon the previous one. The third avenue, interacting, involves providing learners with opportunities to engage with each other and process each chunk. The fourth avenue, pacing, involves teaching each chunk at a proper rate. The final avenue, monitoring, involves assessing learners' understanding during each chunk.

54 Designing and Facilitating Workshops with Intentionality

TABLE 3.2 Background Information Section

Workshop Title	Designing Inclusive Syllabi
Date	Tuesday of the second week in August
Time	This 2-hour workshop will be offered twice. • Morning Session: 9:00-11:00 a.m. • Afternoon Session: 1:00-3:00 p.m.
Location	Zoom (Virtual)
Learning Goals/Objectives	• Examine how the language, policies, materials, and practices in a syllabus may impact students. • Revise your syllabus so that it incorporates more inclusive practices.

TABLE 3.3 Beginning of Workshop Section

Plan	Duration	Materials & Technology Needed
Unofficial Start: • Prior to the official start of the workshop as participants are joining the Zoom room, they will be greeted by a welcome slide with this message: "Welcome to this session! I'm glad you're here. In the chat, please share your name, department, and a thought that completes this sentence: A good syllabus includes ____." This message will also be posted regularly in the chat.	-10 min.	Welcome slide with background music Welcome message to post in the chat Zoom chat
Welcome: • Once we hit the official start time, I will formally welcome all participants to the workshop.	1 min.	
Opening Activity/Warm Up: • Participants will complete a multiple choice Mentimeter poll in response to this question: "Which metaphor best captures what you think the role of a syllabus is? A) Contract, B) Roadmap, C) FAQ, D) Invitation, or E) Other (share in the chat)" • After reviewing the poll results, a few volunteers will be invited to elaborate on why they selected their metaphor. • I will wrap up the activity by explaining that the way we conceptualize our syllabi will influence the way we craft them.	5 min.	Mentimeter poll
Roadmap: • I will review the workshop agenda and learning objectives. • Participants will be invited to share their personal goals for attending the workshop in the chat.	3 min.	Agenda & Objectives slides

Although Marzano's (2009) article was written for teachers, I have also found his framework valuable in the design of professional learning workshops. When designing workshops, I ensure that I chunk and scaffold the content, provide numerous opportunities for participants to interact throughout, carefully pace each activity, and check in with learners along the way to ensure that they are making progress toward the learning goals. Figure 3.2 provides a visual overview of how I incorporate Marzano's "Five Avenues" into the middle portion of my workshops.

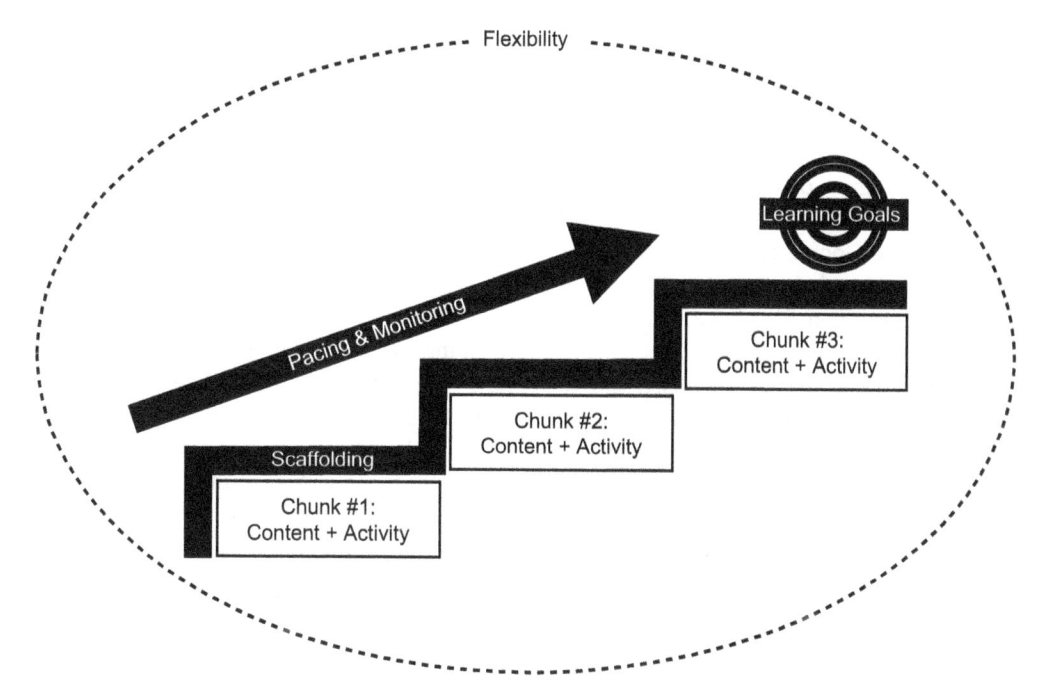

FIGURE 3.2 Tolu's "Marzano in the Middle" Workshop Structure (Based on Marzano, 2009)

Chunking, Scaffolding, and Interacting

I break up the middle of the workshop into multiple chunks that include manageable amounts of content along with interactive activities. The content portion of each chunk may involve direct instruction (where I briefly explain a concept or model a skill), or it may involve participants using media to learn about the content (such as reading an article, watching a video, or listening to a podcast clip). During the activity portion of each chunk, participants have the opportunity to interact with the content and/or with each other. This may involve participants doing a practice activity, engaging in discussions, completing a reflective exercise, doing a collaborative task, or engaging in other active learning activities. The chunks are scaffolded so that each one builds upon the previous one, helping learners progressively deepen their understanding of the topic or develop their skill set. This structure is also designed with self-determination theory in mind, helping learners build competence as they engage with increasingly complex concepts or skills, exercise autonomy through choosing what they do and how they do it, and foster relatedness as they engage with each other.

It is important to note that the order of the content and activities within each chunk can vary. For example, when I'm facilitating technology workshops where the goal is to help learners build competence in using a particular tool, I often do a sequence of content-activity-content-activity-content-activity where I model a small set of skills and then give learners time to try it on their own. Sometimes, I will blend the content and activity portions, having learners do tasks right along with me. In other workshops, I might flip the sequence, with learners doing an activity before I explain the content. This can be a great way to spark curiosity, promote inquiry and exploration, and help surface key ideas and themes in a more learner-directed way.

Pacing and Monitoring

Throughout the middle of the workshop, I monitor participants' understanding and adjust the pacing of the session accordingly. For example, when facilitating on-site workshops, I walk around the room from time to time, asking questions, listening to discussions, observing work, and checking participants' progress on tasks. During virtual workshops, I monitor understanding in various ways, including conducting polling activities (like Mentimeter polls), viewing participants' collaborative online work (in Google Docs, Google Slides, or Padlet), reading participants' comments in the chat, and watching their Zoom reactions. For example, I might ask participants to send reactions to let me know when they have completed an activity and are ready to move on, and I invite participants to ask questions and share their thoughts in the chat or by unmuting.

As I monitor participants, I am checking to see how well they are understanding the content, if there are any areas of misunderstanding that need to be addressed, what is resonating with them or challenging their thinking, and if we need to speed up, slow down, or revisit anything. I also aim to balance checking in with participants with giving them space to work. For example, during on-site workshops, I do not walk around the room the entire time. Rather, I choose strategic points to check in (such as at the beginning of an activity to ensure that everyone is off to a good start, during the middle of the activity to see how they are progressing, and at the end of the activity to prepare them to transition back to the whole group).

Flexibility

Finally, as I design the middle of the workshop, I keep a flexible mindset, knowing that there may be things I need to tweak or toss during the live session. Bell and Goodman (2023) explain that "the flexibility to make needed design adjustments based on what is happening in the moment is an essential skill" (p. 70). For example, based on participants' needs and interests, I might need to spend more time on a particular chunk, hop back a chunk, jump ahead a chunk, or omit a chunk altogether. I might also need to adjust the timing, frequency, or placement of breaks. Developing a solid plan while remaining open to change is critical, and I find it helpful to have an idea of what I can adjust in the moment if needed.

Micro Workshop Plan Update

Let's revisit the Micro Workshop Plan template and complete the middle of the workshop section for the "Designing Inclusive Syllabi" workshop (see Table 3.4). Note that this section of the plan is divided into three main chunks:

- Chunk 1: "The Worst Syllabus Ever" (This chunk addresses common issues/challenges with syllabi and how they can impact students.)
- Chunk 2: Inclusive Syllabus Features (This chunk offers recommendations from the literature about how to design more inclusive syllabi.)
- Chunk 3: Syllabus Tune Up (This chunk gives participants the chance to apply their learning by revising their own syllabi.)

End of Workshop

At the end of each workshop, I typically include my six Rs: recap, reflection, resources, reminders, reactions, and recognition. I previously wrote about this in an *EDUCAUSE Review* article entitled

TABLE 3.4 Middle of Workshop Section

Plan	Duration	Materials & Technology Needed
Chunk 1: "The Worst Syllabus Ever" • Activity (12 min.): Participants will complete a breakout room activity where each group will be assigned a different page of "The Worst Syllabus Ever." [a] Participants will spend the first few minutes silently reading and annotating the page using the commenting tool in Google Docs. Afterward, they will discuss the page as a group, noting content that may create barriers for students and interfere with the goal of fostering inclusivity. (There will also be a non-breakout room option for participants who prefer to engage with the document independently in the main room.) • Activity (12 min.): Participants will return to the main room, and a representative from each group will do a 1-minute share about their assigned page of the syllabus. Afterward, we will debrief the overarching themes of the syllabus. • Content (5 min.): I will share a bit about my personal journey with inclusive syllabus design, noting mistakes I made in the past and how I learned to do better. Afterward, participants will listen to a podcast clip [b] where guest, Cate Denial, shares an experience that challenged her to incorporate more kindness into her syllabus. I will share a link to the podcast transcript in the chat. • Content (3 min.): I will explain that a common factor that impacts syllabus design is instructors' conceptions of "rigor," and I will share Kevin Gannon's distinction between logistical and cognitive rigor. [c] • Activity (3 min.): Participants will reflect on the following question and post their anonymous responses in Padlet: "What is one thing you've learned so far that is resonating with you, challenging you, or stretching your thinking?"	35 min.	"The Worst Syllabus Ever" Google Doc (in "commenter" mode) Slides showing each page of "The Worst Syllabus Ever" along with a 1-minute countdown timer Personal Journey slide Cate's Journey slide with podcast clip & link to transcript Slides about rigor Padlet board
Break	5 min.	Break slide with countdown timer & background music

Chunk 2: Inclusive Syllabus Features
• Content (12 min.): I will share recommendations from the literature for designing a more inclusive syllabus. These recommendations will address three focus areas:
  • Tone & Language
  • Course Materials & Content
  • Assignments & Scheduling
• Activity (6 min.): Participants will engage in a hashtag discussion [d] about the three focus areas by sharing a #thought, #question, #epiphany, [e] or #example from their own syllabus in the chat. They will start their response with the appropriate hashtag so that it's clear which topic they're addressing. Participants will also have the option to share their response by unmuting.
	36 min.	Slides about the six inclusive syllabus focus areas
		
		Hashtag discussion slides
		
		Zoom chat
		
		Inclusive Syllabus handout

(Continued)

TABLE 3.4 (Continued)

Plan	Duration	Materials & Technology Needed

• Content (12 min.): I will share additional recommendations for designing a more inclusive syllabus. These recommendations will address three focus areas:
  • Grading Scheme
  • UDL & Accessibility
  • Policies & Statements
• Activity (6 min.): Participants will engage in another hashtag discussion about the final three focus areas. Afterward, they will receive a digital handout of all the recommendations.		

Break	5 min.	Break slide with countdown timer & background music

Chunk 3: Syllabus Tune Up
• Activity (22 min.): Participants will begin reviewing and revising their syllabus to make it more inclusive. They will choose their workspace via the self-select breakout rooms feature. [f]
  • Main Room: Ask me questions.
  • Breakout Rooms 1–4: Discuss ideas with colleagues.
  • Breakout Room 5: Work silently.
• Activity (3 min.): Participants will add a post to a Padlet board describing a change they made to their syllabus and identifying which of the six inclusive syllabus focus areas the change aligns with. Participants may describe the change they made via text, audio, video, images, and/or other media.
	25 min.	Syllabus Tune Up slide with the workspace options listed and a countdown timer
		
		Padlet board

[a] Syllabus developed by Masland (2020).
[b] Podcast episode from Mason (2024).
[c] Content from Gannon (2023).
[d] Hashtag discussion strategy inspired by Kelly (2024).
[e] Strategy adapted from Thompson's (n.d.) TQE (Thoughts, Questions, Epiphanies) method.
[f] Breakout room format inspired by Western (2020).

"Designing Virtual Edtech Faculty Development Workshops That Stick: 10 Guiding Principles" (Noah, 2023a). This article is also linked in this chapter's Workshop Toolkit. Below, I provide a brief summary of each "R."

Recap

During the summer of 2018, I had the incredible opportunity to co-facilitate a series of faculty workshops in three different states with Tasha Souza. One helpful strategy I learned from her is to recap the learning goals at the end of the workshop. This way, participants are reminded of the aims of the session, and they can self-assess to see if they have made progress toward those goals. The recap also provides a good lead-in to reflection or action planning activities. Since co-facilitating with Tasha, I have continued the practice of recapping the learning goals at the end of each workshop. If the workshop also included time at the start of the session for participants to set their own learning goals, I invite them to revisit those goals at the end, too.

Reflection

After recapping the workshop goals, I facilitate a brief reflection activity (Noah, 2023a). For example, I might invite learners to share their takeaways, remaining questions, and/or next steps via a Mentimeter poll or via a physical or digital exit ticket. (We will take a deep dive into reflection and action planning activities you can use in your workshops in Chapter 7.)

Resources

Following the reflection activity, I give learners access to a curated collection of resources they can use to review and continue their learning after the session (Noah, 2023a). (We will explore concrete resources and strategies you can use to encourage ongoing learning in Chapter 8.)

Reminders

After providing learners with resources, I share reminders about upcoming programs I'll be facilitating and how learners can receive one-on-one support (Noah, 2023a). For example, I offer pedagogical consultations where I can meet with instructors individually to discuss their specific questions and areas of interest. (We will discuss pedagogical consultations further in Chapter 8.)

Reactions

At the end of every workshop, I provide a way for learners to share their reactions to the experience, as their feedback is critical to improving and strengthening the workshop for future learners. Typically, I collect participant feedback through an online tool, such as a Qualtrics or Google Forms survey (Noah, 2023a). In designing the feedback survey, I keep Kirkpatrick and Kirkpatrick's (2016) evaluation model and Zakrajsek's (2018) outline of the different types of evaluation data (discussed in Chapter 2) in mind, including questions that go beyond evaluating satisfaction. For example, one of the open-ended feedback survey prompts that Tasha and I used during our co-facilitation experience was, "What changes, if any, do you plan to make in your instructional practices and/or work with students?" I have included this question (or some version thereof) in all of my feedback surveys since, as a way to capture data about participants' planned implementation of the ideas and skills learned during the workshop. If you are interested in taking a deeper dive into feedback survey design, *Kirkpatrick's Four Levels of Training Evaluation* offers a variety of sample survey tools, many of which include Likert scale questions and open-ended prompts that can easily be used or adapted for workshop feedback surveys.

Recognition

I end every workshop with recognition, thanking participants for their time and their contributions to the session (Noah, 2023a). I know that by choosing to say yes to this workshop, learners had to say no to something else, and I want them to know that I deeply appreciate their presence and engagement. Oftentimes, I highlight things I learned from participants during the learning experience and express my joy in partnering with them. I also reiterate my sincere hope that they will reach out should they wish to keep the conversation going.

TABLE 3.5 End of Workshop Section

Plan	Duration	Materials & Technology Needed
Closing Activities/Cool Down	5 min.	Objectives slide
• **Recap**: I will review the workshop learning goals and encourage participants to revisit their personal goals.		Slide with quote
• **Reflection**: I will share a powerful quote from the book, *A Pedagogy of Kindness*,[a] about the important role of the syllabus. Afterward, participants will complete an open-ended Mentimeter poll where they will share one commitment they will make moving forward.		Mentimeter poll Workshop Wakelet page
• **Resources**: I will share a link to the workshop resources Wakelet page.		Upcoming Programs & Pedagogical Consultations slides
• **Reminders**: I will remind participants of upcoming programs I'll be facilitating and invite them to schedule a pedagogical consultation with me.		Feedback form
• **Reactions**: I will share a link to a short feedback form.		
• **Recognition**: I will thank participants for their presence and engagement.		

Note:
[a] Book by Denial (2024).

Micro Workshop Plan Update

Let's revisit the Micro Workshop Plan template for the "Designing Inclusive Syllabi" workshop one last time and complete the end of workshop section (see Table 3.5).

Additional Workshop Structures

While my personal workshop structure is one way to organize a professional learning workshop, it is not the only option. There are *endless* ways to structure a workshop based on your unique goals, personal preferences, participants' needs/interests, and other factors. Below, I highlight several workshop structures that can be helpful. Additional resources about these structures are included in the Workshop Toolkit at the end of this chapter.

The 4A Learning Sequence

Global Learning Partners (2023) created a useful and memorable workshop structure called the 4A Learning Sequence (see Figure 3.3). This structure involves four steps (Global Learning Partners, n.d., 2023):

1. **Anchor**: Participants do an activity that helps them surface what they know about the topic.
2. **Add**: Participants learn new information about the topic.
3. **Apply**: Participants apply the new information they learned through practice activities or other tasks.
4. **Away**: Participants develop a commitment or plan for how they will use what they learned during the session in the future.

ANCHOR

A task that has the learner access their own prior knowledge or experience with the topic / content / or similar experience (e.g., "Describe your best learning experience of...")

ADD

A task that has the learner hear / see / experience a substantive new piece of content: information, research, theory, skill (e.g., this can be with PowerPoint, film clip, demonstration, etc.)

APPLY

A task that has the learner do something (there and then) with the new content (e.g., practice, application, case studies, compare, etc.)

AWAY

A task that connects the new learning back to the life of the learner and its future use (e.g., a personal action plan, commitment, projection into future, etc.)

FIGURE 3.3   The 4A Learning Sequence (Used with permission from Global Learning Partners, 2023, www.globallearningpartners.com)

The 4A Learning Sequence can be a helpful and versatile structure for designing workshops in a way that actively engages participants throughout the session. Another similar model is Bowman's (2009) 4 Cs (Connections, Concepts, Concrete Practice, and Conclusions), which you can learn more about in her book, *Training from the BACK of the Room!*

Connect, Instruct, Apply (CIA)

In his book, *PRESENTING*, Eng (2019) shares a three-part structure called CIA. This stands for:

1. **Connect**: Start with a "hook" that draws learners in and helps them connect with the topic. This can be a "provocative question, anecdote, striking statistic or fact, analogy, scenario/problem, [or] quotation or aphorism" (Eng, 2019, p. 45).
2. **Instruct**: Explain the key concepts about the topic, being sure to include relevant examples along the way.
3. **Apply**: Provide a way for learners to apply what they have learned.

Eng notes that during each step of the CIA process, it's important to actively involve all learners through activities such as discussions, writing tasks, and polling exercises.

Sparkshops

The Sparkshop model was developed by staff at Boise State University's Center for Teaching and Learning (Boise State University, 2018). Sparkshops are "mini workshops...facilitated in department meetings with the purpose of 'spark'ing interest in a topic" (Focarile et al., 2024, p. 19). Two key characteristics of Sparkshops are that they are brief (approximately 15–20 minutes in length) and that they are conducted during department meetings (meaning that educational developers go to department meetings to facilitate workshops rather than having faculty come to them) (Focarile et al., 2024; Frary & Focarile, 2018).

Each Sparkshop focuses on a specific teaching-related topic, and the session typically follows this process (Focarile et al., 2024):

1. The facilitator provides some data related to the topic, and faculty share their observations.
2. The facilitator describes a specific teaching strategy related to the topic and how it benefits students.
3. Faculty engage in a practice activity using the approach.
4. Faculty reflect on how they might apply the strategy to their teaching.
5. The facilitator concludes the session by providing faculty with a handout about the workshop topic and sharing how faculty can follow up with the CTL to learn more.

The Sparkshop model is also growing in popularity among CTLs at other universities. You can learn more about the model and the various ways universities are implementing it via the links in this chapter's Workshop Toolkit.

What? So What? Now What?

In *Teaching for Diversity and Social Justice*, Bell and Goodman (2023) offer the "What? So What? Now What?" format as one helpful approach to structuring learning experiences about social justice topics. The "What?" portion of the session helps participants develop "knowledge and awareness" about the topic (Bell & Goodman, 2023, p. 70). The "So What?" portion of the session addresses why the content matters. Finally, the "Now What?" portion of the session prompts participants to consider how they will apply what they learned.

Inform-Create-Evaluate (ICE)

Hokanson et al. (2019) developed the inform-create-evaluate (ICE) model to structure synchronous online workshops and mini workshop series for graduate students and postdocs about relevant topics (such as how to craft a teaching philosophy statement). The ICE model has three main components (Hokanson et al., 2019):

1. **Inform**: Prior to the live workshop, participants engage in asynchronous pre-workshop activities that prime them for the experience and help them develop their background knowledge about the topic. The beginning of the live workshop also includes a brief overview of important information related to the workshop topic.
2. **Create**: During the live workshop, participants engage in activities and create products related to the topic of the session (such as crafting the first draft of a teaching statement). These activities aim to help participants apply what they are learning about the workshop topic in a concrete way.
3. **Evaluate**: During the live session, participants engage in peer review and receive feedback about their work. They also reflect on their learning.

The ICE model offers a helpful structure for virtual workshops that are skills-based. It maximizes the benefits of asynchronous and synchronous learning, using the pre-workshop time to frontload content about the topic so that the live workshop time can be devoted to "creation, interaction, feedback, and reflection" (Hokanson et al., 2019, p. 388). In essence, this model leverages the power of a flipped approach to workshop design. The ICE model also helps participants apply their learning and develop relevant products that they can continue to iterate afterward.

Soiree Style

Another workshop format that leverages the benefits of synchronous and asynchronous learning is the soiree style, which was developed by professional development leaders at Michigan State University (Tetu et al., 2024). This format can be used for on-site and virtual workshops, and it involves three parts. First, participants engage in a synchronous meeting. Then, they break for independent work time. Finally, participants reconvene in small groups to share their progress. Tetu et al. (2024) note that "a soiree-style workshop may take place over a matter of hours or days, depending on the amount of time needed to complete the individual asynchronous work" (p. 39).

Cafeteria Learning

In their book, *Let Them Choose*, Douglas and McKenzie (2016) share a workshop model called "Cafeteria Learning," which emphasizes participant choice. In these workshops, participants learn about the same content; however, they're given the freedom to choose how they do so. Cafeteria Learning workshops include the following parts (Douglas, 2018; Douglas & McKenzie, 2016):

1. **Primer**: An activity that sparks participants' thinking about the workshop topic as they wait for the session to begin
2. **Foundational Content**: A mini lesson where the facilitator briefly introduces any essential background information participants need to know about the topic
3. **Activities**: Station activities where participants spend the bulk of the workshop completing self-paced tasks of their choice in order to construct their knowledge of the workshop topic
4. **Debrief**: A closing activity where participants debrief what they learned and how they might apply their learning to their work

The Cafeteria Learning model offers a unique approach to structuring workshops in a way that prioritizes "active, social, and experiential learning that focuses on choice" (Douglas & McKenzie, p. 2). It also shifts the role of the workshop facilitator in important ways. As Douglas and McKenzie (2016) explain, "Cafeteria Learning relies on facilitation, not presentation. As a facilitator, your role is to be a guide during the experience, helping learners to learn from the provided content, one another, and their experiences" (pp. 78–79).

Create Your Own Structure

As mentioned earlier, there is no one "right" way to structure a professional learning workshop. You might decide to follow one of the structures outlined in this chapter, piece together elements of different structures, or create an entirely new structure that better suits your needs. When developing a new workshop structure, be sure to keep the learning goals at the forefront and consider how you can provide learners with active learning opportunities.

It is also important to note that the structures used may vary depending on the purpose and scope of the workshop. For example, in Spring 2024, I designed and facilitated a six-part virtual professional learning series for instructors and staff at my university called the AI "No Prep" Book Club. This series focused on the book, *ChaptGPT Assignments to Use in Your Classroom Today* by

Yee et al. (2023), and it blended elements of a traditional workshop with a book club discussion. Because my purpose for the series was to provide a space where instructors and staff could build a sense of community while engaging in inquiry and self-directed exploration of artificial intelligence tools (such as ChatGPT and Microsoft Copilot), I designed a new structure for this series. Each session in the series focused on a particular section of the book (such as writing assignments), and we followed a four-part structure that I called the Four Ts:

1. **Touch Base**: Participants did a warm-up activity related to the topic of the session.
2. **Tinker Time**: Participants had independent work time, where they chose assignments from the book to read about and try in an AI tool of their choice. (Shout out to Anna Haney-Withrow and Heather Olson for the "Tinker Time" phrase. While they used that phrase for a different professional learning program they developed, I found it to be a perfect fit for this series.)
3. **Talk**: We engaged in a whole-group discussion of the reading and what we discovered during our independent exploration time.
4. **Transition**: We wrapped up the session with a reflection activity, and I shared an AI-related resource each week, provided reminders for future sessions, and obtained feedback from participants.

So get creative with your workshop structure! Think about what you want participants to learn and consider how to design the learning experience accordingly. The only limit is your imagination!

Timing

Regardless of the structure you choose for your workshop, timing is an important element to consider during the planning process (i.e., how long each part of the workshop will take). Planning the duration in advance will help you to keep the session on track and proceed at a good pace. While there are no hard and fast rules about how long each part of your workshop should be, I wanted to share a few examples of general time breakdowns based on my personal experience.

- For 60-minute virtual workshops using my typical workshop structure, I devote approximately 5–10 minutes to the beginning, 40–50 minutes to the middle, and 5–10 minutes to the end.
- For the 60-minute virtual AI "No Prep" Book Club series, I devoted approximately 5 minutes to Touch Base, 20 minutes to Tinker Time, 30 minutes to Talk, and 5 minutes to Transition.
- For a 3-hour on-site workshop entitled "Maximizing Active Learning Classrooms for Student Engagement," I devoted approximately 10 minutes to the beginning, 2 hours and 40 minutes to the middle, and 10 minutes to the end. (The middle portion of the workshop also included a formal break.)

In addition to these general guidelines, I allocate a specific amount of time to the content and activities within each part of the workshop (see Tables 3.3, 3.4, and 3.5). While this is helpful for planning the pacing of the session, it is important to remember that things may take more or less time during the actual live session. Thus, the timing serves more as a helpful guide than as a rigid requirement. As we discussed earlier, flexibility is key, and we need to be open to adjusting things

A Facilitator-Heavy Approach

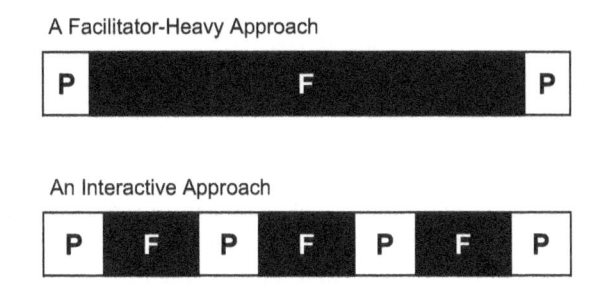

| P | F | P |

An Interactive Approach

| P | F | P | F | P | F | P |

FIGURE 3.4 Facilitator (F) Versus Participant (P) Zones

in the moment based on the needs of the group. This may include spending more or less time on an activity or skipping it altogether.

Also, be sure to include formal breaks during your workshop, whether you are facilitating virtually or on-site. This is a critical way to honor the physical needs of participants and give them the time and space to rest, stretch, and attend to other needs. (We will discuss the importance of breaks further in Chapter 4.)

Finally, as you solidify the timing for your workshop, be sure to reflect on how much of the workshop is spent in the facilitator zone (F) versus the participant zone (P) (see Figure 3.4). The facilitator zone refers to times during the workshop where you are explaining content or demonstrating skills while participants are listening. The participant zone refers to times when participants are actively engaging with the content and/or with each other. Too often, workshops look like the first bar in the figure where participants spend the majority of the session listening to the facilitator present information, and their only opportunities for active engagement are during a brief opening activity and a closing Q&A session. If you notice that your workshop is facilitator-heavy, consider how to break it up to include more opportunities for participant engagement, interaction, and voice throughout the session, as depicted in the second bar in the figure. "In other words, design your content for contribution—not consumption" (Littlefield & Wise, 2021, p. 8).

The specific amount of time spent in each zone can vary throughout the session. A helpful rule of thumb is the "ten-minute rule" (Bowman, 2009), where you aim to keep the facilitator zone portions to approximately 10 minutes at a time, with participant zone activities between each part. Some participant zone activities may be shorter (e.g., turn-and-talk or responding to a poll), whereas other participant zone activities may be longer (e.g., case study analysis or planning time). Additionally, consider how you can offer variety in how participants engage by incorporating different types of activities (Cohn & Greer, 2023) and "[including] a mix of individual, [paired], small-group, and large-group" tasks (Cougler Blom, 2021, p. 94). (We will discuss specific collaborative activities and active learning techniques you can use in Chapters 5 and 6.)

Materials

Along with planning the structure and timing of your workshop, you also need to develop and curate the materials that will be used throughout the session. This may include things such as slides, handouts, videos, articles, props, signs, office supplies (like sticky notes, index cards, chart paper, and markers), feedback forms, supplementary resources, and more. Next, we will explore several important design considerations for two common types of workshop materials: handouts and slides.

Handouts

Handouts can be helpful resources for participants to use during workshops. Common types of handouts include graphic organizers, guided notes, readings, data sets, infographics, activity/assignment directions, assessments, workshop summaries/key points, resource lists, workbooks, and more.

Interactive handouts, such as guided notes and graphic organizers, can help participants follow along with the main points of the workshop while providing a structured space where they can capture their notes and ideas. Guided notes can be provided in different formats, such as a skeletal outline that includes blanks in strategic places for participants to fill in key words or phrases (Biggers & Luo, 2020; Kiewra, 1985). Graphic organizers are visuals that can help participants understand the relationship between ideas. Common graphic organizer formats include Venn diagrams, hierarchy charts, and timelines. These types of handouts also support UDL. Guideline 3, "Design options for building knowledge," prompts practitioners to "highlight and explore patterns, critical features, big ideas, and relationships (3.2)," and tools such as graphic organizers can help learners better determine important information and how those ideas are related (CAST, 2024b). Also, guideline 6, "Design options for strategy development," prompts learners to "organize information and resources (6.3)," and guided notes and graphic organizers can be helpful organizational tools (CAST, 2024b).

Regardless of the type of handout you are designing for your workshop, it is important to ensure that it is accessible. In fact, UDL guideline 4, "Design options for interaction," explicitly prompts practitioners to "optimize access to accessible materials... (4.2)" (CAST, 2024b). Before proceeding, I must make it clear that I am not an expert in accessibility, and I know I still make mistakes and have much to learn. In fact, I wrote an Edutopia article that was aptly titled "Mistakes I Used to Make in Digital Accessibility—and How to Fix Them" (Noah, 2023b). When I recognized several years ago that there was a gap in my understanding of accessibility, I became much more intentional about developing my knowledge, skills, and awareness in this area by attending webinars, reading articles, and listening to the wisdom of my incredible professional learning network. Special thanks to sarah currie, Ann Gagné, Cait S. Kirby, Michael McCreary, Mandy Penney, and Sarah Silverman, who have greatly challenged and expanded my thinking in this area.

Gray (2023) at BCcampus offers the following definition of accessibility:

> Accessibility is the need for us to design and create resources, experiences, tools, and spaces that allow for and support the diversity of our bodies and minds. Although accessibility can benefit everyone, the needs of disabled people should be centered.

Cawthon (2024) emphasizes the importance of "accessibility by intentional design not retrofit" (p. 179), meaning that accessibility should be considered from the very start. Thus, when creating workshop handouts, we should be intentional about designing them in an accessible way. The following list offers tips for creating accessible documents. While it is important to remember that accessibility is "a mindset and not a checklist or a to-do list" (Cawthon, 2024, p. 190), my hope is that these recommendations will offer a helpful place to start.

- Use the built-in heading styles of your word processing platform to format the document so that it will be accessible to participants using screen readers.
- Ensure that images have alternative text (alt text) so that participants who are blind or have low vision will have access to the content.

- If the document includes hyperlinks, be sure to use descriptive text that clearly conveys the destination of the links instead of pasting the full "raw" links or using generic language (like "click here"). (Example: "Learn about the UDL guidelines" vs. "Learn about the UDL guidelines: https://udlguidelines.cast.org/")
- Avoid underlining text for emphasis as this makes it unclear what is a link and what is not. Instead, use other formats for emphasis (e.g., bold).
- Format lists using the built-in bullet points or numbered list tools in the word processing platform.
- Avoid sprinkling emojis throughout the text and using emojis as bullet points, as this can make the text difficult to understand for participants who are using screen readers (Finke, n.d.).
- If the document includes color-coded information, be sure that the information is also conveyed in another way that will be perceivable to participants with color vision deficiency.
- Offer options for how participants can access the handout. Instead of providing only a printed copy, be sure to also provide access to a digital copy that participants can customize to their liking. This is an important way to reduce barriers to perception (CAST, 2024b).

For additional guidance about how to design accessible documents, please check out the digital accessibility resources linked in this chapter's Workshop Toolkit.

Slides

When designing slides for your workshop, be mindful of how much text you are including. Oftentimes, facilitators will fall into the trap of using their slides as speaker notes, where they write out everything they plan to say on their slides. This practice not only results in text-heavy slides that can be difficult for participants to read and process, but it can also lead to the facilitator simply reading their slides to participants, which is not engaging.

Rather than treating your slides as your script, treat them as your sidekick. In other words, think of your slides as something that complements and supports learning during the session rather than being the main focus of the session. For example, instead of writing out everything you plan to say verbatim on your slides, consider how you can use related images and short text (such as words, phrases, and short bullet points) that you can elaborate on. Conveying ideas using multiple modes (beyond text alone) supports UDL guideline 2, "Design options for language & symbols," which encourages practitioners to "illustrate through multiple media (2.5)" (CAST, 2024b). Additionally, research shows that conveying information through a combination of words and relevant images enhances learning (Clark & Mayer, 2024). This is known as the "multimedia principle," and it is a foundational concept of effective multimedia design (Clark & Mayer, 2024, p. 57).

In *Multimedia Learning*, Mayer (2021) shares 15 research-based principles for designing effective multimedia content (such as the multimedia principle), and in *e-Learning and the Science of Instruction*, Clark and Mayer (2024) discuss what many of these principles look like within the context of e-learning (such as virtual professional learning). A few examples of additional principles that can shape our slide design practices include (Clark & Mayer, 2024; Mayer, 2021):

- **Coherence Principle**: Omit irrelevant and/or unnecessary text, images, and audio that are not aligned with the learning goals.
- **Signaling Principle**: Use cues (such as arrows, circles, and bold words) to highlight important information.
- **Spatial Contiguity Principle**: Place words near corresponding parts of images.

I have included links to related resources about these principles in this chapter's Workshop Toolkit. (Norman Eng's book, *PRESENTING*, and Echo Rivera's YouTube channel, More Than PowerPoint, also offer helpful insight into how to design effective slides.)

Just like with handouts, it is essential to be intentional about accessibility in your slide design. Below are some tips for ensuring slide accessibility:

- When selecting slide templates, avoid those that are "busy" (i.e., those that have distracting decorative elements). If necessary, you can edit the master slides to delete distracting elements.
- Use a legible font and a large font size. Avoid decorative fonts and small font sizes that are difficult to read.
- Include alt text for the images on your slides.
- Ensure appropriate color contrast between the foreground and background elements on your slides to improve legibility.
- Avoid overcrowding your slides with content. It's better to distribute the content across multiple slides than to pack too much content onto one.
- Consider using simple animations (like "appear") to reveal relevant text or images on your slides as you discuss them. This can help learners manage the amount of content they have to process at once and keep the focus on what is being discussed at the time. When using animations, be sure to keep them simple; extravagant animations (such as "fly in" and "spin") can not only be distracting for participants but also create challenges for those with motion sensitivity.
- If you plan to show a video during your workshop, be sure that it has accurate captions and that the captions are enabled during viewing.
- If you plan to play a podcast clip during your workshop, be sure to share an accurate transcript.
- Consider giving participants access to your slides and/or handout in advance.

To learn more about how to design accessible slides, please visit the digital accessibility resources linked in this chapter's Workshop Toolkit.

Technology

So far, we have discussed the important roles that structure, timing, and materials play in workshop design. Digital technology is another area to consider. We can use technology for many purposes: to check in with participants, activate prior knowledge, foster collaboration, promote multiple forms of expression, assess learning, cultivate creativity, prompt reflection on learning, and much more. We can also use technology to offer participants "choice (what to learn, when, and how to learn it)" (Briggs & Ouellett, 2023, p. 394). The NLC principle, "Protect participant time," notes the importance of "effectively deploying new digital technologies to engage participants" (Bass et al., 2019, p. 35). Thus, we need to make intentional decisions about what tools to use, when, and how.

One framework that I find helpful in thinking about technology integration is the Technological Pedagogical Content Knowledge (TPACK) model (Figure 3.5), which highlights three connected bodies of knowledge that are essential for educators: content knowledge (knowledge of the subject one is teaching), pedagogical knowledge (knowledge of instructional strategies and the science of learning), and technological knowledge (knowledge of the various applications of technology, including its possible uses and limitations) (Koehler & Mishra, 2009). The authors of the TPACK framework also highlight the important role of context, noting that "a one-size-fits-all approach to technology integration" dismisses the fact that educators "operate in diverse contexts of teaching and learning" (Koehler & Mishra, 2009, p. 62). Within the context of professional learning workshops, the TPACK model can prompt us to think about the content we're addressing, the

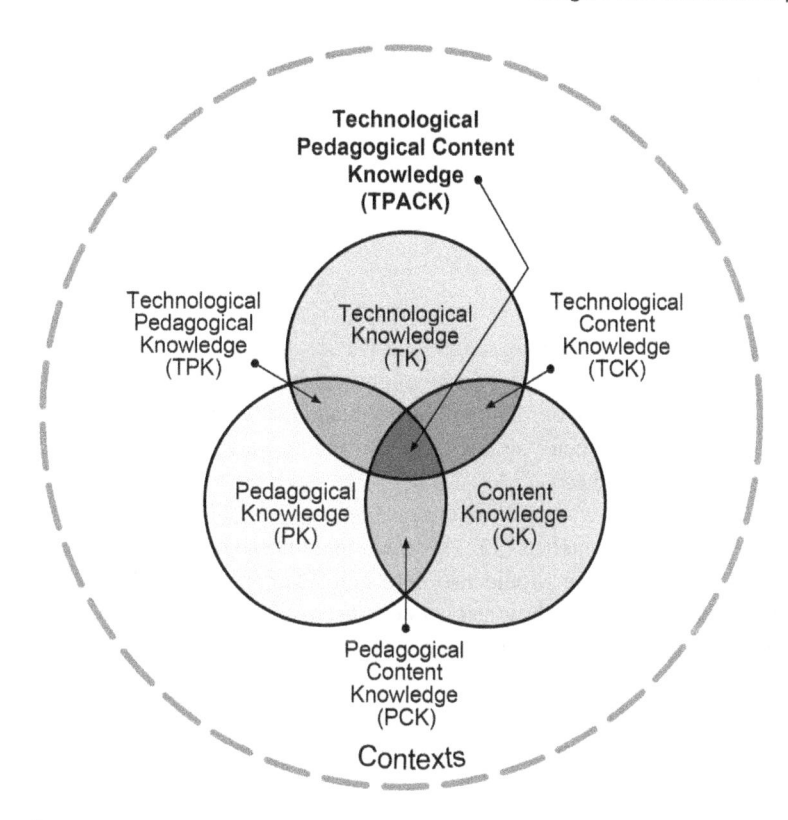

FIGURE 3.5 The TPACK Model (Reprinted by permission of the publisher, © 2012 by tpack.org, http://tpack.org)

methods and activities we're using to facilitate learning, and the ways in which we can employ technology to enhance the learning experience. The TPACK model also prompts us to consider the unique contextual factors that may impact our decisions.

Below, I offer some general tips to consider when determining which digital tools (if any) to incorporate into a workshop.

Selecting Technology

- Review the digital tools that participants have access to at your university, as these tools have already been vetted and paid for by the campus. For example, does your university have a subscription to Hypothesis or Slido? If so, consider using these tools in your workshops, as participants may already be familiar with them.
- When deciding whether to adopt a new tool, be sure to consider factors such as the cost of the tool, how accessible it is, and "whether the technology needs high-speed internet" (Briggs & Ouellett, 2023, p. 394). As UDL guideline 4, "Design options for interaction," states, it is important to "optimize access to accessible materials and assistive and accessible technologies and tools (4.2)," and this includes ensuring that the tools we use can be navigated well by assistive technologies (CAST, 2024b).
- For new tools, be sure to consider how much time it will take to "onboard" participants. Some tools have a big learning curve, where it may take significant time and practice for participants to become adept at using them, whereas others are low friction, allowing participants to be

ready to go within seconds or minutes. My personal preference is to stick with low-friction tools that people can use with little explanation (such as Padlet and Mentimeter). This way, we are not losing precious workshop time doing onboarding of tech tools when that is not the main focus of the session.
- Select digital tools that are versatile rather than those that can only be used for a singular purpose.

Using Technology

- Let decisions about technology integration be driven by the learning goals of the session rather than the technology itself. There should be alignment between the content of the session, the facilitation methods and activities that will be used, and the technologies that will be employed. There may also be times when you decide *not* to incorporate digital tools into a session and instead use analog approaches.
- Leverage technology in ways that promote *participants'* use of technology rather than solely facilitator use. Briggs and Ouellett (2023) explain that instead of focusing on using technology to "deliver information," you should use it to help learners "create knowledge together, in community" (p. 394). Consider how learners can use technology for the 4Cs: communication, collaboration, critical thinking, and creativity (Partnership for 21st Century Learning, 2015, 2019).
- For virtual workshops, consider how to leverage the built-in features of the virtual conferencing platform (such as the chat, polls, reactions, annotation tools, and breakout rooms).

Facilitating Participant Comfort with Technology

- Limit how many digital tools you use within a given workshop. Each new tool you introduce is something that participants will have to learn, and this can make things feel overwhelming (especially if participants are not as comfortable with technology). Lovett et al. (2023) also note that learning how to use new tools "imposes additional cognitive load" on learners (p. 126). Less is more.
- If the workshop itself is focused on teaching people how to use a particular digital tool (e.g., how to create videos in Loom), keep the focus on that tool.
- Find ways to use the same tools across different workshops in a variety of ways. This can help participants become more comfortable with the tools and expose them to their various applications. Additionally, your creative use of the tools can serve as a model for participants of how they can maximize the potential of the tools in their own work.

Throughout the remainder of this book, I will share specific examples of digital tools you can incorporate into your workshops. However, it is important to note that the lifespan of tools can be short, and new tools are being released all the time. The tools in existence at the time of writing this book may very well be gone, go by a different name, or have different features in the future. To keep things more evergreen, in Table 3.6, I outline different categories of tools that can be useful, along with specific examples of tools that fall within each category. (Links to all technologies referenced in this book can be found in the Appendix and in this chapter's Workshop Toolkit.)

While I placed each tool in only one category for simplicity's sake, many tools have features that span multiple categories. For example, Padlet can be used for polling, video recording, audio recording, content curation, digital whiteboarding, and more. Also, as we discussed earlier, it is essential to consider cost, accessibility, and other factors when determining which tools to use.

TABLE 3.6 Digital Tools Library

Types of Digital Tools	Sample Tools
Collaborative Documents	**Apple**: Keynote, Notes, Numbers, & Pages documents shared via iCloud **Google**: Docs, Drawings, Sheets, & Slides **Microsoft**: Excel, PowerPoint, & Word files shared via OneDrive or SharePoint
Collaborative Whiteboards	Canva Whiteboard, FigJam, Freeform, Miro, Mural, Padlet Sandbox, Zoom Whiteboard
Other Collaborative Boards	Padlet
Polling Tools	Mentimeter, Poll Everywhere, Slido
Video Creation Tools	Clips, Edpuzzle, iMovie, Loom, PlayPosit, Screencastify, ScreenPal
Audio Recording Tools	Adobe Podcast, GarageBand, Mote, Voice Memos
Assessment Tools	GoReact, Kahoot, Plickers, Quizizz
Interactive Presentation Tools	Butter Scenes, Nearpod, Pear Deck
Survey Tools	Google Forms, Qualtrics, SurveyMonkey
Social Annotation Tools	Hypothesis, Kami, Perusall, VoiceThread
Messaging Tools	Discord, Mighty Networks, Slack
Design Tools	Adobe Express, Canva
Interactive Content Tools	Genially, ThingLink
QR Code Generator Tools	Bitly, Google Chrome, Shortcuts
Content Curation & Digital Portfolio Tools	Bulb, Wakelet
Scavenger Hunt Tools	Goosechase
Generative Artificial Intelligence (AI) Tools	Adobe Firefly, ChatGPT, Claude, DALL-E, Goblin Tools, Google Gemini, Microsoft Copilot, Midjourney, Padlet TA, Perplexity
Learning Management System Tools	Canvas, Blackboard, Brightspace, Moodle
Virtual Conference Platforms	Adobe Connect, Butter, Engageli, Google Meet, Microsoft Teams, Webex, Zoom

Some of the tools on this list are free, whereas others are freemium or require paid subscriptions. Additionally, it is recommended that you check in with your campus' information technology office and disability resource center to ensure the accessibility of the tools. While the list in Table 3.6 is not exhaustive, my hope is that as technology changes and tools come and go, this table will serve as a helpful guide that you can return to for different options. I also encourage you to continue adding on to the table as new tools arrive on the scene.

Recap

- Develop a well-structured micro plan that details the content participants will learn and the activities they will do throughout the workshop.
- Plan how much time will be devoted to each component.

- Determine the materials you will need for the workshop and ensure that resources (such as handouts and slides) are designed in an accessible way.
- Consider the role that digital technologies will play in the workshop.

Sticky Note Reflection

Choose Your Own Adventure: Choose one of the following questions to reflect on:

A) What is one new workshop structure you would like to try in the future? What do you find appealing about this structure?
B) Think about a workshop you recently facilitated. Draw a bar representing the amount of time spent in the facilitator and participant zones. What do you notice?
C) What are 1–2 digital accessibility practices you would like to be more intentional about when designing workshop handouts and slides?
D) Reflect on how you currently use technology in your workshops. What is an area of strength? What is an area for growth?

Workshop Toolkit

Scan the QR code or visit the URL to access additional resources related to this chapter.

www.tolunoah.com/workshop-toolkits

Design Time

Create a micro plan for your workshop using whichever structure you feel would work best. If you're interested in using my personal workshop structure, you can find an editable planning template in the Workshop Toolkit. The toolkit also includes a link to SessionLab's Session Planner, which is a helpful drag-and-drop tool that can be used to craft a micro plan in any structure. The planner automatically updates the timing as you develop your plan, and it allows you to color-code different sections so that you can ensure there is enough variety in the session.

Facilitators' Lounge

Join the Facilitators' Lounge to connect with other readers and share your takeaways, strategies, and next steps!

www.tolunoah.com/facilitators-lounge/

References

Bass, R., Eynon, B., & Gambino, L.M. (2019). *The New Learning Compact: A framework for professional learning and educational change*. Every Learner Everywhere. www.everylearnereverywhere.org/resources/the-new-learning-compact/

Bell, L.A., & Goodman, D.J. (2023). Design and facilitation. In M. Adams, L.A. Bell, D.J. Goodman, & D. Shlasko (with R.R. Briggs & R. Pacheco) (Eds.), *Teaching for diversity and social justice* (4th ed., pp. 57–96). Routledge.

Biggers, B., & Luo, T. (2020). Guiding students to success: A systematic review of research on guided notes as an instructional strategy from 2009–2019. *Journal of University Teaching & Learning Practice, 17*(3), 1–14. https://doi.org/10.53761/1.17.3.12

Boise State University. (2018, December 5). *Center for teaching and learning*. Boise State News. www.boisestate.edu/news/2018/12/05/center-for-teaching-and-learning/

Bowman, S.L. (2009). *Training from the BACK of the room! 65 ways to step aside and let them learn*. Pfeiffer.

Briggs, R.R., & Ouellett, M.L. (2023). Social justice education online. In M. Adams, L.A. Bell, D.J. Goodman, & D. Shlasko (with R.R. Briggs & R. Pacheco) (Eds.), *Teaching for diversity and social justice* (4th ed., pp. 383–408). Routledge.

CAST. (2024a). *Address biases, threats, and distractions*. https://udlguidelines.cast.org/engagement/interests-identities/biases-threats-distractions/

CAST. (2024b). *Universal Design for Learning guidelines version 3.0*. https://udlguidelines.cast.org/

Cawthon, S.W. (2024). *Disability is human: The vital power of accessibility in everyday life*. TSPA.

Clark, R.C., & Mayer, R.E. (2024). *e-Learning and the science of instruction: Proven guidelines for consumers and designers of multimedia learning* (5th ed.). Wiley.

Cohn, J., & Greer, M. (2023). *Design for learning: User experience in online teaching and learning*. Rosenfeld Media.

Cougler Blom, B. (2021). *Design to engage: How to create and facilitate a great learning experience for any group*. FriesenPress.

Denial, C.J. (2024). *A pedagogy of kindness*. University of Oklahoma Press.

Douglas, J. (2018, May 6). *Introduction to Cafeteria Learning: Let them choose*. ATD. https://www.td.org/content/video/introduction-to-cafeteria-learning-let-them-choose

Douglas, J., & McKenzie, S. (2016). *Let them choose: Cafeteria Learning Style for adults*. ATD Press.

Eng, N. (2019). *PRESENTING: The professor's guide to powerful communication*. EDUCATIONxDESIGN.

Fink, L.D. (2013). *Creating significant learning experiences: An integrated approach to designing college courses* (2nd ed.). Jossey-Bass.

Finke, B. (n.d.). *Emojis and accessibility: The dos and don'ts of including emojis in texts and emails*. https://blog.easterseals.com/emojis-and-accessibility-the-dos-and-donts-of-including-emojis-in-texts-and-emails/

Focarile, T., Earl, B., & Frary, M. (2024). The Sparkshop: Making faculty development timely and department-based. In D.D. Chapman & M.E. Bartlett (Eds.), *Faculty development on a shoestring: Programs to support higher education faculty using little or no resources* (pp. 17–31). Information Age Publishing.

Frary, M., & Focarile, T. (2018, September 21). *The "Sparkshop": Making faculty development timely and department-based* [Webinar]. POD Network. https://podnetwork.org/the-sparkshop-making-faculty-development-timely-and-department-based/

Gannon, K. (2023, May 22). *Why calls for a 'return to rigor' are wrong*. The Chronicle of Higher Education. www.chronicle.com/article/why-calls-for-a-return-to-rigor-are-wrong

Global Learning Partners. (n.d.). *The 4-A learning sequence: Designing effective adult learning*. www.globallearningpartners.com/wp-content/uploads/migrated/resources/The_4As_Template.pdf

Global Learning Partners. (2023, December 14). *4 steps for learning that lasts*. www.globallearningpartners.com/blog/4-steps-for-learning-that-lasts/

Gray, J. (2023, September 28). *Accessibility bites: Assistive technologies*. BCcampus. https://bccampus.ca/event/accessibility-bites-assistive-technologies/

Hokanson, S.C., Grannan, S., Greenler, R., Gillian-Daniel, D.L., Campa III, H., & Goldberg, B.B. (2019). A study of synchronous, online professional development workshops for graduate students and postdocs reveals the value of reflection and community building. *Innovative Higher Education, 44*, 385–398. https://doi.org/10.1007/s10755-019-9470-6

Hughes, L. (2023). *The 2-hour workshop blueprint: Design fast. Deliver strong. Without stress*. Big Charlie Press.

Kelly, K. (2024). *Making college courses flexible: Supporting student success across multiple learning modalities*. Routledge.

Kiewra, K.A. (1985). Providing the instructor's notes: An effective addition to student notetaking. *Educational Psychologist, 20*(1), 33–39. https://doi.org/10.1207/s15326985ep2001_5

Kirkpatrick, J.D., & Kirkpatrick, W.K. (2016). *Kirkpatrick' four levels of training evaluation*. ATD Press.

Koehler, M.J., & Mishra, P. (2009). What is technological pedagogical content knowledge? *Contemporary Issues in Technology and Teacher Education, 9*(1), 60–70. https://www.learntechlib.org/p/29544/

Littlefield, C., & Wise, W. (2021). *How to make virtual engagement easy: A practical guide for remote leaders and educators*. We and Me.

Lovett, M.C., Bridges, M.W., DiPietro, M., Ambrose, S.A., & Norman, M.K. (2023). *How learning works: 8 research-based principles for smart teaching*. Jossey-Bass.

Marzano, R.J. (2009, October 1). The art and science of teaching/helping students process information. *Educational Leadership, 67*(2). www.ascd.org/el/articles/helping-students-process-information

Masland, L. (2020). *Worst syllabus ever workshop – Syllabus*. https://docs.google.com/document/d/1B0XLubyZ3qI0GVsUQDJY0k1ct4yH5hlR29hGdGKuxjk/edit

Mason, D. (Host). (2024, January 10). What is a pedagogy of kindness? (No. 5) [Audio podcast episode]. In 3QTL. https://taylorinstitute.ucalgary.ca/resources/podcast/3qtl#cate-denial

Mayer, R.E. (2021). *Multimedia learning* (3rd ed.). Cambridge University Press.

Noah, T. (2023a, March 14). *Designing virtual edtech faculty development workshops that stick: 10 guiding principles*. EDUCAUSE Review. https://er.educause.edu/articles/2023/3/designing-virtual-edtech-faculty-development-workshops-that-stick-10-guiding-principles

Noah, T. (2023b, September 15). *Mistakes I used to make in digital accessibility – And how to fix them*. Edutopia. www.edutopia.org/article/creating-accessible-digital-content

Parker, P. (2018). *The art of gathering: How we meet and why it matters*. Riverhead Books.

Partnership for 21st Century Learning. (2015, May). *P21 framework definitions*. Battelle for Kids. https://static.battelleforkids.org/documents/p21/P21_Framework_Definitions_New_Logo_2015_9pgs.pdf

Partnership for 21st Century Learning. (2019). *Framework for 21st century learning definitions*. Battelle for Kids. https://static.battelleforkids.org/documents/p21/P21_Framework_DefinitionsBFK.pdf

Playmeo. (n.d.). *Unofficial starts*. https://www.playmeo.com/unofficial-starts/

Playmeo. (2024, October 14). *Brilliant 'UNOFFICIAL START' ideas to engage groups quickly* [Video]. YouTube. https://youtu.be/XN_hCHkY1J8?feature=shared

Tetu, I.C., Kelly, S., Fu, J., Kirby, C.K., Schopieray, S., & Thomas, S. (2024). Developing asynchronous workshop models for professional development. *Communication Design Quarterly, 12*(1), 37–43. https://cdq.sigdoc.org/wp-content/uploads/2024/04/CDQ-12.1.pdf

Thompson, M.E. (n.d.). *TQE: Thoughts, questions, and epiphanies*. Unlimited Teacher. www.unlimitedteacher.com/tqe

TPACK.org. (2012). *Using the TPACK image*. https://tpack.org/tpack-image/

Western, N. [@nswestern]. (2020, September 24). *Using the campfire/watering hole/cave breakout room strategy in Design Multimedia this morning as my students get started on* [Tweet]. Twitter/X. https://twitter.com/nswestern/status/1309168631243313152

Wiggins, G., & McTighe, J. (2005). *Understanding by design* (2nd ed.). ASCD.

Yee, K., Whittington, K., Doggette, E., & Uttich, L. (2023). *ChaptGPT assignments to use in your classroom today*. UCF Created OER Works. https://stars.library.ucf.edu/oer/8

Zakrajsek, T. (2018). Documenting and assessing the work of the CTL. *Journal on Centers for Teaching and Learning, 10*, 59–71. https://openjournal.lib.miamioh.edu/index.php/jctl/article/view/198

4
ADOPT AN INCLUSIVE MINDSET

Guiding Question:
How can you create an inclusive, welcoming, and equitable learning experience?

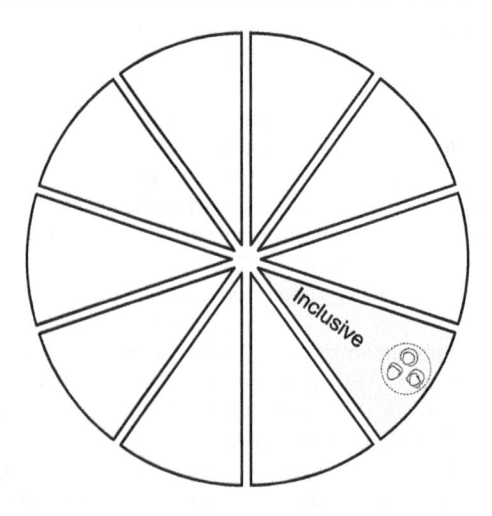

One of the benefits of workshops is the incredible opportunity they provide to gather with people from diverse backgrounds and experiences to explore topics and discuss ideas together. For example, in pedagogical workshops, you often have instructors from different disciplines and departments, with different years of teaching experience. In addition to their unique professional backgrounds, participants also have "multiple social identities, interests, expectations, needs, prior experiences, lived realities" and more (Bell & Goodman, 2023, p. 61). As facilitators, we must consider how we can foster an inclusive, welcoming, and equitable learning experience for the diverse participants in our workshops.

In *Inclusive Teaching*, Hogan and Sathy (2022) discuss the importance of educators adopting an "inclusive teaching mindset," where choices are guided by two questions: "1. Who might be left behind as a result of my practice? 2. How can I invite those students in?" (p. 11). These questions apply not only to the college classroom setting but also to professional learning spaces. As facilitators, we should also consider who we might be excluding through our workshop design and facilitation practices and how we can bring those people in.

It is important to note that the concept of inclusive practice is broad and incorporates many different topics. For instance, Silverman (2024a) frames inclusive teaching as an "umbrella concept" that includes multiple areas, such as accessibility, Universal Design for Learning (UDL), and belonging. As such, it is beyond the scope of this book to address every possible aspect of inclusion. Additionally, the journey toward becoming a more inclusive facilitator is lifelong and requires ongoing learning, unlearning, listening, and introspection.

In this chapter, we will focus on inclusive practices that you can use during the design and facilitation stages of a workshop. The next chapter will discuss ways to foster an inclusive learning community that promotes a sense of belonging. My hope is that these chapters will offer some helpful principles and practices that you can continue to expand on throughout your facilitation journey.

It Starts with Design

The creation of an inclusive, welcoming, and equitable workshop experience begins before we enter the physical or virtual room with participants. It starts with our design. Let's explore some important factors to consider when you are in the planning and preparation stages of a workshop.

Be Mindful of Scheduling and Modality

When scheduling workshops, be intentional about the dates you select. Scheduling workshops during major religious holidays may exclude certain people from participating (especially during work-restricted holidays such as Rosh Hashanah and Eid). Be sure to check multifaith calendars when planning out the schedule for your workshops.

Additionally, consider offering workshops at different times of the day to be more inclusive of learners' schedules. As I shared in Chapter 1, when facilitating virtual workshops, I typically facilitate one session in the morning and a repeat session in the afternoon. You might also consider offering some evening and/or weekend workshops, which can expand professional learning opportunities for learners (such as adjunct instructors who may not be able to attend daytime or weekday sessions). Furthermore, as we discussed in the Introduction, offering solely on-site workshops can exclude many would-be participants. Be sure to provide virtual options, too. Being intentional about the scheduling and modality of professional learning events supports the New Learning Compact (NLC) principle, "Protect participant time" (Bass et al., 2019, p. 35), and it increases the potential reach of your programs.

Use Inclusive Materials and Methods

The materials and methods we use in our workshops can play an important role in fostering a welcoming, inclusive, and equitable climate. As you prepare your workshop, be sure to reflect on the voices, perspectives, and approaches that are included in and excluded from your workshop.

The UDL principle, "Design multiple means of representation," highlights the importance of using inclusive materials and methods. For example, guideline 1, "Design options for perception," prompts practitioners to "represent a diversity of perspectives and identities in authentic ways (1.3)" (CAST, 2024b). Guideline 2, "Design options for language & symbols," prompts practitioners to "cultivate understanding and respect across languages and dialects (2.3)" and to "address biases in the use of language and symbols (2.4)" (CAST, 2024b). Additionally, guideline 3, "Design options for building knowledge," prompts practitioners to "cultivate multiple ways of knowing and making meaning (3.3)" (CAST, 2024b).

In the book, *Teaching for Diversity and Social Justice*, Bell and Goodman (2023) offer five helpful questions to consider when selecting materials and methods: "Who is included? What is included? How is it included? From whose perspective? and Using what sources?" (p. 61). The authors also emphasize the importance of not using content that perpetuates stereotypes; instead "seek materials that reflect the diversity of experiences within a social identity group" (Bell & Goodman, 2023, p. 61). As Belzer and Dashew (2023) explain, "It is important that learners see themselves in the materials they encounter; it is also important that they see authors with identities that are different from their own" (p. 7). As you select the readings, videos, and other content that participants will engage with during the workshop, be intentional about including diverse voices and perspectives.

We also need to be cognizant of the images we use in our workshop materials. Conduct an audit of the images on your slides and handouts by reflecting on these questions:

- Do the images in your workshop materials mostly or only show people of a particular race, gender, age, ability, etc.?
- Do the images show people doing stereotypical roles (e.g., only showing white male scientists), or do they show people from various backgrounds doing various roles?
- Are the images reflective of the diversity of our society?

Being more critical and intentional about the images you use in your workshop materials can be a helpful step in fostering a more inclusive environment where participants see themselves and others represented in multifaceted and positive ways. This chapter's Workshop Toolkit includes links to several helpful websites for diverse and inclusive images, such as Disabled and Here (which features images of disabled people of color) and the Centre for Ageing Better (which features images of people over the age of 50).

Mitigate Barriers

CAST (the organization that created the UDL guidelines) hosts an annual conference, and in 2023, I had the opportunity to be a first-time presenter at their online conference. When submitting my proposal to present, one of the prompts I had to respond to was this: "What barriers do you anticipate participants might face in achieving the goal during your session? How are you proactively designing to minimize those barriers?" This prompt encouraged me and other potential presenters to hold a magnifying glass up to our session plans and examine what could impede participants at each step and how we could design the session to reduce those barriers.

As we design our workshops, we should keep CAST's questions in mind. Take the time to carefully review your workshop plans, considering the barriers that participants might face and how you can proactively address them. For example, the workshop I proposed and later facilitated at the UDL conference was entitled "Empowering Learners and Minimizing Barriers with iPad Accessibility Tools." My goal was to help participants learn how they could leverage five iPad accessibility features to minimize barriers to learning. My plan for the workshop was to share my iPad screen via Zoom so that I could model how to enable and use each feature as participants followed along on their own devices. One barrier I anticipated participants might face was difficulty following along and/or keeping up with each step. For example, participants could miss a step if they needed more time to navigate their device, happened to look away, were distracted, or were less experienced with their device. I proactively designed to minimize that barrier by using an on-screen pointer on my iPad to draw attention to each action I was taking on the screen, demonstrating the process for using each accessibility tool twice, and pasting a brief written summary of the steps in the chat.

Another barrier I anticipated participants might face was difficulty with some of the iPad gestures. To address this barrier, I created a cardboard cutout of an iPad that I used to clearly model gestures on camera that would be difficult to show on the iPad screen alone. Additionally, I intentionally sequenced the workshop so that I taught participants about AssistiveTouch first, as this accessibility feature provides users with additional options for controlling and navigating their device (beyond using gestures).

A third barrier I anticipated was that participants might have difficulty remembering all of the steps for each accessibility feature after the session. I proactively designed to minimize that barrier by creating a Wakelet page that included text-based directions and video tutorials for each iPad accessibility feature so that participants would have multiple means for reviewing the content. I also created a cheat sheet document that provided participants with a brief summary of the steps for enabling and using each accessibility tool.

When anticipating potential barriers in workshop plans, CAST's (2024b) UDL guidelines offer a helpful place to start. Earlier in this chapter, we explored the "Design multiple means of representation" principle, with a particular focus on considerations related to inclusive materials and methods. Let's revisit the three guidelines from that principle and explore additional questions to consider as we aim to reduce barriers to learning:

- **Guideline 1: "Design options for perception" (considerations 1.1 and 1.2)**: What barriers might participants face in terms of their ability to perceive information during the workshop? How can you proactively minimize these barriers by offering ways for learners to customize how information is displayed and by offering information in multiple formats (e.g., providing verbal descriptions of visual content, providing directions verbally and in writing, etc.)?
- **Guideline 2: "Design options for language & symbols" (considerations 2.1, 2.2, and 2.5)**: What barriers might participants face in terms of their comprehension of the language and symbols that are used during the workshop? How can you proactively minimize these barriers by clearly explaining the meaning of any specialized terms, acronyms, or symbols, and by supporting the use of text-to-speech tools? Also, how can you use media (such as images) to represent important concepts in different ways (instead of using text alone)?
- **Guideline 3: "Design options for building knowledge" (considerations 3.1, 3.2, and 3.4)**: What barriers might participants face as they try to construct meaning of what they are learning in the workshop? How can you proactively minimize these barriers by designing opportunities for participants to draw connections to their prior knowledge, explore relationships between ideas, and transfer their learning to new situations?

While the questions above focus on the UDL "representation" principle, it is also important to consider the "engagement" and "action and expression" principles. However, trying to address every single UDL guideline when designing a workshop can be very overwhelming. CAST (n.d.) notes that it is not necessary to address every guideline every time; instead, practitioners should focus on the guidelines that are most relevant to the learning goals. Additionally, it can be helpful to start with one thing and continue to build from there. In their book, *Reach Everyone, Teach Everyone,* Tobin and Behling (2018) suggest the following:

> Instead of focusing on the three brain networks, think of UDL as merely plus-one thinking about the interactions in your course. Is there just one more way that you can help keep learners on task, just one more way that you could give them information, just one more way that they could demonstrate their skills?
>
> *(p. 134)*

Tobin and Behling's (2018) plus-one approach can be very helpful when designing professional learning workshops. Start by identifying one barrier that participants might face during your workshop. Then, identify one additional way that you can engage participants, convey information, or have them demonstrate their learning in order to minimize that barrier. For example, if your workshop is addressing a complex topic, one barrier that participants might face is difficulty keeping all of the ideas organized or understanding how they are related. Using the plus-one approach, you might consider one additional way that you can convey information. For example, you can provide participants with a graphic organizer, guided notes sheet, concept map, sketchnote, or infographic to help them better understand the key ideas and how they are related.

Design Accessible Spaces

The physical or virtual spaces we use for our workshops can also play a critical role in fostering a welcoming, inclusive, and equitable climate. In Chapter 3, we discussed the importance of digital accessibility, with a focus on how to design accessible workshop handouts and slides. However, accessibility doesn't stop there; we also need to ensure that the space where the workshop will be held is accessible. This is a critical way that we can act on UDL guideline 6, "Design options for strategy development," which prompts practitioners to "challenge exclusionary practices (6.5)" (CAST, 2024b). As I mentioned in Chapter 3, I am not an expert in accessibility; however, I want to share some general guidance based on what I have been learning over the past few years. Special thanks to Mandy Penney who offered additional insight into these topics and helpful recommendations.

Access Needs

One way to create a more accessible workshop experience is by providing a way for participants to share their access needs prior to the workshop. Access needs may include the need for sign language interpretation, captions, regular breaks, specific seating, dietary options, flexibility in positioning (e.g., freedom to stand), and flexibility in camera usage (Montague-Asp et al., 2023; Reinholz & Ridgway, 2021). Adams et al. (2023) note that "everyone has access needs, it's just that some needs are already met by default while others are not" (p. 34). By intentionally inviting participants to share their needs prior to the workshop and working proactively to address them, we can design professional learning experiences that are more inclusive, equitable, and responsive. It is also important to note that there may be times when the needs of some participants contrast with the needs of others, such as when participants request different degrees of lighting in an on-site session (Montague-Asp et al., 2023). This situation is commonly referred to as "access friction" (Calling Up Justice, 2023; Silverman, 2024b), and it may require facilitators to consider "creative" solutions (Montague-Asp et al., 2023).

One helpful strategy for learning about participants' access needs is including a question about this on the workshop registration form. For example, during the 2024 Virtual Gathering for Educational Developers, the lead organizers (Cait S. Kirby, Liz Norell, Michael McCreary, Carly Lesoski, and Brooke Shafar) included this prompt on the conference registration form: "Please describe any accessibility needs or personal preferences that would support you in participating fully and comfortably in this event." Responses to this question were shared with conference presenters (sans identifying information) so that they could proactively design their sessions with these needs in mind (Nave, 2024).

At my university, our department's workshop registration form includes an optional question about accommodations where registrants can specify their needs. Completion of this question automatically triggers an email to the workshop facilitator, informing them of the person's need for accommodations. Our university also has an access center with which we can partner for assistance with accommodations (such as American Sign Language [ASL] interpretation).

On-Site Spaces

The physical settings in which we facilitate our on-site workshops can make a big difference in terms of accessibility. Below are some general recommendations for selecting and setting up accessible on-site workshop spaces. This is not an exhaustive list, but it will hopefully offer a helpful place to start.

- Visit different rooms to see which space would best serve the needs of the workshop based on the number of participants expected and the activities they will engage in. (I prefer to choose slightly larger rooms where participants can spread out and work in different areas of the room as desired.)
- Choose a location that is close to a parking lot so that people will not need to travel long distances to reach the workshop.
- Check the main doors to the building. Are they wheelchair accessible (e.g., ramp, doors that open automatically or with a push button, etc.)?
- Avoid hosting workshops in buildings that can only be accessed or navigated via stairs.
- Select a room with easy access to restrooms.
- Choose a room with tables and chairs that are adjustable, movable, and suitable for a range of body types and mobility aids (e.g., wheelchairs). Set up the tables and chairs in a way that ensures that pathways are clear and easy to navigate and that participants can see from wherever they may be sitting.
- Adjust the lighting in the room to ensure greater visibility.
- Test your slides on the projector system before the workshop to ensure that they are displaying clearly and with appropriate color contrast.
- Use a portable microphone during the session to ensure that participants can hear you from wherever they may be seated. During Q&A time(s), pass the mic to participants so that everyone can hear the questions and answers.
- Place air purifiers in the room and prop open the doors and windows (if possible) for ventilation purposes.
- Consider having masks available for participants who might choose to wear one.

Virtual Spaces

Accessibility also matters in virtual spaces. Whether you are using Zoom or another virtual platform, ensuring that the right settings are enabled and that you model inclusive practices during the session is key. For example:

- Ensure that closed captioning is enabled. (Note: Automatic captions are not always accurate; some facilitators pursue funding for professional captioners instead.)
- If any participants have requested sign language interpretation, be sure that the virtual conferencing platform is appropriately set up in the sign language interpretation view.
- Inform participants about the accessibility features that are available (e.g., captions).
- Plan to describe any important graphics on your slides verbally so that participants who are blind, have low vision, or are participating in the workshop while in transit can still access the content.
- Invite participants to make their own decisions regarding camera usage.

- Encourage participants to take care of their needs as needed (e.g., eating, drinking, stretching, taking breaks, etc.).

Additional resources for designing accessible virtual and on-site events are linked in this chapter's Workshop Toolkit.

Offer Options for Movement

When designing workshops (particularly on-site workshops), it is common to incorporate activities that involve movement. While the research on embodied cognition highlights the many benefits of movement for learning (Hrach, 2021; Paul, 2021), it is also important to be mindful of those with mobility-related access needs. In keeping with UDL guideline 4, "Design options for interaction," consider how you can "vary and honor the methods for response, navigation, and movement (4.1)" (CAST, 2024b). This can include offering options for how participants can engage in movement-based learning activities (e.g., "You can take a stroll outside with a colleague to discuss these questions or remain here in the room to chat.").

Silverman (2022) suggests that professional learning programs can be made more accessible to instructors with disabilities by "limit[ing] activities that assume certain capabilities," such as those which require participants to stand for extensive periods of time or move around the room (p. 74). Additionally, Briggs and Ouellett (2023) suggest that when incorporating activities that involve movement, we should tell learners to "do what works for their own bodies and learning experience" (p. 397). As a UDL practice, consider how to offer participants at least one additional option for participation that can be done with or without movement.

Send Pre-Workshop Communication

Pre-workshop communication provides a valuable opportunity to convey a sense of welcome and care to workshop participants. When designing your communication, it can be helpful to keep Parker's (2018) notion of "priming" in mind. She explains:

> Your gathering begins at the moment your guests first learn of it. …The intentional gatherer begins to host not from the formal start of the event but from that moment of discovery. This window of time between the discovery and the formal beginning is an opportunity to prime your guests. It is a chance to shape their journey into your gathering.
>
> *(Parker, 2018, pp. 145–146)*

In my educational development work, priming occurs in a few different ways. One is through an introductory video. When I first started my current role, my amazing colleague at the time, Michael Sanchez, had the brilliant idea of recording a video to introduce me to instructors. I wrote a short script in which I shared my passion for pedagogy; my prior experiences working in K-12, higher education, and corporate edtech; and my excitement to partner with instructors in this new role. Michael helped me record and edit the video. Afterward, he had another brilliant idea. (Michael was full of these!) He thought it would be helpful to include my introductory video on the registration page for each workshop I was facilitating. That way, instructors could play the video and get to know a bit about me, their facilitator, beforehand. This idea has been a hit with instructors! Some have even emailed me to say that they enjoyed watching the video and to thank me for sharing my experience and being "present" and "personable." Although the introductory video is just about me (rather than the particular workshop I am facilitating), this strategy has worked well for priming participants for their experience with me.

Another way that I prime instructors for workshops is by scheduling a reminder email to be sent to registrants the day before the workshop (Noah, 2023). This email reminds instructors of the date, time, topic, and location of the workshop; provides the Zoom link (if it is a virtual workshop); and includes information about anything instructors need to bring or prepare in advance. I also convey that I am looking forward to our time together.

Parker (2018) recommends that priming go beyond logistics to preparing people and getting them in the right mindset for the types of things they will do during the gathering. As such, you might consider including a workshop-related question, a point to ponder (such as a fact or quote), or an action to take in your pre-workshop emails to get participants thinking about the topic before the session begins. During a Slido webinar, the invited speaker, Leanne Hughes, shared the idea of sending a Slido poll to participants prior to the workshop so that you can display the results on the screen when participants arrive as a way of "priming a conversation" (Slido, 2023). Inspired by this strategy, I have recently begun including an "In the Meantime" section in some of my pre-workshop emails that asks participants to respond to a quick, anonymous one-question poll about the workshop topic. For example, the pre-workshop poll for my Padlet Sandbox workshop asks, "How often do you use digital whiteboard activities in your teaching or other professional work?," and participants can select one of four options: frequently, occasionally, rarely, or never. The pre-workshop poll strategy can also be useful for gaining insight into participants' prior knowledge of the workshop topic before the session. You might ask, "What do you already know about this topic?" or "What skills do you already possess as related to this topic?" (Aguilar & Cohen, 2022, p. 147).

You could also send a one-question survey or poll to solicit participants' questions about the workshop topic and learn about their reasons for attending. For example, you can ask, "What questions do you have about this topic?," "What do you wonder about this topic?," "What is your goal for attending this workshop?," or "What do you hope to learn during this workshop?" You can then use the responses to shape your workshop plans (e.g., by intentionally addressing those questions and goals during the workshop, including related activities or discussion opportunities, and/or providing supplementary resources related to learners' questions and goals). This is a simple yet powerful way to be responsive to learners' needs and interests.

If you have more time and wish to put a more creative spin on your pre-workshop communication, you could create a brief workshop trailer video to prime participants and build excitement for the workshop. In the video, you could highlight some of the topics participants can expect to learn about, pose questions or share interesting facts to get them thinking about the topics, and include other content to pique their interest. There are a variety of tools you can use to create workshop trailer videos, including Loom, Clips, Zoom, and iMovie. To keep the workshop trailers evergreen and reusable, be sure to avoid mentioning the specific date, time, and location of the workshop in your video. Instead, you can communicate this information in the body of your pre-workshop email or via the workshop registration page. For accessibility purposes, ensure that the video includes accurate captions.

Inclusive Practices for Live Events

Now that we have explored some important things to consider during the design and preparation stages of a workshop, we will turn our attention to how you can foster a welcoming and inclusive climate during a live (on-site or virtual) event.

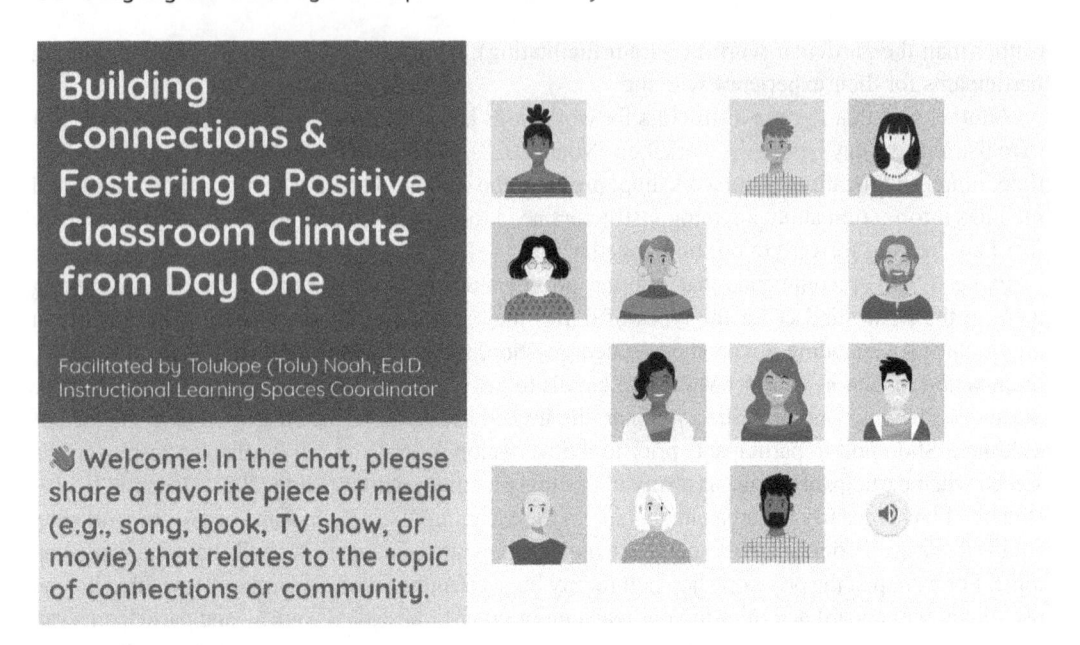

84 Designing and Facilitating Workshops with Intentionality

FIGURE 4.1 Sample Welcome Slide from Tolu's "Building Connections & Fostering a Positive Classroom Climate from Day One" Workshop

Note: Slides template from Slidesgo.

Greet Learners

Adams et al. (2023) explain that "how the class or workshop begins and the tone that is established at the outset sets the stage for the rest of the learning experience" (p. 39). This includes how we greet learners and welcome them into the workshop space.

Whenever I am facilitating a virtual workshop, I join the Zoom room early and put up a welcome slide that greets participants upon arrival (Noah, 2023). The welcome slide includes the title of the workshop, my name, a welcome message, and an "unofficial start" activity (see Chapter 3 for more information). Typically, the unofficial start is a low-stakes workshop-related prompt for participants to respond to in the chat (see Figure 4.1). I also play some background music to set a positive mood (Noah, 2023). As participants join the virtual session, I greet them each by name (typically via the chat).

For on-site workshops, I set up a sign-in table with a welcome sign, name tags, and other materials at the entrance. As participants enter the room, I greet them personally. I also have a welcome slide on the screen with soft music playing in the background and an unofficial start activity for participants to do.

Provide Options for Engagement

In August 2023, I had the opportunity to attend a virtual "Climate Action Pedagogy" workshop by Karen Costa. During the beginning of the workshop, she shared this powerful invitation:

> You are invited to **adapt** this learning experience to your needs today.
> You are invited to keep your **camera on or off**, or switch between the two.
> You are invited to set lofty **productivity** goals, or join us in quiet **reflection**.

You are invited to be a **novice or an expert**, and everything in between.
You are invited to show up as your **whole human self**.
(K. Costa, personal communication, August 16, 2023, emphasis in original)

Karen's invitation demonstrated her understanding that every participant in the session had unique needs and preferences, and it honored our autonomy as adults to make choices that worked best for us. Her invitation also made space for whatever place participants were in. She understood that some people may have been ready to go full force and be super productive, while others may have been in a space where they needed to simply listen and reflect. Additionally, Karen's invitation explicitly acknowledged the range of expertise in the room, making it clear that participants did not need to be experts to engage. In all, Karen's invitation demonstrated that all participants were welcome as they were and that the ways they chose to engage were welcome, too.

Within the virtual workshop space, a commonly contested topic is camera usage. Some facilitators feel that participants should keep their cameras on, whereas others feel that decisions about camera usage should be left to the individual. While as a facilitator, I certainly *prefer* when people have their cameras on, I never require it. It is always an invitation that people are free to accept or reject without judgment.

There are many reasons why participants may choose to leave their cameras off in virtual sessions. Some may find it much easier to focus on the workshop if they don't have to worry about how they're appearing on the screen. Others may prefer to keep their personal setting private, or they may be joining the session while in transit. Still others may be grabbing a bite to eat while attending the workshop. Others may not have the bandwidth (emotionally or technically) to be on camera that day.

A common pushback that some facilitators share with respect to camera usage is that requiring people to have their cameras on makes it easier for them to see nonverbal cues and check if participants are engaged. However, Cohn and Greer (2023) offer this important food for thought:

> When you judge participation based on how someone looks or acts on the call, you may be lured into acting upon implicit biases that you may have about the people on your calls. To put it more bluntly, judging participation and engagement based on whether participants are smiling, nodding, or looking "focused" may reinforce a whole set of biases that could be ableist, ageist, sexist, and racist. …As a facilitator, it might feel good for you to see faces, but for your participants, putting on appearances in front of the camera could cause a bundle of worries that might distract them from the learning experience.
>
> We know it feels strange to talk to a bunch of blank squares or still image avatars. However, if you design a real-time online learning experience with varied activities, multiple ways to participate, and a variety of options to get learners actively involved in the conversation, you shouldn't need to worry about having the camera turned on at all. You'll be able to understand whether learners are present simply by their engagement in the activities you've designed to capitalize upon the precious value of shared time together.
>
> *(p. 57)*

During the 2024 Virtual Gathering for Educational Developers, Jenae Cohn put these principles into action beautifully. She led a fantastic community-building session that modeled inclusive camera practices along with well-designed activities that offered participants multiple ways to engage. Jenae began her session by explicitly sharing several different participation options, one of which was the following: "There's no pressure to have your camera 'on' at any point during this time. Do what's most comfortable for you, and please abstain from commenting on the presence (or absence) of others' videos" (J. Cohn, personal communication, June 24, 2024). This simple statement not only honored participants' autonomy to decide what worked best for them but also set a tone in the session for participants to not question or judge others' camera choices. Throughout the remainder of the session, Jenae facilitated a series of community-building activities that offered participants a choice of what they discussed and how they discussed it. Using some well-structured Google Docs, participants were able to choose which questions they wanted to discuss in breakout rooms and whether they wanted to participate in the discussions by speaking, typing in the Zoom chat, or adding notes to the Google Docs. Additionally, participants had the option to opt out of the breakout room discussions and simply share their thoughts via the Google Docs in the main room if they wished. As we engaged in these activities, people frequently commented on how impressed they were with Jenae's design and facilitation of the session, how impactful it was, and how they planned to adopt similar approaches in their own educational development work. Jenae showed everyone that you don't need to mandate camera usage or breakout room participation to build community and engage participants in meaningful ways.

In sum, we need to "be flexible about how the participants choose to engage. It's their learning experience after all" (Cohn & Greer, 2023, p. 122).

Use Participants' Names

A key way that we can foster a welcoming and inclusive environment in our workshops is by learning participants' names, correctly pronouncing their names, and using their names throughout the workshop. Names are a critical part of people's identities, and saying participants' names properly is a simple yet powerful way that we can acknowledge and honor them. As someone with a name that is frequently mispronounced, this practice is especially personal and pivotal to me.

I am the proud daughter of Nigerian immigrants, and my Yoruba heritage is core to my being. While on a day-to-day basis, I typically go by the shortened version of my name (Tolu Noah), it is the extended version that brings me much joy to say (Tioluwaniope Omolara Esther Noah). In our culture, every name has a meaning and tells a unique story.

- My first name, Tioluwaniope ("TEA-oh-loo-wah-KNEE-oh-pay"), means "Thanks be to God." I was given this name because my parents were grateful to have made it to the United States.
- My middle name, Omolara ("OH-mo-la-rah"), means "My child is my family." I was given this name because when my parents immigrated to the United States, they had no familial connections here. It was just the two of them and me (until my two sisters came along).
- Esther is a name I chose. In the Nigerian–American church I grew up in, when you were baptized, you chose someone in the Bible you wanted to emulate. As a teen, I was obsessed with the story of Queen Esther, so I chose her name.
- My last name, Noah, comes from the Bible, too.

While I don't expect anyone to memorize the extended version of my name (although some of my close friends in high school certainly did and would say the entire thing whenever they saw me walking down the hall!), I do appreciate it when people make a sincere effort to get my day-to-day name (Tolu) right.

Hogan and Sathy (2022) explain that "not saying a student's name correctly can be perceived as a racial microaggression" (p. 96), and I believe that this applies beyond the college classroom setting, too. Whether it is a colleague at work or the facilitator in a workshop who frequently mispronounces your name, the sting is real. For many people, their name is strongly tied to their cultural background or heritage. However, they often experience the pain of others mispronouncing their name, avoiding using their name, or trying to give them a nickname because their name is "too hard to learn." As workshop facilitators, it is important for us to be aware of this and to proactively avoid causing harm.

One strategy I have found helpful in my work is reviewing the workshop registration list beforehand and practicing pronouncing unfamiliar names (Noah, 2023). For example, I will often search for YouTube videos or websites that have audio recordings of people's names to learn how to pronounce them correctly. You might also invite participants to record the pronunciation for their name via tools such as Namecoach, NameDrop, or Padlet. (Links to these and other name-related resources are included in this chapter's Workshop Toolkit.)

During on-site workshops, I provide participants with name tags and/or name tents so that I can match names with faces and help participants learn and use each other's names, too. One helpful practice Hogan and Sathy (2022) recommend is inviting learners to include the phonetic spelling for their name as well. I do this for my own name tags and name tents by always writing the phonetic spelling, "TOE-loo," below my first name (Tolu). For virtual workshops, I include the phonetic spelling as part of my Zoom name.

Throughout my workshops, I also aim to use participants' names as much as possible. For example, if a participant raises their physical or virtual hand to ask a question, I will call on them by name. Or, if they share an idea in the chat, I will attribute the idea to them by name (e.g., "Chinyere shared a great idea in the chat" instead of "There's a great idea in the chat."). Furthermore, I explicitly ask participants to correct me if I mispronounce their name (Noah, 2023). This simple act of inviting corrections is an important way to convey to participants that I really do care about getting it right.

Construct Group Agreements

The NLC principle, "Create supportive professional communities," highlights the importance of building a climate of "trust, openness, and respect across difference" (Bass et al., 2019, p. 36). Eynon and Iuzzini (2020) also note that "to take full advantage of the power of peer learning, professional development leaders and facilitators must create environments shaped by an ethos of mutual support, where it is safe to discuss difficulties as well as triumphs" (p. 80). Thus, as workshop facilitators, we must consider how to foster a space where participants can be open and vulnerable with each other while operating with care and respect.

One strategy we can use during the beginning of our workshops to clarify expectations for engagement is developing what are commonly referred to as "norms," "guidelines," or "ground rules" (Adams et al., 2023, p. 39; Gorski, n.d.). In my personal work, I prefer to call them "group agreements" (Noah, 2017; Noah & Souza, 2018). The National Equity Project (n.d.) distinguishes "agreements" from "norms" and "rules," explaining that "agreements are an aspiration, or collective vision, for how we want to be in relationship with one another." Additionally, creating agreements can be a helpful way to "cultivate empathy and restorative practices (9.4)" as UDL guideline 9 ("Design options for emotional capacity") suggests (CAST, 2024a).

There are a variety of protocols and processes that can be used to generate group agreements with participants. For example, the National Equity Project (n.d.) offers a helpful guide entitled "Developing Community Agreements," which outlines a process where participants do a journaling activity about their needs, followed by small-group and large-group discussions where they reach a consensus on the agreements. Additionally, the Center for Leadership & Educational Equity

(CLEE) offers a variety of protocols, including "Affinity Mapping" (adapted by Ross Peterson-Veatch; CLEE, n.d.-a), "Forming Ground Rules (Creating Norms)" (developed by Marylyn Wentworth; CLEE, n.d.-b), and "Norms Construction—A Process of Negotiation" (developed by Betty Bisplinghoff; CLEE, n.d.-c). (These and other resources are linked in this chapter's Workshop Toolkit.)

While it is ideal to create agreements with participants, there may be occasions when, because of limited time or other factors, you might decide to prepare some agreements in advance (Aguilar & Cohen, 2022; Gorski, n.d.). In this case, Gorski (n.d.) recommends checking in with participants to see if they agree with the agreements, and if time permits, inviting them to add additional ideas to the list.

Furthermore, when developing group agreements, it is important to be mindful of how the agreements themselves may unintentionally reinforce power dynamics (Sensoy & DiAngelo, 2014). For example, Sensoy and DiAngelo (2014) explain how common agreements such as "Assume good intentions" can actually "allow members of dominant groups to avoid responsibility" for the impact of their words (p. 4). The authors share examples of alternative agreements that they have used in their work, such as "Strive for intellectual humility. Be willing to grapple with challenging ideas" and "Recognize how your own social positionality (e.g., race, class, gender, sexuality, ability) informs your perspectives and reactions" (Sensoy & DiAngelo, 2014, p. 8).

Encourage Disturbance

Bell and Goodman (2023) describe the importance of facilitating learning spaces that offer both "challenge and support" (p. 72). UDL guideline 8, "Design options for sustaining effort & persistence," similarly encourages practitioners to "optimize challenge and support (8.2)" (CAST, 2024b). Bell and Goodman (2023) use the terms "comfort zone" and "learning edge" as a way to help participants conceptualize the different feelings they may have during a learning experience (p. 76). The comfort zone is the realm of "familiar beliefs and experiences," whereas the learning edge encompasses "moments of discomfort" that people may experience as they learn about new ideas and perspectives (Bell & Goodman, 2023, p. 73). The authors encourage facilitators to help participants learn how to recognize and remain engaged when they are on their learning edge instead of returning to their comfort zone.

One resource that I have found useful in helping learners embrace the discomfort of being on their "learning edge" is Wheatley's (2009) essay, "Willing to Be Disturbed." In this essay, Wheatley highlights the value of being challenged, listening to different viewpoints, and operating with curiosity. When I was a teacher education professor, I had my students read and discuss portions of "Willing to Be Disturbed" on the first day of my Diversity in the Classroom course to set the tone for our discussions and encourage them to embrace the challenging thoughts and emotions they might experience as we discussed complex diversity and social justice topics throughout the semester (Noah, 2017). I have also used portions of this essay in my professional learning workshops.

Manage Difficult Dynamics

In *The Art of Gathering*, Parker (2018) discusses the importance of conducting gatherings with "generous authority," which includes facilitating gatherings in a way that protects guests (pp. 81–87). The UDL guidelines also highlight the importance of protecting learners. For example, guideline 7, "Design options for welcoming interests & identities," prompts practitioners to "address biases, threats, and distractions (7.4)" (CAST, 2024b). In the context of professional learning workshops, the need to protect participants might arise when someone is repeatedly dominating or derailing discussions or when someone is committing microaggressions or making other problematic remarks. As facilitators, we should intervene in order to reduce harm.

One framework that can be helpful in addressing challenging situations is the Open the Front Door (OTFD) communication framework, which Tasha Souza introduced me to during our co-facilitation experience. The framework was developed by Quantum Learning Network's SuperCamp program, and it's an approach to managing conflict in a positive way (DePorter, n.d.). The OTFD framework includes four steps (DePorter, n.d.):

1. **Observation (O)**: Explain what occurred in an objective way.
2. **Thought (T)**: Explain your thoughts/opinions about the situation.
3. **Feeling (F)**: Explain how you feel about the situation.
4. **Desire (D)**: Explain what you would like the person/people to do moving forward.

The OTFD framework encourages the use of "I" statements and offers these sentence starters for each step of the process: "I noticed…," "I think…," "I feel…," and "I would like…" (DePorter, n.d.; SuperCamp, 2013).

During our co-facilitated workshops, Tasha shared that the OTFD framework can be used in a direct manner (where you address a particular person/group of people) or in an indirect manner. Here is an example of an indirect OTFD response:

> *I noticed **(Observe)** the volume of some people's voices rising. I think **(Think)** there were some strong reactions to what was said. I feel uncomfortable **(Feeling)** moving forward with the discussion until we explore this. I am hoping some of you can share **(Desire)** what you are thinking/feeling right now so we can have a conversation and learn from each other.*
>
> (Souza, 2017, Communication Framework section, emphasis in original)

Using the OTFD framework can be a helpful way to address difficult situations during workshops. You can learn more about this framework and read additional examples of OTFD responses via the links in this chapter's Workshop Toolkit.

Provide Breaks

Whether you are facilitating on-site or virtual workshops, providing formal breaks is critical. Breaks allow participants time to stretch, rest, reenergize, and take care of personal needs. They are especially crucial in virtual workshops and conferences where participants are often expected to sit for extensive periods of time and "Zoom fatigue" can easily set in. Briggs and Ouellett (2023) explain that we should be mindful of learners' bodies "and encourage them to move, take breaks, and take care of themselves" (p. 393). Be sure to anticipate participants' needs and include breaks during your workshops.

Recap

- Design with inclusivity in mind by being intentional about scheduling and modality, using inclusive materials and methods, proactively addressing barriers to learning, designing accessible learning spaces, offering options for movement, and sending pre-workshop communication.
- Facilitate with inclusivity in mind by greeting learners, providing options for engagement, using participants' names, constructing group agreements, encouraging disturbance, managing difficult dynamics, and providing breaks.

Sticky Note Reflection

Commitment: What is one commitment you will make to create a more inclusive, welcoming, and equitable workshop experience?

Workshop Toolkit

Scan the QR code or visit the URL to access additional resources related to this chapter.

www.tolunoah.com/workshop-toolkits

Design Time

Review your workshop plans, and identify a potential barrier that participants might experience. Use Tobin and Behling's (2018) "plus-one approach" to determine one additional option to address it.

Facilitators' Lounge

Join the Facilitators' Lounge to connect with other readers and share your takeaways, strategies, and next steps!

www.tolunoah.com/facilitators-lounge/

References

Adams, M., Briggs, R.R., & Shlasko, D. (2023). Pedagogical foundations for social justice education. In M. Adams, L.A. Bell, D.J. Goodman, & D. Shlasko (with R.R. Briggs & R. Pacheco) (Eds.), *Teaching for diversity and social justice* (4th ed., pp. 27–55). Routledge.

Aguilar, E., & Cohen, L. (2022). *The PD book: 7 habits that transform professional development.* Jossey-Bass.

Bass, R., Eynon, B., & Gambino, L.M. (2019). *The New Learning Compact: A framework for professional learning and educational change*. Every Learner Everywhere. www.everylearnereverywhere.org/resources/the-new-learning-compact/

Bell, L.A., & Goodman, D.J. (2023). Design and facilitation. In M. Adams, L.A. Bell, D.J. Goodman, & D. Shlasko (with R.R. Briggs & R. Pacheco) (Eds.), *Teaching for diversity and social justice* (4th ed., pp. 57–96). Routledge.

Belzer, A., & Dashew, B. (2023). Foundational concepts and commitments for adult learning. In A. Belzer & B. Dashew (Eds.), *Understanding the adult learner: Perspectives and practices* (pp. 3–19). Routledge.

Briggs, R.R., & Ouellett, M.L. (2023). Social justice education online. In M. Adams, L.A. Bell, D.J. Goodman, & D. Shlasko (with R.R. Briggs & R. Pacheco) (Eds.), *Teaching for diversity and social justice* (4th ed., pp. 383–408). Routledge.

Calling Up Justice. (2023, May 7). *Access friction explained*. https://callingupjustice.com/access-friction-explained/

CAST. (n.d.). *Frequently asked questions*. https://udlguidelines.cast.org/more/frequently-asked-questions/

CAST. (2024a). *Cultivate empathy and restorative practices*. https://udlguidelines.cast.org/engagement/emotional-capacity/empathy-restorative-practices/

CAST. (2024b). *Universal Design for Learning guidelines version 3.0*. https://udlguidelines.cast.org/

Center for Leadership and Educational Equity. (n.d.-a). *Affinity mapping*. www.clee.org/resources/affinity-mapping/

Center for Leadership and Educational Equity. (n.d.-b). *Forming ground rules (creating norms)*. www.clee.org/resources/forming-ground-rules-creating-norms/

Center for Leadership and Educational Equity. (n.d.-c). *Norms construction – A process of negotiation*. www.clee.org/resources/norms-construction-a-process-of-negotiation/

Cohn, J., & Greer, M. (2023). *Design for learning: User experience in online teaching and learning*. Rosenfeld Media.

DePorter, B. (n.d.). *Communication series by SuperCamp: #1 – Open the front door*. The Teen Mentor. https://theteenmentor.com/2019/08/30/communication-series-by-supercamp-1-open-the-front-door/

Eynon, B., & Iuzzini, J. (2020). *ATD teaching & learning toolkit: A research-based guide to building a culture of teaching & learning excellence*. Achieving the Dream. https://achievingthedream.org/teaching-learning-toolkit/

Gorski, P.C. (n.d.). *Guide for setting ground rules*. www.edchange.org/multicultural/activities/groundrules.html

Hogan, K.A., & Sathy, V. (2022). *Inclusive teaching: Strategies for promoting equity in the college classroom*. West Virginia University Press.

Hrach, S. (2021). *Minding bodies: How physical space, sensation, and movement affect learning*. West Virginia University Press.

Montague-Asp, H., Piepzna-Samarasinha, L.L., Shlasko, D., & Siegel, L.L. (2023). Ableism and disability justice. In M. Adams, L.A. Bell, D.J. Goodman, & D. Shlasko (with R.R. Briggs & R. Pacheco) (Eds.), *Teaching for diversity and social justice* (4th ed., pp. 303–344). Routledge.

National Equity Project. (n.d.). *Developing community agreements*. www.nationalequityproject.org/tools/developing-community-agreements

Nave, L. (Host). (2024, August 2). Virtual gathering, real inclusion with Cait Kirby and Liz Norell (No. 130) [Audio podcast episode]. In *Think UDL*. https://thinkudl.org/episodes/virtual-gathering-real-inclusion-with-cait-kirby-and-liz-norell

Noah, T. (2017). Encourage, enlighten, engage: Using the three E's to build students' intercultural competence. *International Christian Community of Teacher Educators Journal, 12*(1), 1–7. https://digitalcommons.georgefox.edu/icctej/vol12/iss1/6/

Noah, T. (2023, March 14). *Designing virtual edtech faculty development workshops that stick: 10 guiding principles*. EDUCAUSE Review. https://er.educause.edu/articles/2023/3/designing-virtual-edtech-faculty-development-workshops-that-stick-10-guiding-principles

Noah, T., & Souza, T. (2018). *What to do before, during, and after difficult dialogues about diversity*. Best of the 2018 Teaching Professor Conference Report. https://scholarworks.boisestate.edu/ctl_teaching/11/

Parker, P. (2018). *The art of gathering: How we meet and why it matters*. Riverhead Books.

Paul, A.M. (2021). *The extended mind: The power of thinking outside the brain*. Mariner Books.

Reinholz, D.L., & Ridgway, S.W. (2021). Access needs: Centering students and disrupting ableist norms in STEM. *CBE-Life Sciences Education, 20*(3), 1–8. https://doi.org/10.1187/cbe.21-01-0017

Sensoy, O., & DiAngelo, R. (2014). Respect differences? Challenging the common guidelines in social justice education. *Democracy & Education, 22*(2), 1–10. https://democracyeducationjournal.org/home/vol22/iss2/1/

Silverman, S. (2022). Instructors are learners too: Making faculty development accessible to faculty. *New Directions for Teaching and Learning, 2022*(172), 69–77. https://doi.org/10.1002/tl.20526

Silverman, S. (2024a, April 9). *The inclusive teaching umbrella*. https://sarahemilysilverman.com/2024/04/09/the-inclusive-teaching-umbrella/

Silverman, S. (2024b, May 23). Navigating "access friction" in teaching. *Beyond the Scope*. https://beyondthescope.substack.com/p/navigating-access-friction-in-teaching

Slido. (2023, June 28). *Best practices for truly inclusive meetings with Leanne Hughes: Slido Webinars* [Video]. YouTube. https://youtu.be/QR7mqGa0QgA?feature=shared

Souza, T. (2017, August 19). *Managing hot moments in the classroom: Concrete strategies for cooling down tension*. Faculty Focus. www.facultyfocus.com/articles/effective-classroom-management/managing-hot-moments-in-the-classroom-concrete-strategies-for-cooling-down-tension/

SuperCamp. (2013, November 13). *OTFD – A powerful communication technique*. https://prezi.com/tszt1slnknpa/otfd-a-powerful-communication-technique/

Tobin, T.J., & Behling, K.T. (2018). *Reach everyone, teach everyone: Universal Design for Learning in higher education*. West Virginia University Press.

Wheatley, M.J. (2009). *Turning to one another: Simple conversations to restore hope to the future* (2nd. ed.). Berrett-Koehler Publishers.

5
CULTIVATE CONNECTION

Guiding Question:
How can you foster a sense of belonging, build trust, and promote relationship building in your workshop?

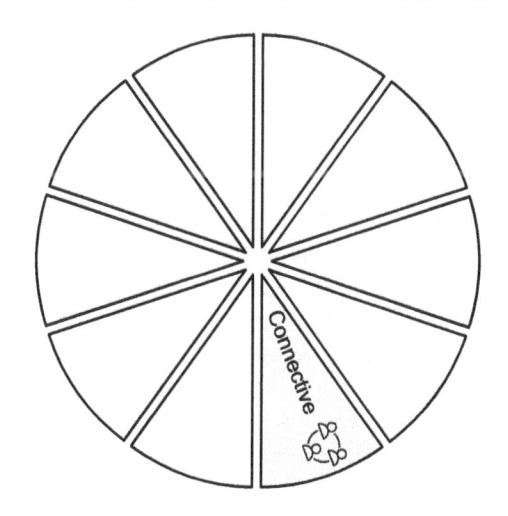

When designing and facilitating workshops, it is essential to consider how we can help foster relatedness and a sense of belonging. Cohen (2022) defines belonging as "the feeling that we're part of a larger group that values, respects, and cares for us—and to which we feel we have something to contribute" (p. 5). Belonging is a core need of all human beings (Strayhorn, 2019), and its importance is also reflected in Universal Design for Learning (UDL) guideline 8, "Design options for sustaining effort & persistence," which prompts practitioners to "foster belonging and community (8.4)" (CAST, 2024). As facilitators, we need to be intentional about designing learning experiences that convey to participants that they and their contributions matter. Many of the strategies we discussed in Chapter 4 (such as using inclusive materials, learning participants' names, and designing accessible spaces) are also helpful strategies for fostering belonging. In this chapter, we will take a deeper dive into ways to promote belonging through the interpersonal interactions that take place during the workshop.

Connections with others play a vital role in the learning process. Eyler (2018) explains that sociality is a key way that people learn, and Adams et al. (2023) note that "building real relationships deepens the possibilities for learning and is also a valued outcome in itself" (p. 37). The professional learning literature highlights the importance of relationships, too. The New Learning Compact (NLC) principle, "Create supportive professional communities," states that "social

DOI: 10.4324/9781003482963-6

94 Designing and Facilitating Workshops with Intentionality

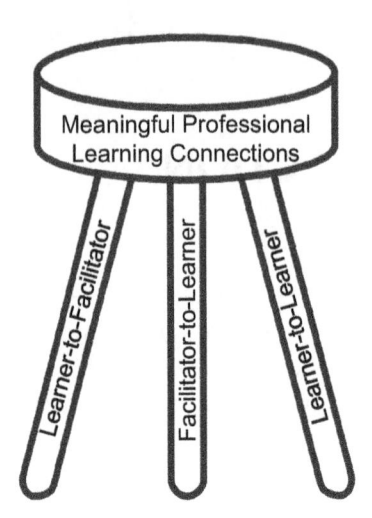

FIGURE 5.1 Professional Learning Connections Stool

learning and community support are essential to professional learning" (Bass et al., 2019, p. 36). Additionally, Steinert et al. (2016) note that "intentional community-building" is an important component of effective faculty development programs (p. 777). Furthermore, a study by Bouwma-Gearhart (2012) found that faculty members' desire to connect with others about teaching and have a "safe and supportive place for their pedagogical discussions" was a key motivating factor for their participation in professional learning events (p. 563).

So far, we have established that belonging and connection are critical components of effective professional learning experiences. However, connection is not guaranteed simply because you have gathered a group of people together in a physical or virtual room. Rather, "you have to design your gatherings for the kinds of connections you want to create" (Parker, 2018, p. 94). In this chapter, we will explore ways to tap into the power of sociality, promote a sense of belonging, and foster meaningful connections with and among participants. We'll do this by examining three important types of connections: learner-to-facilitator, facilitator-to-learner, and learner-to-learner connections (see Figure 5.1).

Learner-to-Facilitator Connections

The relationships we form with participants in our workshops can play a meaningful role in their learning experience. By giving participants insight into who we are, we can establish trust and rapport with them. Next, we'll explore strategies for fostering learner-to-facilitator connections.

Share Your Professional Journey

One way to help participants connect with you is by sharing information about your professional journey. In Chapter 4, I described how the introductory video Michael Sanchez helped me create has allowed instructors at my university to get to know me prior to attending my workshops. Whenever I am facilitating workshops externally (e.g., at conferences, online events, and invited events), I will often take a moment to share about my professional background during the "roadmap" portion of the session so that participants know about the experiences I bring to my work. For example, I share how many years I've been working in the field of education (a little over 20 years as of the publication date of this book), and I briefly highlight the professional roles that have been part of my career (teacher, college professor, Apple professional learning specialist, and educational developer). I share these details to offer a point of connection to participants. The two main groups for whom I facilitate workshops are college professors and K-12 teachers, so by mentioning my own prior teaching experiences in both of these realms, I can convey to participants that I understand where they're coming from because I have done that work myself.

If you choose to share your professional background, be sure to keep it as brief as possible. I typically take no longer than 60 seconds to share a few key aspects of my background. Also, rather than starting the workshop by introducing yourself, consider saving your introduction until after the opening activity. As we discussed in Chapter 3, the beginning of a gathering is a critical period when participants' attention is high and when they are most likely to remember what has occurred (Bowman, 2009; Parker, 2018). Rather than using those opening minutes to talk about yourself, use them to spark participants' thinking about the workshop topic, and then introduce yourself afterward.

Share Your Personal Story

Another way to help participants connect with you is by sharing personal anecdotes or other experiences related to the workshop topic. For example, you might share challenges you've experienced, lessons learned, or areas for growth. Adams et al. (2023) note that self-disclosure can help participants feel comfortable enough to share, too.

In previous chapters, I mentioned my experience co-facilitating workshops with Tasha Souza. These workshops focused on helping instructors learn how to facilitate dialogue about challenging topics. To personalize the workshops, I shared some of my own fears around facilitating discussions about challenging topics. Examples of fears I shared included "What if a student says something offensive or completely off base? How should I respond? Worse yet, what if I inadvertently say something offensive…?" and "My students are coming from various backgrounds, experiences, and levels of exposure to and comfort with these topics. How do I navigate all of these different dynamics in the room?" (Noah, 2017, p. 2). As I shared each fear, I asked participants to snap along (like they were in a poetry reading) if they could relate. This simple exercise of laying my personal fears out on the table and asking participants to snap if they could relate not only humanized me as a facilitator but also normalized the fears we often face when facilitating difficult conversations. By seeing and hearing others snap, participants knew that they were not alone. Additionally, sharing my fears modeled the vulnerability that I knew would be essential for our conversations throughout the remainder of the day.

It is important to note that what you choose to share about yourself in your workshops is completely up to you, based on your context and comfort level. Your social identities may influence what you choose to disclose (or not disclose), too. For example, as a young Black woman, I am often navigating additional dynamics related to power and privilege that shape what and how much I choose to share in different settings. Cavanagh (2016) suggests that if you choose to use self-disclosure, you should "do it selectively, and in ways that are relevant" (p. 88). "Don't self-disclose too frequently, don't self-disclose randomly, and don't self-disclose inappropriate information" (Cavanagh, 2016, p. 88). Adams et al. (2023) also recommend "[using] disclosure planfully, with careful consideration of the desired and likely impacts on participants and yourself" (p. 37). Ultimately, you should only share what you feel comfortable sharing while also avoiding oversharing.

Share Other Personal Tidbits

In addition to planned disclosure, you can also offer participants insight into who you are in more informal and organic ways. For example, in Chapter 4, I shared the strategy of displaying a welcome slide with a low-stakes workshop-related prompt for participants to respond to in the chat. Sharing your own response to the prompt can be an informal way to connect with learners. Additionally, you can incorporate personal tidbits about your interests, hobbies, and passions into your workshop through the stories you share, the examples you provide, the metaphors you use, the references you make, the images you include, and more.

Consider Your Personal Presence

Our presence and tone during workshops can affect how comfortable participants are in engaging with us. While there is no one "right" way to be or operate as a facilitator, below, I highlight several traits that can make a difference:

- **Dynamic and Enthusiastic**: The energy and enthusiasm we emit during workshops impacts the "feel" of the session. Eyler (2018) explains, "To some degree, simply displaying our own delight and enthusiasm for our subjects creates an atmosphere of happiness that cultivates learning. Enthusiasm is one of the most underestimated teaching tools at our disposal" (p. 128). Consider how you can convey interest and enthusiasm about the workshop topic in a way that feels genuine and authentic to you.
- **Warm and Approachable**: Being approachable during workshops is essential. If participants are fearful of us or feel uncomfortable asking questions or seeking help, that will impact their learning experience. Displaying a positive attitude, inviting questions and input, checking in with participants regularly, and being patient can help convey a warm, approachable, and supportive tone. Modeling vulnerability through appropriate self-disclosure can help, too.
- **Joyful and Humorous**: Eyler (2018) explains that happiness, humor, and other positive emotions can enhance learning. Additionally, UDL guideline 7, "Design options for welcoming interests & identities," encourages learning experiences that "nurture joy and play (7.3)" (CAST, 2024). One way to leverage the power of positive emotions and foster a joyful learning experience in workshops is to incorporate appropriate humor into the session. When using humor, Cavanagh (2016) suggests connecting the humor to the content, steering clear of humor that perpetuates stereotypes, and using humor in a way that feels authentic. This may mean finding examples of existing humorous materials (such as readings, images, or videos) that you can use (Cavanagh, 2016). For example, one of the virtual workshops I facilitate is about how to leverage QR codes for teaching and learning. During this workshop, I invite participants to scan a sample QR code on one of my slides, and then I wait. Within moments, laughing face reactions start appearing on the screen, and comments such as "LOL" and "You got me!" start filling up the chat. That's because the QR code links to a music video of Rick Astley's popular song, "Never Gonna Give You Up." (Yes, I am still Rickrolling people. Sorry, not sorry.).
- **Encouraging and Affirming**: Providing encouragement is an important way to build up and celebrate workshop participants. For me, this looks like affirming participants on a regular basis (Noah, 2023). I am constantly thanking participants for their contributions, highlighting the great ideas they're sharing, and expressing gratitude for the ways they're stretching my thinking. I want participants to know that I see, value, and appreciate them.
- **Caring and Kind**: Operating with care and kindness is key. Eyler (2018) explains that "caring is a vital ingredient for learning" (p. 132), and a key way to demonstrate care is by being kind.

Within the context of workshops, kindness and care look like many of the inclusive practices we discussed in Chapter 4. By showing learners that we care about them as people and by demonstrating kindness in our approach, we can foster trusting relationships with them.

Facilitator-to-Learner Connections

As facilitators, we should seek to learn about the participants in our sessions. Facilitator-to-learner connections not only help us connect on a personal level but also help us tailor the workshop to participants' unique interests and needs. Next, we'll explore strategies for fostering this type of connection.

Do Introductory Activities

A simple way to begin getting to know participants is by inviting them to introduce themselves. During virtual workshops, I blend introductions into the welcome slide prompt or opening activity by having participants use a workshop-related topic to introduce themselves. For example, the welcome slide prompt for my "Ending the Semester Well" workshop invites instructors to share the following in the chat: their name, department, and three words or short phrases that capture how they want their students to feel on the last day of class.

During on-site workshops, I have participants do paired or small-group introductory activities, and I walk around the room and listen in on their conversations as they introduce themselves. For example, during my "Maximizing Active Learning Classrooms for Student Engagement" workshop, instructors do a suit partner greeting. Prior to the workshop (before instructors arrive), I place a playing card at each seat. Then, during the suit partner greeting, instructors pair up with another person in the room who has the same suit on their card (e.g., a person with a heart on their playing card would pair up with another person who has a heart on their card). Instructors then introduce themselves to their suit partner by sharing their responses to these questions:

- What is your name?
- What is your department?
- Why did you come to this workshop?
- What do you hope to give?
- What do you hope to gain?

(The last three questions come from a virtual workshop I attended by Maha Bali, where we used the Impromptu Networking Liberating Structure developed by Lipmanowicz and McCandless, 2013, for introductions.)

You can also invite participants to bring a personal item to the workshop and use it as the basis for introductions. For example, if you're facilitating an on-site workshop, you can ask participants to bring an object that represents what the workshop topic means to them. During the session, participants can have small-group discussions and share who they are, what they brought, and why. If you're facilitating a virtual workshop, you can do a brief scavenger hunt activity where you challenge participants to find an object in their environment that represents or relates to the workshop topic. Participants can then share via breakout rooms as you pop into each room, or they can post photos and explanations of their objects in a shared online space (such as Padlet, Wakelet, or Google Slides).

When doing introductions, be mindful of which activities you use and how much time they will take. Participants often have mixed feelings about traditional icebreaker activities that are typically unrelated to the topic of the session. Additionally, introductory activities that require people to go around the physical or virtual room one by one to introduce themselves can often be very time consuming. Consider the size of the group and the goals and duration of the session as you decide how to incorporate introductory activities into your workshop. For example, if you're doing a workshop series where people will be meeting repeatedly, you might decide to dedicate more time to introductions during the first session in order to establish a strong foundation. In shorter workshops, you often need to use quick introductory activities.

Another option is to provide a way for participants to introduce themselves *before* the workshop. For example, you could include questions in your workshop registration form that invite participants to share about themselves and their goals for attending the session. Or, you could do Padlet Introductions. Create a new Padlet board dedicated to the workshop, share the link with participants prior to the session, and invite them to record a brief video where they introduce themselves and explain their personal goals, hopes, or intentions for the workshop. You (and participants) can watch and comment on the videos before the session to get to know each other better. Alternatively, you could use your campus' learning management system to foster connections. For example, you could create a discussion board post in Canvas and invite participants to do introductory posts there.

Use Polling Activities

Polling tools (such as Mentimeter, Poll Everywhere, Slido, and Butter Scenes) offer quick, interactive ways to get to know participants. You can ask participants questions about their roles and responsibilities, feelings about the workshop topic, prior knowledge of or experiences with the topic, goals for the session, comfort level with the topic, concerns about the topic, and more. This can help you develop a deeper understanding of the group, identify important trends, empathize with participants, and tailor the learning experience accordingly.

Acknowledge Expertise

When participants come to our workshops, they are not blank slates. Rather, they have valuable knowledge, skills, backgrounds, and experiences that they bring. Acknowledging their expertise and providing space for them to share their knowledge and lived experiences with the group can help promote connection and a sense of belonging. The NLC principle, "Respect educators' knowledge," also encourages the use of professional learning approaches that "leverage the pedagogical and leadership knowledge and skill of your educators" and that "surface all participants' expertise (pedagogical, cultural, etc.) and apply it to engaging the challenge at hand" (Bass et al., 2019, p. 32).

One way that I center participants' expertise is by including frequent discussion opportunities in my workshops, where participants can share their experiences, strategies, resources, and ideas. Also, when a participant asks a question, I sometimes invite the group to respond first. These actions reinforce that workshops are spaces of *multidirectional* learning where we can all learn from each other and not just from the facilitator.

Listen Well

The activities we incorporate into our workshops can provide numerous organic opportunities to get to know participants. This requires deep and active listening on our part. As participants engage in discussions, participate in collaborative activities, and share comments, we as facilitators need to be attentive and listen to what is being said along with what is *not* being said. Through listening well, we can learn more about participants' values, experiences, hopes, needs, and challenges.

Invite Ongoing Conversations

While connecting with participants during workshops is important, the connections don't have to end there. We can also connect after our workshops by hanging out to chat for a few minutes, sending follow-up emails, and doing consultations. For example, during the closing of every workshop, I remind participants that I'm available for pedagogical consultations, and I invite them to schedule time to meet with me. (We will discuss pedagogical consultations further in Chapter 8.)

Learner-to-Learner Connections

One of the best ways to foster connections between workshop participants is to incorporate low-stakes partner and small-group activities where they can think together. Interactive activities tap into the power of sociality for learning (per Eyler's, 2018, themes), allowing participants to cultivate deeper relationships as they share their knowledge, perspectives, and experiences with each other. In fact, participants often find that one of the most meaningful aspects of a workshop is the opportunity they have to engage in dialogue with others and learn from the ideas and experiences they share. Interactive activities also support the UDL guidelines. Guideline 8, "Design options for sustaining effort & persistence," prompts practitioners to "foster collaboration, interdependence, and collective learning (8.3)" (CAST, 2024). Additionally, guideline 9, "Design options for emotional capacity," encourages learners to "develop awareness of self and others (9.2)" and "cultivate empathy and restorative practices (9.4)" (CAST, 2024). Next, we'll explore strategies you can use to foster connection and collaboration among workshop participants.

Connect from the Start

Provide an opportunity for learners to connect during the beginning of each workshop, as this can help foster a sense of community and support participants in building rapport. The introductory activities I described earlier serve not only to help facilitators get to know learners but also to help learners get to know each other.

You can also use tools such as Chad Littlefield's (2024a) We! Connect name tags to spark connections among learners. Unlike traditional name tags which only have space to record names, these name tags also include brief prompts. There are six different prompts in the set, which include, "I am curious about…," "I am trying to solve the challenge of…," "I would love to learn more about…," "I have been thinking a lot about…," "I love talking about…," and "I wish I had more time for..." There are many ways you can use the name tags, such as by having participants record a response that relates to the workshop topic and then share their answer with a partner (Littlefield, 2024b). (Links to additional strategies for using the name tags are included in this chapter's Workshop Toolkit.)

Incorporate Interactive Activities Throughout

While it's important for participants to connect with each other at the start of the workshop, that should not be the *only* opportunity for connection. Consider how you can include interactive opportunities *throughout* the workshop. This ties back to Chapter 3's discussion of structure. We want to break up the facilitator zone with participant zone activities to allow active engagement with the content and connection with each other. The NLC principle, "Create supportive professional communities," also highlights the importance of providing space for participants to "support and learn from each other" (Bass et al., 2019, p. 36). Luckily, many strategies from the education world also work well for professional learning workshops. In the following sections, I highlight specific interactive activities you can use in your workshops. (Additional information about many of these strategies is included in this chapter's Workshop Toolkit.)

Turn-and-Talk

With the turn-and-talk technique, you pose a question or prompt to learners and then give them a minute or two to turn and talk to a partner about it (Eng, 2019). For example, in a pedagogical workshop about student engagement techniques, you might invite instructors to do a turn-and-talk in response to this question: "What is one strategy you use to engage students in learning?" Turn-and-talk is a quick and simple activity that can be used with any content. It also works well in on-site and virtual sessions. For example, participants in virtual workshops can engage in turn-and-talk via breakout rooms.

You can also adapt this strategy by doing a turn-talk-type. After the discussions, ask one person from each pair to grab their mobile device and submit the top ideas they discussed via a polling tool, such as Mentimeter (Noah, 2024). This way, you can glean insights from every pair and review the overarching themes as a whole group without having to dedicate extensive periods of time to having each pair share verbally.

Stop-Jot-Share

Eng's (2018, 2019) stop-jot-share technique incorporates writing into the sharing process. Here, you do a mini lesson about a topic, and then you stop and ask learners to jot down what they can recall. Afterward, learners share what they wrote with a partner. For example, during a pedagogical workshop about alternative grading techniques, you might first explain the characteristics of a few different models of grading (such as standards-based grading and specifications grading). Then, pause and give participants 1–2 minutes to record what they can remember about the models. Finally, invite them to share their responses with a partner.

Stop-jot-share leverages the benefits of retrieval practice by prompting participants to recall what they learned (Eng, 2018). It also taps into the power of sociality, as participants discuss ideas and help each other clarify areas of misunderstanding. Like turn-and-talk, this strategy can also be used in on-site and virtual workshops. In virtual settings, you might have participants do the stop and jot parts in the main room before transitioning to breakout rooms for the share. Or, you might have participants remain in the main room and share their response in the chat by sending a direct message to another participant.

Discussion Diamond

The discussion diamond (also referred to as the placemat) is a group discussion technique from the education world (Collaborative for Teaching & Learning, n.d.; University of Washington Institute for Science + Math Education, 2016). This technique lends itself well to professional learning workshops, too. The way it works is you divide participants into groups of four, and give each group a sheet of chart paper or a slide that is divided into five spaces: four independent writing

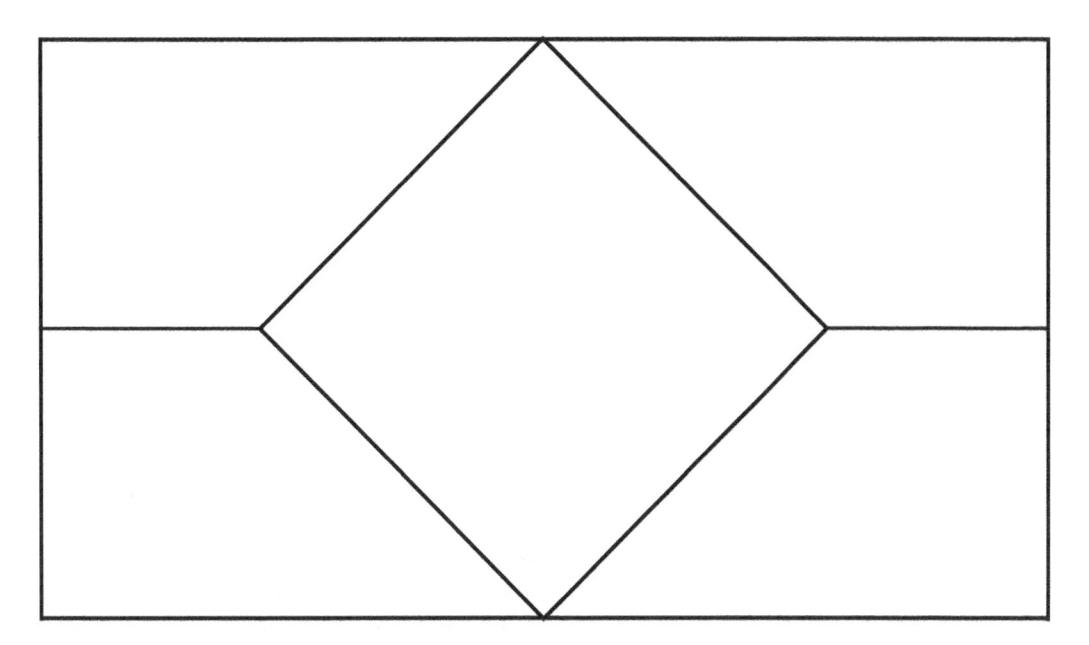

FIGURE 5.2 Sample Discussion Diamond Template

spaces in the corners or along the sides of the paper or slide, plus one common writing space in the center. (See Figure 5.2 for one way to set up the paper or slide.)

In on-site workshops, participants sit around the paper so that each person can easily access their independent writing space. In virtual workshops, you can assign participants to breakout rooms, and have each participant type their name in one of the independent spaces on a slide to "claim" their spot. You then pose a workshop-related question, prompt, or scenario to participants and have them record their responses in their spaces. Afterward, participants take turns sharing their responses with the group. Then the group discusses the responses, comes to a consensus, and records this in the center of the paper or slide.

Social Annotation

Social annotation is a collaborative learning strategy that "enables learners to add multimodal notes to digital and online resources for the purposes of information sharing, peer-to-peer interaction, collaboration, and knowledge production" (Kalir & Garcia, 2021, pp. 149–150). A variety of tools can be used for social annotation, including Google Docs, Hypothesis, Perusall, Kami, and VoiceThread. For example, during my virtual "Designing Inclusive Syllabi" workshop (discussed in Chapters 2 and 3), instructors do a social annotation activity in Google Docs, where they annotate "The Worst Syllabus Ever," a mock syllabus developed by Lindsay Masland (2020). The syllabus is full of noninclusive language, policies, and practices. Instructors join breakout rooms where they spend the first few minutes independently reading and annotating an assigned page of the syllabus using the commenting feature in Google Docs. Afterward, they discuss their observations and impressions. We then return to the main room where a representative from each group does a brief share of what they noticed. This social annotation activity is one of the most powerful aspects of the workshop, helping instructors interact with others as they reflect on the explicit and implicit messages in syllabi and how these messages can impact students.

Other Collaborative Digital Tasks

There are many other collaborative digital tasks that participants can engage in, whether the workshop is on-site or online. Participants can crowdsource ideas, strategies, and resources about the workshop topic via collaborative documents and spaces (such as Google Docs and Padlet). They can also draft workshop-related documents or plans together in Google Docs. Or, they can work in small groups to create a resource in Canva or Google Slides that relates to the workshop topic. If each group creates a resource for a different subtopic, at the end of the workshop, all participants can leave the session with a collection of resources that they can immediately use or adapt.

Four Corners

Four corners is an instructional strategy in which learners express their opinions about a prompt by moving to the corner of the room that best reflects their thoughts. This strategy works well for exploring multiple perspectives about a topic. Imagine that a facilitator is doing an on-site workshop about artificial intelligence (AI). Before the session begins, the facilitator tapes up signs labeled "Strongly Agree," "Agree," "Disagree," and "Strongly Disagree" in the four corners of the room. During the workshop, the facilitator begins the activity by reading aloud a statement such as, "The benefits of AI outweigh the drawbacks." Participants are then asked to move to the corner of the room that best reflects their opinion, and they discuss their rationale with the people in the same corner. Afterward, a representative from each corner shares a summary of their group's rationale with the whole group. Participants are also told that they can switch corners if they change their mind during the discussion. As we discussed in Chapter 4, it's important to keep participants' needs in mind when doing movement-based activities such as this. For example, you might consider having chairs available in each corner so that participants don't have to stand for extensive periods of time. Or, you might decide to do a non-movement-based version of this activity (described next).

Four corners can be adapted as a digital activity for use in both on-site and virtual settings. Simply use a collaborative online tool (such as Google Slides, Padlet Sandbox, FigJam, Miro, Mural, or Zoom Whiteboard) to divide the space into four quadrants, and label the sections "Strongly Agree," "Agree," "Disagree," and "Strongly Disagree." Then, let participants use the sticky note or text box features of the tool to add their name to the quadrant that best captures their opinion. If facilitating on-site, participants can engage in a whole group discussion from where they are seated and move their digital names around as their opinions shift. If facilitating virtually, participants can join breakout rooms based on where they placed their name. After discussing their rationale with others in the same breakout room, participants can return to the main room where a representative from each group shares what they discussed with the whole group.

Discussion Protocols

Discussions can be a valuable way to foster connections and promote curiosity about the workshop topic. In *How Humans Learn*, Eyler (2018) notes that "one of the most basic mechanisms for engaging curiosity is through asking questions" (p. 64). However, we must be mindful of the types of questions we ask, being sure to leverage "more open-ended questions than closed-ended ones" so that discussions move beyond simple, surface-level responses to deeper, more thoughtful responses (Eyler, 2018, pp. 46–48). Discussion protocols offer helpful tools for structuring discussions. They use open-ended questions and prompts that encourage curiosity and help people think about the topic deeply.

One of my favorite sources for discussion protocols is the Center for Leadership & Educational Equity (CLEE) website. They offer dozens of free protocols for many purposes. These include:

- **Text Rendering Experience** (revised by Angela Breidenstein; CLEE, n.d.-b): Participants independently read and annotate a text, and then they engage in a three-round small-group discussion where they share a sentence, phrase, and word from the text that they found most important or meaningful. After the three rounds, participants discuss the overall themes and trends they noticed, along with any additional insights.
- **ATLAS: Looking at Data** (adapted by Dianne Leahy; CLEE, n.d.-a): The facilitator provides participants with a dataset and leads them through a four-step process to discuss their observations, interpretations, implications of the data, and reflections on the experience.

Liberating Structures are also helpful tools for structuring group interactions in a way that includes all voices in the conversation (Lipmanowicz & McCandless, 2013). There are over 30 different Liberating Structures which you can read about in the book, *The Surprising Power of Liberating Structures,* or by visiting the Liberating Structures website. These include:

- **1-2-4-All** (Lipmanowicz & McCandless, 2013): Participants first respond to a question or prompt independently in writing. Afterward, they pair up to discuss their responses. Then each pair joins another pair to discuss their thoughts in groups of four. Finally, each small group shares a key thought from their discussion with the whole group.
- **TRIZ** (Lipmanowicz & McCandless, 2013, pp. 187–190): Begin by posing an "unwanted result" to participants and having each group brainstorm how they could make it a reality. For example, in a pedagogical workshop about assignment design, a facilitator might ask instructors to brainstorm responses to this question: "How could we ensure that students submit LOW quality work?" Following the brainstorm, have groups make another list of things they are currently doing that reflect the items on the original list. Finally, have groups reflect on how they could stop doing the actions on their second list.
- **25/10 Crowdsourcing** (Lipmanowicz & McCandless, 2013): This interactive brainstorming strategy begins with each participant writing an idea on an index card. Then, participants are given a few minutes to exchange cards until time is up; they should no longer have their original card and should not know whose card they have. Participants pair up to discuss the idea on the card they're holding, and afterward, they independently rate the card on a scale of 1 (low) to 5 (high) and write this score on the back of the card. (Alternatively, you could skip the paired discussion and simply have participants independently read and rate the card.) The exchange, discussion, and rating process is repeated for a total of five rounds. Afterward, participants add up the scores on the card they have to obtain a grand total, and the facilitator asks the people who are holding the top ten highest rated cards to read aloud the ideas.
- **User Experience Fishbowl** (Lipmanowicz & McCandless, 2013): This Liberating Structure can be particularly helpful for centering participants' expertise. Invite participants who have experience with the workshop topic to sit in an inner circle and have a conversation with each other about their experiences. The remaining participants sit in an outer circle, listening to the conversation. Afterward, the participants in the outer circle form small groups to discuss their observations and generate questions for the inner circle. The activity concludes with Q&A time. In a virtual workshop, you can replicate the inner/outer circle structure by spotlighting the

inner circle participants during the conversation and using breakout rooms for the small-group discussions.

If you're seeking even more discussion ideas, check out *The Discussion Book* by Brookfield and Preskill (2016), which offers 50 discussion techniques. (All of the aforementioned discussion resources are linked in this chapter's Workshop Toolkit.)

Gamified Tasks

You can nurture a spirit of collaborative play in your workshops by gamifying tasks. A simple way to do so is by incorporating spinners or dice into an activity. For example, you might provide each small group with a list of discussion questions, scenarios, topics, or tasks and have them roll dice or use a spinner to determine which questions, scenarios, or topics to discuss or which tasks to complete. While physical dice and spinners can be used, there are also free randomization tools available online. For example, in Google Chrome, you can search for "Google spinner" to bring up a virtual spinner, "Google coin flip" to bring up a virtual coin, or "Google dice roller" to bring up virtual dice. There are also websites with free randomization tools that you can easily customize and share.

You might also use popular games and activities in your workshops. For example, I've seen facilitators use bingo, digital escape rooms, LEGO blocks, Play-Doh, and word games (such as word searches) to promote play. Additionally, apps such as Goosechase can be used to create scavenger hunts that participants can complete whether they are meeting on-site or virtually. By incorporating gamified tasks into workshops, we can "nurture joy and play (7.3)" as UDL guideline 7 ("Design options for welcoming interests & identities") encourages (CAST, 2024).

Card Sort Matching Activity

Card sort matching activities involve participants working in pairs or small groups to match physical or digital cards that are related to the workshop topic. For example, participants can match key terms with their definitions, examples with categories, terms with images, and more.

During my on-site "Maximizing Active Learning Classrooms for Student Engagement" workshop, instructors engage in a card sort matching activity about Lovett et al.'s (2023) cycle of self-directed learning, which involves five metacognitive processes. Each small group receives an envelope containing 26 cards. Five of the cards have the names of the five metacognitive processes (assess, evaluate, plan, monitor, reflect). The remaining cards have guiding questions that I developed based on Lovett et al.'s descriptions of the metacognitive processes (e.g., "What are the goals of the task?," "How will I do this task?," "What did I learn?"). Instructors work in small groups to sort the cards into five categories, matching each guiding question with the metacognitive process they think it aligns with. Afterward, we review the answers as a whole group.

Card sort matching activities can also be adapted for virtual workshops. You could create a digital card sort via Padlet Sandbox, Flippity, FigJam, or Google Slides, and have participants sort the cards in breakout rooms.

Carousel

With the carousel strategy, you put chart paper around the room with questions, problems, images, text, or other workshop-related content that you want participants to engage with. Then, divide participants into small groups and have each group start at a particular station. Participants discuss the content at their station and record their thoughts on the chart paper. After a set period of time (e.g., 3–5 minutes), groups rotate clockwise to the next station and repeat the process until they have visited all of the stations.

The carousel strategy can also be done digitally. For example, in Google Slides, you can create a slide for each station (e.g., slide 1 = station 1, slide 2 = station 2, etc.). On each slide, include the content you want participants to engage with, along with a designated space for each group to record their thoughts. Have each group start on a different slide, and use a timer to signal when they should proceed to the next one. If participants are working in Zoom breakout rooms, you can use the "broadcast" feature to alert them when it's time to proceed to the next slide.

Jigsaw

Jigsaw is a popular cooperative learning strategy developed by Aronson (n.d.). The gist of this strategy is that learners are divided into small groups, and each learner in the group is responsible for learning about a specific topic which they will later teach their peers. The jigsaw technique is often used with readings, and multiple variations of the approach have emerged over the years (Gonzalez, 2015, Cult of Pedagogy, 2015; K. Patricia Cross Academy, n.d.). Here is one way that you could use the jigsaw approach in an on-site workshop:

- Prior to the workshop, select the readings or other materials you want participants to engage with, and consider how you can divide the content into 4–6 parts. For example, if I were planning a workshop for 16 participants, I would select four different articles related to the workshop topic or a long article that I can break up into four sections.
- During the workshop, divide participants into "expert groups," and assign each group a text (see Figure 5.3). Provide time for participants to independently read and annotate the text. Afterward, they should discuss the text with their "expert group" and determine the key ideas they want to share with others.
- Have participants form new "jigsaw groups" that are made up of one person from each of the "expert groups" (see Figure 5.4). Participants should then take turns teaching their "jigsaw group" about what they read.

Jigsaws are a great way to structure small-group learning and encourage deeper thinking and discussion about the workshop topic. They can also be used in virtual workshops. (You can find information on how to adapt jigsaws for online settings in this chapter's Workshop Toolkit.)

Group 1	Group 2	Group 3	Group 4
A	B	C	D
A	B	C	D
A	B	C	D
A	B	C	D

FIGURE 5.3   "Expert Groups"

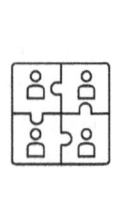

	Group 1	Group 2	Group 3	Group 4
	A	A	A	A
	B	B	B	B
	C	C	C	C
	D	D	D	D

FIGURE 5.4 "Jigsaw Groups"

Grouping Techniques

When using interactive activities in workshops, it's essential to consider how you will group participants. I prefer to use grouping techniques that are quick, easy, and don't leave anyone out. I also try to mix participants throughout the session so that they can hear more diverse perspectives, glean new ideas, and hopefully expand their professional learning network. Because grouping techniques look different in on-site and virtual workshops, we'll explore strategies based on each modality next.

On-Site Techniques

One of my favorite ways to quickly group workshop participants is by using physical objects, a practice I used extensively when I was a teacher education professor (Noah, 2019). For example, I distribute playing cards and have participants group by suit or number; distribute image cards and have participants group with others who have the same image; or write letters or numbers in the corner of the workshop handouts (e.g., A, B, C) and have participants group with others who have the same or different letters/numbers. In the past, I frequently used color as a grouping strategy, with participants forming groups based on the color of their index card, dot sticker, marker, sticky note, or handout. However, as I've learned more about accessibility, I've become more intentional about avoiding the use of color alone as a grouping strategy so as to not create barriers for participants with color vision deficiency.

Another strategy I developed to group participants is discussion partners cards. Prior to the workshop, I create cards that include space for participants to write their name at the top, along with a two-column table below. The first column lists the main topics we'll be discussing during the workshop, and the second column has space for participants to record other participants' names. For example, cards for a pedagogical workshop about self-determination theory might list these topics in the first column of the table: "intrinsic & extrinsic motivation," "competence," "autonomy," and "relatedness" (see Figure 5.5).

At the beginning of the workshop, I give each participant a discussion partners card, and I ask them to write their name at the top. Then, I give them a few minutes to mingle and select a partner for each topic. I encourage participants to select partners they do not know well or have not worked with before, and I tell them that they should only record each other's names for a particular topic if they both have that slot available. Once participants are fully booked (i.e., they have a partner listed for each topic on their card), they return to their seats. Then, throughout the workshop, we pause for activity breaks where participants meet with their topical partners to discuss ideas and complete related tasks. For example, after learning about what autonomy entails, participants might meet

Discussion Partners Card

Your Name: _____

Topic	Partner's Name
Intrinsic & Extrinsic Motivation	
Competence	
Autonomy	
Relatedness	

FIGURE 5.5   Sample Discussion Partners Card

with their autonomy partner to discuss a case study related to the topic or to brainstorm appropriate instructional strategies.

Online Techniques

In virtual workshops, you can use breakout rooms to group participants. For example, Zoom allows you to automatically assign participants to breakout rooms of specific sizes (e.g., four participants per room), manually assign participants to specific rooms, or let participants choose their own rooms based on their personal interests or backgrounds (e.g., topical rooms, discipline-based rooms, etc.). (Breakout rooms will be discussed further in Chapter 11.)

Provide Clear Structure

Regardless of the activities you use to foster connection and collaboration in your on-site and virtual workshops, it's important to provide a clear structure so that participants understand what to do. When designing activities, keep the 5Ws in mind:

- **Who?** Explain who participants will be working with. In on-site workshops, consider using a grouping strategy or providing verbal prompts such as, "Pair up with the person sitting across from you" in order to ensure that no one is left out.
- **What?** Describe the specific task that participants should complete. Be sure to provide the directions in multiple formats as well. I always display directions on a slide and/or handout in addition to explaining them verbally. This way, participants can look back at the slide or handout for a reminder of what to do. Providing directions in multiple formats also supports UDL guideline 1, "Design options for perception," by "[supporting] multiple ways to perceive information (1.2)" (CAST, 2024).
- **Where?** Explain where the task should be completed (e.g., on a handout, an assigned Google slide, etc.).

- **When?** Specify how much time participants will have to complete the task (and adjust accordingly as needed).
- **Why?** Make the purpose of the task clear and relevant so that participants understand the rationale for doing it.

One helpful framework for crafting clear activity guidelines is the Transparency in Learning and Teaching (TILT) framework, which involves specifying the purpose of the activity, the specific tasks to be completed, and the criteria for success (Winkelmes et al., 2019). By providing a clear structure for interactive activities, you can minimize participants' confusion and maximize the time they have to learn from and with each other.

Recap

- Foster learner-to-facilitator connections by sharing appropriate parts of your professional journey and/or personal story and by being mindful of your personal presence.
- Nurture facilitator-to-learner connections by doing introductory activities, engaging in active listening, and inviting the expertise of the group.
- Promote learner-to-learner connections through interactive activities.
- Use grouping techniques to mix participants.
- Provide clear guidelines for interactive tasks.

Sticky Note Reflection

Top Three: Which three connection ideas from this chapter resonated with you most? Why?

Workshop Toolkit

Scan the QR code or visit the URL to access additional resources related to this chapter.

www.tolunoah.com/workshop-toolkits

Design Time

Review your workshop plans. Do you include ways to foster learner-to-facilitator, facilitator-to-learner, and learner-to-learner connections? If not, design activities that can help participants connect with you and each other.

Facilitators' Lounge

Join the Facilitators' Lounge to connect with other readers and share your takeaways, strategies, and next steps!

www.tolunoah.com/facilitators-lounge/

References

Adams, M., Briggs, R.R., & Shlasko, D. (2023). Pedagogical foundations for social justice education. In M. Adams, L.A. Bell, D.J. Goodman, & D. Shlasko (with R.R. Briggs & R. Pacheco) (Eds.), *Teaching for diversity and social justice* (4th ed., pp. 27–55). Routledge.

Aronson, E. (n.d.). *History of the jigsaw*. Jigsaw Classroom. www.jigsaw.org/history/

Bass, R., Eynon, B., & Gambino, L.M. (2019). *The New Learning Compact: A framework for professional learning and educational change*. Every Learner Everywhere. www.everylearnereverywhere.org/resources/the-new-learning-compact/

Bouwma-Gearhart, J. (2012). Research university STEM faculty members' motivation to engage in teaching professional development: Building the choir through an appeal to extrinsic motivation and ego. *Journal of Science Education and Technology, 21*, 558–570. https://doi.org/10.1007/s10956-011-9346-8

Bowman, S.L. (2009). *Training from the BACK of the room! 65 ways to step aside and let them learn*. Pfeiffer.

Brookfield, S.D., & Preskill, S. (2016). *The discussion book: 50 great ways to get people talking*. Jossey-Bass.

CAST. (2024). *Universal Design for Learning guidelines version 3.0*. https://udlguidelines.cast.org/

Cavanagh, S.R. (2016). *The spark of learning: Energizing the college classroom with the science of emotion*. West Virginia University Press.

Center for Leadership & Educational Equity. (n.d.-a). *ATLAS: Looking at data*. www.clee.org/resources/atlas-looking-at-data/

Center for Leadership & Educational Equity. (n.d.-b). *Text rendering experience*. www.clee.org/resources/text-rendering-experience/

Cohen, G.L. (2022). *Belonging: The science of creating connection and bridging divides*. W.W. Norton & Company.

Collaborative for Teaching & Learning. (n.d.) *Placemat*. https://ctlonline.org/placemat-2/

Cult of Pedagogy. (2015, April 15). *The jigsaw method* [Video]. YouTube. https://youtu.be/euhtXUgBEts?feature=shared

Eng, N. (2018, April 23). *Introducing stop-jot-share*. https://normaneng.org/introducing-stop-jot-share/

Eng, N. (2019). *PRESENTING: The professor's guide to powerful communication*. EDUCATIONxDESIGN.

Eyler, J.R. (2018). *How humans learn: The science and stories behind effective college teaching*. West Virginia University Press.

Gonzalez, J. (2015, April 15). *4 things you don't know about the jigsaw method*. Cult of Pedagogy. www.cultofpedagogy.com/jigsaw-teaching-strategy/

Kalir, R., & Garcia, A. (2021). *Annotation*. The MIT Press.

K. Patricia Cross Academy. (n.d.). *Teaching technique 04: Jigsaw*. https://kpcrossacademy.org/techniques/jigsaw/

Lipmanowicz, H., & McCandless, K. (2013). *The surprising power of Liberating Structures: Simple rules to unleash a culture of innovation*. Liberating Structures Press.

Littlefield, C. (2024a, June 4). *3 fun ways to start a meeting* [Video]. YouTube. https://youtu.be/Q6MXf6Q6WMY?feature=shared

Littlefield, C. (2024b, June 5). *5 creative ways to start a meeting* [Video]. YouTube. https://youtu.be/bGwtaYJhERA?feature=shared

Lovett, M.C., Bridges, M.W., DiPietro, M., Ambrose, S.A., & Norman, M.K. (2023). *How learning works: 8 research-based principles for smart teaching*. Jossey-Bass.

Masland, L. (2020). *Worst syllabus ever workshop – Syllabus*. https://docs.google.com/document/d/1B0XLubyZ3qI0GVsUQDJY0k1ct4yH5hlR29hGdGKuxjk/edit

Noah, T. (2017). Encourage, enlighten, engage: Using the three E's to build students' intercultural competence. *International Christian Community of Teacher Educators Journal, 12*(1), 1–7. https://digitalcommons.georgefox.edu/icctej/vol12/iss1/6/

Noah, T. (2019). *10 easy grouping techniques for the college classroom*. The Scholarly Teacher. www.scholarlyteacher.com/post/10-easy-grouping-techniques-for-the-college-classroom

Noah, T. (2023, March 14). *Designing virtual edtech faculty development workshops that stick: 10 guiding principles*. EDUCAUSE Review. https://er.educause.edu/articles/2023/3/designing-virtual-edtech-faculty-development-workshops-that-stick-10-guiding-principles

Noah, T. (2024, October 14). *I tried a slight adaptation of the Think, Pair, Share strategy today in a hybrid workshop where I was facilitating* [Image attached] [Post]. LinkedIn. www.linkedin.com/posts/tolu-noah_facilitationthoughts-professionallearning-activity-7251719381133508608-Rwcm?utm_source=share&utm_medium=member_desktop

Parker, P. (2018). *The art of gathering: How we meet and why it matters.* Riverhead Books.

Steinert, Y., Mann, K., Anderson, B., Barnett, B.M., Centeno, A., Naismith, L., Prideaux, D., Spencer, J., Tullo, E., Viggiano, T., Ward, H., & Dolmans, D. (2016). A systematic review of faculty development initiatives designed to enhance teaching effectiveness: A 10-year update: BEME guide no. 40. *Medical Teacher, 38*(8), 769–786. http://dx.doi.org/10.1080/0142159X.2016.1181851

Strayhorn, T.L. (2019). *College students' sense of belonging: A key to educational success for all students* (2nd ed.). Routledge.

University of Washington Institute for Science + Math Education. (2016). *Student talk flowchart and protocols.* STEM Teaching Tools. https://stemteachingtools.org/assets/landscapes/FullSet_StudentTalkProtocolsandFlowchart1_c.pdf

Winkelmes, M.-A., Boye, A., & Tapp, S. (2019). *Transparent design in higher education teaching and leadership: A guide to implementing the transparency framework institution-wide to improve learning and retention.* Routledge.

6
USE ACTIVE LEARNING STRATEGIES

Guiding Question:
How will participants actively engage with the workshop topics?

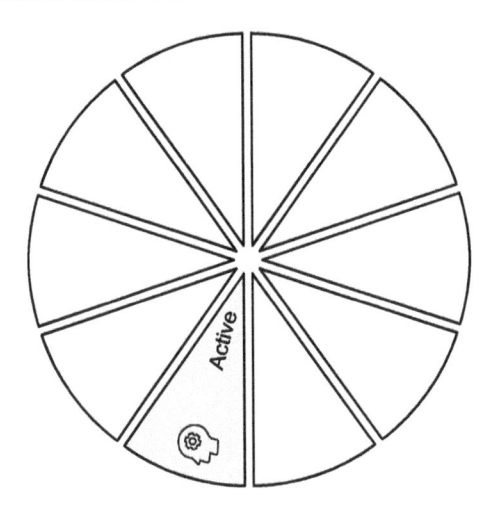

A popular working definition of active learning from the educational research literature is as follows: "Active learning engages students in the process of learning through activities and/or discussion in class, as opposed to passively listening to an expert. It emphasizes higher-order thinking and often involves group work" (Freeman et al., 2014, pp. 8413–8414). One common misconception about active learning is that it requires engaging in some sort of physical activity; in reality, it is more about how students are mentally engaging with the material (Oakley et al., 2021). Active learning is recognized as an "evidence-based pedagogy" that can enhance student learning (Eynon & Iuzzini, 2020, p. 26). However, Silverman (2024) notes that, in some cases, active learning activities could inadvertently create barriers for students and that "deliberate attention to inclusion and accessibility" when designing and facilitating active learning activities is key. (Please revisit Chapter 4 for recommendations about how to leverage Universal Design for Learning [UDL] to identify and address potential barriers.)

Active learning matters not only in classroom contexts but also in professional learning contexts. Steinert et al. (2016) note that "experiential learning and opportunities for practice and application" are critical components of effective faculty development programs (p. 777). Similarly, Zakrajsek (2010) lists "inclusion of some form of collaborative or active learning on the part of the participants" as an important element of workshops (pp. 95–96). Additionally, Bowman (2009) emphasizes that participants need "time to discuss, question, move, act, participate, teach and learn from each other" in order to retain and apply their learning (p. 11).

DOI: 10.4324/9781003482963-7

In short, participants need to *do* something with the information they're learning rather than simply being expected to take it all in.

While the COVID-19 pandemic has prompted educational developers to be more intentional about using and modeling active learning techniques in their workshops (Kuntz et al., 2022), it is still common to experience workshops where the facilitator spends most of the time talking while participants sit and listen. Put another way, some workshops continue to prioritize time in the facilitator zone rather than the participant zone.

The "sit-and-get" form of professional learning represents what Clark and Mayer (2024) call a "receptive" or "information acquisition" approach, where the goal is to convey information to participants as they simply listen (pp. 14, 23–24). Such approaches to workshop facilitation can pose a variety of challenges for participants. First, the sheer amount of information conveyed can increase participants' cognitive load. Sweller et al. (2011) explain that "when processing novel information, the capacity of working memory is extremely limited," and when we have to process a lot of new information, "our working memory processing system tends to break down" (p. 43). In other words, "learning slows and frustration grows" (Clark & Mayer, 2024, p. 32). An important implication of this as workshop facilitators is to be mindful of the amount of information we are conveying at once.

Other challenges posed by lecture-dominant workshop approaches relate to Eyler's themes of authenticity and sociality. Eyler (2018) explains that "prolonged lecturing" is inauthentic and does not create space for the "social engagement" that contributes to learning (pp. 164–168). Additionally, Cougler Blom (2021) notes that presentation-based approaches often do not create space for learners to share their own expertise. This can ultimately limit opportunities for participants to learn from each other.

Rather than using receptive or transmissive approaches, Clark and Mayer (2024) encourage the use of a "guided discovery" or "knowledge construction" approach, where we engage learners as "active sense makers" (pp. 14, 24). They explain:

> Simply telling learners what you want them to know is not enough. You also need to help learners process the information, based on what we know about how the human mind works. You can fill the screen with all kinds of information, but productive learning will not happen unless the learner pays attention to the relevant material, mentally organizes it into a meaningful structure, and integrates it with relevant prior knowledge.
>
> *(Clark & Mayer, 2024, pp. 25–26)*

CAST (2024a) adds that "**building usable knowledge...depends not upon merely perceiving information, but upon active skills** like making connections, synthesizing information, asking questions, selective attending, integrating new information with prior knowledge, strategic categorization, and active memorization" (emphasis in original). By incorporating these types of active learning opportunities into workshops, we can help participants better understand, retain, and apply their learning.

From a professional learning standpoint, the strategies we use in our workshops can also serve as important models for participants. This is particularly true for educational developers who facilitate professional learning for instructors about effective teaching. As instructors observe and experience the techniques we use in our workshops, they may reflect on their own instructional practices and consider implementing similar techniques in their teaching. In fact, the New Learning Compact (NLC) principle, "Connect with practice," highlights the importance of ensuring that "your professional development methods model the pedagogies and practices you hope to encourage" (Bass et al., 2019, p. 33). If we promote the use of active learning pedagogies but fail to use those techniques in our professional learning workshops, what message does that send to instructors?

Additionally, *who* participates in active learning in our workshops matters just as much as *how*. Bowman (2009) and Eng (2019) encourage the use of techniques that engage everyone, not just a few people. Within the realm of education, Himmele and Himmele (2017) refer to this as a "total-participation mindset," where educators leverage "techniques that allow for all students to demonstrate, at the same time, active participation and cognitive engagement in the topic being studied" (p. 4). Bruff (2019) refers to this as "all-skate," where all students have the opportunity to participate in activities (pp. 44–51). As we design professional learning workshops, we should consider how to incorporate activities that allow every participant to engage. Many of the interactive strategies we explored in Chapter 5 (such as turn-and-talk and jigsaw) are also active learning techniques that embody a "total-participation"/"all-skate" approach.

In this chapter, we will explore additional active learning strategies that you can use, whether you're facilitating on-site or virtually. We'll use APA format (no, not that one!) as our guiding framework. Here, APA stands for:

- **Activate** prior knowledge
- **Process** new information
- **Apply** learning

Additionally, we'll explore the importance of offering choices as participants engage in active learning activities.

Activate Prior Knowledge

One way to incorporate active learning into workshops is to include activities during the beginning of the workshop that help participants activate their prior knowledge of the topic. As Brown et al. (2014) explain, "Learning always builds on a store of prior knowledge. We interpret and remember events by building connections to what we already know" (p. 100). UDL guideline 3, "Design options for building knowledge," also prompts practitioners to help learners "connect prior knowledge to new learning (3.1)" (CAST, 2024c). Next, we'll explore practical strategies for activating participants' prior knowledge. (Additional resources about these strategies are linked in this chapter's Workshop Toolkit.)

Entrance Tickets

Entrance tickets are a popular instructional strategy for activating prior knowledge. At the start of your workshop, provide participants with a paper or digital "ticket" where they will respond to a question or prompt related to the workshop topic. An entrance ticket for a pedagogical workshop about metacognition, for example, might ask, "What is metacognition?" For paper-based entrance tickets, participants can write their response on a half sheet of paper, an index card, or a sticky note. For digital entrance tickets, participants can submit their response via Google Forms, or post their response in a collaborative online space (such as Padlet, FigJam, Mural, or Miro). Polling tools (such as Mentimeter, Poll Everywhere, Slido, and Butter Scenes) also work well for digital entrance tickets. Following the entrance ticket activity, you can review the responses as a whole group or have participants discuss their responses in pairs or small groups (as you listen in) to obtain a sense of their initial understanding of the topic.

Three Words

With Three Words, participants share three words or phrases that they associate with the workshop topic. Having participants distill their thoughts into three words or phrases can be a helpful way to obtain a sense of their initial conceptualization of the workshop topic. It can also help you to identify areas that participants may not know about or associate with the topic based on what is missing from their responses. This strategy works particularly well with digital polling tools such as Mentimeter and Poll Everywhere, which can produce a word cloud of the results and make it easier to examine the major themes and trends.

Guess the Stats

If your workshop involves data of some sort, you can use Guess the Stats to activate participants' prior knowledge. Display some data or statistics on a slide or handout that relate to the workshop topic, but replace the numbers and percentages with blanks. Then, have participants guess the numbers that should go in each blank.

During a past on-site session, I displayed four fill-in-the-blank statistics on a slide and provided participants with four colorful index cards labeled with four different numbers. Each participant paired up with a colleague to read the statistics and discuss which number they thought completed each blank and why. Afterward, I read aloud the statistics one at a time and asked participants to hold up the index card with the number they thought was correct. Because the cards were different colors, I could easily see at a glance what the most popular responses were. I then revealed the correct answers.

Guess the Stats works well in virtual workshops, too. In 2023, I attended a workshop at the online Teaching, Learning, and Technology Conference (TLTCon), where the facilitators (April Higgins and Hilary Valentine) used this strategy expertly. Their workshop was about microlearning, and rather than starting the workshop by presenting data about microlearning, April and Hilary had participants guess the results instead. They would put up a statement about microlearning with the number or percentage intentionally left out, ask participants to share their guesses in the chat, and then reveal the correct answer. This process continued for a few statements. The activity not only helped participants activate their prior knowledge of microlearning, but it also resulted in high levels of participant engagement.

Knowledge and Skills Ratings

Knowledge ratings are a common instructional strategy in which students are provided with a list of vocabulary words or concepts related to a reading, lesson, or unit, and they rate their knowledge of each term on a 3–4 point scale that ranges from not knowing what the term means to understanding the term well (Bifield, n.d.; Blachowicz, 1986; Eberly Center, n.d.; Kinsella, 2005; Taylor et al., 2009; Urquhart & Frazee, 2012). You can adapt the knowledge rating strategy for your workshops by having participants rate their knowledge of workshop-related concepts. Figure 6.1 shows a sample knowledge rating for a workshop about the science of learning, where instructors rate their knowledge of the terms "retrieval practice," "spacing," "interleaving," and "metacognition" using this scale (adapted from Kinsella, 2005 & Taylor et al., 2009):

- I don't know what this means.
- I have seen or heard this before, but I don't know the meaning.
- I can explain the meaning of this.

Knowledge Rating

Workshop Topic: The Science of Learning

	I don't know what this means.	I have seen or heard this before, but I don't know the meaning.	I can explain the meaning of this.	I could teach someone else about this.
Retrieval Practice				
Spacing				
Interleaving				
Metacognition				

FIGURE 6.1 Sample Knowledge Rating

- I could teach someone else about this.

If your workshop is skills-based, participants can complete a skills rating instead where they rate their level of proficiency for each skill. For example, in a workshop about digital accessibility, the skills rating might list skills such as "add alt text to images" and "create descriptive hyperlinks." Participants could rate their proficiency for each skill on a scale that ranges from not knowing how to do the skill to being able to teach others how to perform the skill.

Knowledge and skills ratings can be completed on paper, via digital handouts, or via survey and polling tools such as Google Forms, Qualtrics, and Mentimeter. If facilitating virtually via Zoom, you could put a copy of the knowledge or skills rating on a slide and have participants use the stamp tool in the annotation toolbar to mark how they would rate themselves for each concept or skill. This strategy has the added benefit of helping you to quickly identify trends across the entire group.

Pre-Tests

Have participants complete a brief pre-test at the start of the workshop that addresses the main workshop concepts. The pre-test could include multiple choice, fill-in-the-blank, matching, true/false, and/or short answer questions. It can be completed on paper or via digital tools such as Google Forms, Qualtrics, Quizizz, Kahoot, or Mentimeter.

Pre-tests are not only a great way to activate participants' prior knowledge, but they also tap into the power of generation. Brown et al. (2014) explain that "generation is an attempt to answer a question or solve a problem before being shown the answer or the solution" (p. 208). The authors also note that generation strengthens memory. "By wading into the unknown first and puzzling through it, you are far more likely to learn and remember the solution than if somebody first sat you down to teach it to you" (Brown et al., 2014, p. 209).

Flipped Learning Anticipation Guide

Before Workshop True or False?	Statement	After Workshop True or False?	Notes
	One example of flipped learning is moving lectures outside of class time so that students have time during class to do higher-order activities.		
	To do flipped learning, instructors need to record or curate instructional videos that students can watch before class.		
	Flipped learning can only be done in on-site classes.		
	Instructors and students need to have access to high-quality technology in order to do flipped learning well.		
	Flipped learning requires more responsibility on the part of the student.		

FIGURE 6.2 Sample Anticipation Guide for Flipped Learning Workshop

Note: Statements inspired by Talbert (2017)

Anticipation Guides

Anticipation guides are commonly used as pre-reading or pre-unit activities (Duffelmeyer, 1994; Facing History & Ourselves, 2009); however, they can also be used at the beginning of workshops to activate participants' prior knowledge of the workshop topic. Before the workshop, prepare a handout that includes a list of statements related to the workshop topic, along with space for participants to record whether they think each statement is true or false (or whether they agree or disagree with each statement). Be sure to include some statements that address common misconceptions participants may have about the topic. Figure 6.2 shows a sample anticipation guide based on a pedagogical workshop about flipped learning.

At the beginning of the workshop, ask participants to independently read the list of statements and mark whether they think each statement is true or false (or whether they agree or disagree). Then, let them discuss their responses in pairs, small groups, or as a whole group. If facilitating virtually, you can have participants share their responses in the chat or discuss them in breakout rooms. Afterward, proceed with the remainder of the workshop, and at the end of the session, have participants revisit their anticipation guide and mark their thoughts for each statement again to see if/how their thoughts have changed. Participants can also record supporting notes in the last column of the handout.

Process New Information

A second way to incorporate active learning into workshops is to include activities that help participants process the new information they're learning. The interactive activities we discussed

118 Designing and Facilitating Workshops with Intentionality

in Chapter 5 (such as jigsaws, turn-and-talk, and social annotation) also work well as processing activities, but they're just the start! Next, we'll explore additional activities that participants can do to engage with and make sense of the workshop topics. (Resources related to these strategies are linked in this chapter's Workshop Toolkit.)

Quickwrite

Quickwrite is a common instructional strategy that works well as a processing activity in workshops. Pause during the workshop and give participants a brief amount of time (e.g., 1–2 minutes) to write a response to a workshop-related question or prompt. You can then follow up with a brief discussion or proceed to the next part of the workshop.

TQE Method

The TQE method is a discussion strategy developed by educator, Marisa Thompson, to help students engage in deeper discussions of course-related texts and other media (Thompson, n.d.). The general process entails four steps, where students (a) read the text, (b) generate TQEs (i.e., thoughts, questions, and epiphanies), (c) engage in small group discussions about their TQEs, and (d) discuss the top TQEs from each group as a whole class. I have found it helpful to adapt the TQE method as a quick processing activity. For example, after explaining some content, you can pause and invite participants to share a thought, question, or epiphany about the content in the chat, via a polling tool (such as Mentimeter, Poll Everywhere, or Butter Scenes), or via a digital whiteboard tool (such as Padlet Sandbox or Miro) (see Figure 6.3). Afterward, you can review the responses as a group before proceeding to the next part of the workshop.

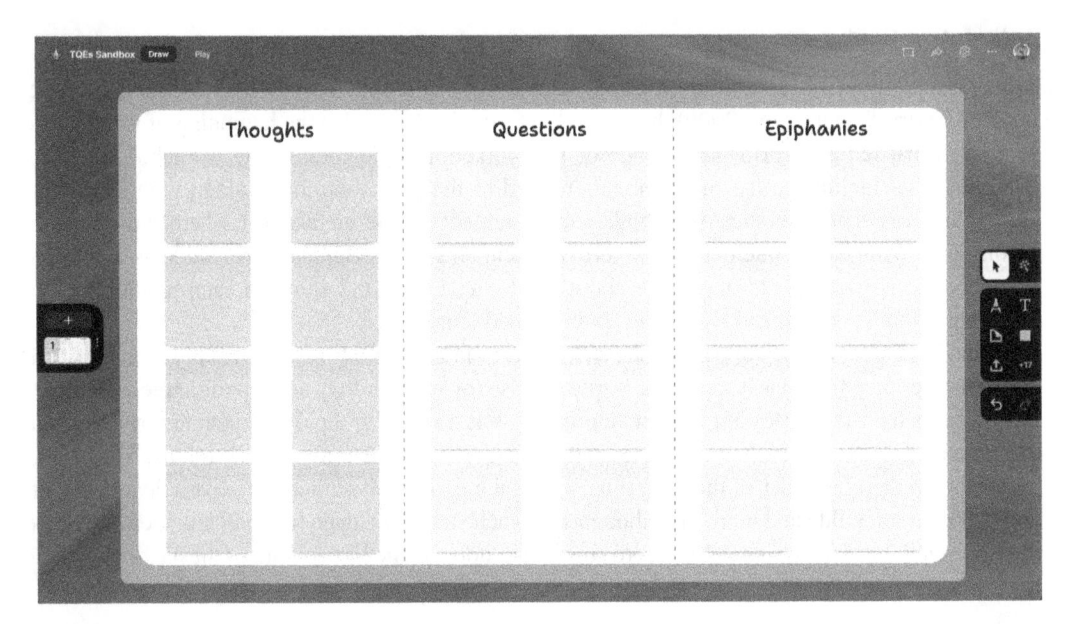

FIGURE 6.3 A TQE Activity in Padlet Sandbox
Note: TQE method adapted from Thompson (n.d.)

Response Cards

Response cards are a popular formative assessment strategy from the education world; they also work well in workshops. Prior to the workshop, prepare a set of cards for each participant. For example, you might prepare a set of true/false cards by writing the letters T and F on index cards. Alternatively, you might create a set of agree/disagree or multiple choice (A, B, C, D) cards. You can even create a set of cards that are more specific to the workshop topic. For example, for a pedagogical workshop about self-determination theory, you might prepare a set of cards labeled "competence," "autonomy," and "relatedness." Symbols (such as thumbs up/thumbs down) and images (such as pictures and icons related to the workshop topic) can also be used.

During the workshop, provide each participant with a set of response cards. Then, pose a series of questions, and ask participants to raise the card that matches their response. In virtual workshops, you can replicate this strategy by asking participants to grab a sheet of paper and create their own cards or by mailing a set of cards to each participant in advance. You could also create slides that represent the response cards (such as a slide with two boxes labeled "True" and "False") and have participants use the Zoom annotation stamp tool to mark their answers on the screen.

Another response card option with a digital twist is Plickers. These are special cards that have unique barcodes, along with four answer choices around the barcode (A, B, C, D). Each participant simply rotates their card so that their answer choice is on top, and then they hold up their card. The facilitator can then use the Plickers app on their phone or tablet to quickly scan all the cards and view the results. For virtual workshops, you can use the Plickers e-learning tool instead, where participants use their devices to submit their answers.

Visualization Activities

Participants can create visualizations (such as concept maps, sketchnotes, or infographics) as another way of processing workshop content. With these types of tasks, participants use a combination of drawings/images and text to synthesize their learning and make connections between ideas.

Retrieval Practice

Agarwal and Bain (2019) define retrieval practice as "bringing information to mind or pulling information out" (p. 36). In other words, it's the process of recalling previously learned information (Agarwal & Bain, 2019). Research shows that retrieval practice enhances learning. Agarwal et al. (2020) explain that "by trying to recall information, we exercise or strengthen our memory, and we can also identify gaps in our learning" (p. 2). In essence, retrieval practice "interrupts forgetting" (Brown et al., 2014, p. 3). Research also shows that retrieval practice (along with feedback) can aid in the transfer of learning to new situations (Pan & Agarwal, 2020).

A simple way to incorporate retrieval practice into workshops is by pausing at strategic points throughout the workshop to have participants write down or explain to a colleague what they have learned so far. (Eng's, 2019, stop-jot-share strategy from Chapter 5 is a perfect example of this.) You could also administer brief quizzes or knowledge checks using paper-based quizzes, Plickers, or other tools (such as Google Forms, Kahoot, Quizizz, or Mentimeter). If the workshop is skills-based, you could have participants do skills checks where you pause and have them complete a short list of tasks using the skills they have learned so far (Noah, 2023). The key is incorporating activities that prompt participants to recall what they previously learned.

Retrieval practice activities work well not only within a specific workshop but also across workshops. In fact, research recommends spacing out retrieval practice for greater impact (Agarwal et al., 2020; Brown et al., 2014). For example, if you're facilitating a workshop series, you can have participants do retrieval practice activities at the start of each session, where they recall what they learned in previous sessions.

Metacognitive Exercises

Designing activities that prompt participants to engage in metacognition is yet another way that we can help them process the new information they're learning. Chick (2013) defines metacognition as follows:

> Metacognition is, put simply, thinking about one's thinking. More precisely, it refers to the processes used to plan, monitor, and assess one's understanding and performance. Metacognition includes a critical awareness of a) one's thinking and learning and b) oneself as a thinker and learner.

Several of the activities discussed in this chapter are also metacognitive strategies that encourage participants to think about their thinking (e.g., knowledge and skills ratings, the TQE method). Another metacognitive strategy you can use is "Aha! & Huh?" I first experienced this strategy in a workshop facilitated by Stephanie Fenwick and Shawna Lafreniere Nist. Since then, I have continued to use and adapt the strategy in my own professional learning work. The way this strategy works is that you pause at strategic points during the workshop and ask participants to jot down an "aha" and a "huh."

"Ahas" can include:

- Revelations or new insights
- Key takeaways
- Ideas for how to apply what has been learned so far
- Something they found interesting, surprising, or engaging
- Important reminders

"Huhs" can include:

- Questions
- Concerns
- Ideas they're grappling with
- Areas they found confusing or challenging
- Things they want to practice further or learn more about
- Areas where they would like additional support

If your workshop is on-site, you can follow up each "Aha! & Huh?" pause with a brief share where participants discuss what they wrote with a partner while you go around the room and listen in. Or, if you're facilitating virtually, you can have participants share their "ahas" and "huhs" in the chat, in a collaborative online space (such as Padlet), or via breakout rooms.

Gallery Walk

Gallery walks are related to the carousel strategy, which we discussed in Chapter 5. While carousels involve participants visiting stations in groups, gallery walks involve participants visiting stations independently.

In on-site workshops, you can set up gallery walk stations on the walls around the room. Each station should contain different workshop-related content, such as photos, graphs, charts, questions, problems, or excerpts from a text. The stations could also include QR codes linked to online content, such as videos, audio clips, or websites (Noah, 2022). During the workshop, give participants a set period of time to walk around the room and silently explore the content. As participants visit each station, they should record their thoughts on a graphic organizer or guided notes sheet. Alternatively, participants could jot down their thoughts on sticky notes that they will place on the wall at each station, or they could write their thoughts on chart paper that is already placed at each station. After the independent exploration time has ended, facilitate a discussion with the whole group.

Gallery walk activities can also be done digitally. For example, you could create a shared Google Slide deck or Padlet Sandbox where each slide/card represents a different station. Or, you could create a Wakelet or Padlet board where each column of the board represents a station. Give participants a set period of time to independently visit the virtual stations and post their thoughts using the built-in tools of the platform. Afterward, facilitate a conversation about the activity.

Self-Explanation

Research shows that explaining what you're learning to yourself or others helps the learning stick (Brown et al., 2014; Lang, 2021; Lovett et al., 2023). You can incorporate self-explanation into workshops through discussions, written exercises, and other activities that prompt participants to explain their thinking. For example, you could invite participants to do a quickwrite, create an audio recording, or do a turn-and-talk where they explain a workshop-related concept in their own words. You could even use the Directed Paraphrasing technique, where you ask learners to gear their explanation toward a particular audience and purpose (Angelo & Zakrajsek, 2024). In a pedagogical workshop about flipped learning, for example, you might ask instructors to respond to this prompt: "Imagine that you're planning to flip your class, and you want to share with your students what flipped learning entails and why you're doing it. What would you tell them?"

Apply Learning

The popular saying goes, "Give a person a fish, and you feed them for a day. Teach a person how to fish, and you feed them for a lifetime." I would argue that the second half of that quote needs to be unpacked further. *How* you teach a person to fish matters. A person who is taught to fish simply by listening to someone explain the process is probably not going to be able to feed themselves as well as someone who is taught how to fish through direct opportunities to practice and receive guidance about their approach. The same is true in the context of professional learning. Simply telling participants what we want them to know or be able to do will not suffice; rather, participants need ample opportunities to practice and receive feedback. As Clark and Mayer (2024) explain, "practice with feedback helps you improve" (p. 217).

This brings us to our third way to incorporate active learning into workshops: include activities that allow participants to practice, or apply, what they are learning. With respect to self-determination theory, application activities can help participants build competence. They can also give participants the chance to learn from their mistakes. As Eyler (2018) notes, failure is a key way in which humans learn, and it "can be one of our biggest allies in learning if we use it appropriately" (p. 196).

When determining what types of application activities to use in workshops, keep these factors in mind:

- **Goals**: The application activities you select should align with the learning goals of the workshop. For example, if one of the workshop goals is to "Design a course assignment using the transparent design (TILT) framework," then participants should have time to practice that skill.
- **Authenticity**: Use authentic, or realistic, tasks when possible. As Eyler (2018) explains, people "learn the most from realistic problems and authentic scenarios" (p. 154). Authentic tasks also support UDL guideline 7, "Design options for welcoming interests & identities," which encourages practitioners to "optimize relevance, value, and authenticity (7.2)" (CAST, 2024c).
- **Relevance**: As we discussed in Chapter 1, it's important for workshops to be relevant to participants. Consider how you can design practice activities in a way that relates to participants' goals, work, and context.
- **Transfer**: Design practice activities for transfer. Cilliers and Tekian (2016) note that providing participants with time to practice and receive feedback during professional learning programs can support them in transferring what they have learned to their work. UDL guideline 3, "Design options for building knowledge," also encourages practitioners to "maximize transfer and generalization (3.4)," and a key way to do so is through practice activities (CAST, 2024c).

Next, we'll explore practical application activities you can use in workshops. (Resources related to these strategies are linked in this chapter's Workshop Toolkit.)

Scenarios and Case Studies

Participants can apply their learning by responding to workshop-related scenarios and case studies where they analyze a situation and determine the best course of action. You can use existing case studies and scenarios or create them with the assistance of AI tools such as ChatGPT. Participants can work independently, in pairs, or in small groups to respond to the case studies or scenarios. Afterward, you can debrief the activity as a whole group.

Role-Play

Role-playing activities can help participants apply their learning and receive feedback in an interactive manner. For example, during the workshops that I co-facilitated with Tasha Souza, Tasha led participants in a series of role-plays where they practiced using the Open the Front Door (OTFD) technique (along with other communication frameworks) to respond to challenging situations (see Chapter 4 for more details about OTFD).

One format that you can use for role-playing activities is the Improv Prototyping Liberating Structure (Lipmanowicz & McCandless, 2013). Here, a group of participants role-plays a challenging scenario while the remaining participants observe. The observers discuss what worked well and what could be improved, and then a new group of participants volunteers to act out a revised response. The process continues with participants iterating on the role-plays until they have developed solid solutions to the scenario.

Practice Activities

Practice activities are another great way to help participants apply their learning. In an *EDUCAUSE Review* article entitled "Designing Virtual Edtech Faculty Development Workshops that Stick: 10 Guiding Principles," I share several ways to structure practice activities. You can do a series of demo/practice cycles where you demonstrate a skill and then pause to give participants time to practice; use the "explore with me" format where participants practice the skills right along with you; do skills checks where you have participants use skills they've learned so far to complete a series of tasks independently; or incorporate sandbox time where you give participants time to independently explore and try out skills of their choice (Noah, 2023).

For example, during the 2024 ISTE Conference, I facilitated a virtual workshop entitled "Digital Accessibility 101: How to Create Accessible Instructional Materials." In this session, I introduced participants to the acronym, C.H.I.L.L., which stands for color, headings, images, links, and lists. I chunked the session into five parts based on the five letters of the C.H.I.L.L. acronym, and each chunk used a demo/practice format:

- Demo: I briefly shared a few important digital accessibility principles related to the topic and why they matter. For example, for images, I explained the importance of adding alt text and demonstrated how to use Chen's (2020) "object-action-context" format to write alt text for a sample image. I also explained the process for adding alt text to images in Google Docs.
- Practice: Participants did a practice activity in Google Docs where they helped a mock teacher educator named Marcella revise a specific part of her syllabus and assignment guidelines using the principles they had just learned. For example, the practice activity for the image topic entailed participants adding alt text to an image in Marcella's syllabus.

We repeated the demo/practice process for each part of the C.H.I.L.L. acronym so that participants not only learned about what the digital accessibility principles are and why they matter, but they also gained hands-on practice implementing each one. By the end of the 50-minute workshop, many participants rated their skill level in creating accessible documents higher than at the start, and several even shared that they would be passing along the information they learned to their colleagues!

As you design practice activities, consider how you can also incorporate interleaving, which involves mixing practice (Agarwal & Bain, 2019; Brown et al., 2014). For example, after learning about each digital accessibility topic separately and gaining some initial practice with each skill, I could have had participants do a culminating activity that involved practicing all of the skills in a mixed fashion if time permitted.

Planning and Application Time

With planning and application time, you give participants time during the workshop to begin creating a lesson plan, activity, assignment, or resource that they can use in their work (Noah, 2023). Consider providing participants with an optional graphic organizer or template they can use for planning purposes, such as a Google Doc or Slide (see Figure 6.4). Since participants are often pressed for time, including dedicated time during the workshop where they can get a head start on planning and creating materials while you are available to provide support can be very helpful (Noah, 2023).

Name: _____	
Lecture Topic or Unit	
Goals (What do you hope students will know or be able to do by the end of the lecture/unit?)	
Assessments (How will you assess students' progress toward the learning goals?)	
Activities (What activities will students do to make progress toward the learning goals? What content will they need to learn?)	
ISPACE Integration (How could you use the 3D Printing Lab, 360° Theater, XR Lab, or Podcast Studio to support engagement, enhancement, or extension of the learning goals?)	

FIGURE 6.4   Sample Google Slides Planning Template for Innovation Space (ISPACE) Workshop

Self-Assessment

For self-assessment activities, you can ask participants to bring a sample document to the workshop that they will evaluate during the session (such as a sample assignment or course syllabus), or you can provide time during the workshop for participants to create an initial draft of a document and then self-assess it. To structure the self-assessment, provide participants with a checklist, rubric, or a set of guiding questions that they can use to evaluate their work. As participants determine their strengths and areas for growth, they can begin revising their work during the workshop or make plans for how they will revise it afterward.

Projects

Application activities can also be in the form of "educational projects" that participants complete (Steinert et al., 2016, p. 777). For example, if you're facilitating a workshop series, you might have participants submit artifacts of learning throughout the series (such as sample course assignments or materials that incorporate the principles learned). Alternatively, participants could complete a culminating task, such as a digital portfolio or exhibition.

The Power of Choice

As you incorporate active learning activities into your workshops, consider how you can offer participants choices. Choice-based activities support participants' autonomy. Additionally, UDL guideline 7, "Design options for welcoming interests & identities," prompts practitioners to "optimize choice and autonomy (7.1)," noting that "embedding authentic choices that align with learning goals can be a meaningful way to enhance learner engagement" (CAST, 2024b).

Next, we'll explore options for providing choice in terms of three Ts: topics, tasks, and tools. (Additional resources about choice-based activities are linked in this chapter's Workshop Toolkit.)

Topics

One way to offer choices during workshops is to give participants options for what they learn about during the session. This can be as simple as letting participants choose which topics to explore, which readings to complete, or which subjects to discuss.

Choice boards are a great tool for this purpose. For example, if you're facilitating a pedagogical workshop about active learning, you could create a choice board in Padlet with links to different active learning techniques (see Figure 6.5). Participants can select at least one technique from each column that they are interested in learning more about and "like" each post to indicate their choice. Then, participants can explore the linked resources and add comments to the Padlet posts describing how they could use the active learning techniques in their courses.

Another adaptation of this strategy is QR Code Tic-Tac-Toe boards (Noah, 2022; Noah, 2023). The QR Code Tic-Tac-Toe board is divided into nine squares, each of which contains a QR code and hyperlink to different workshop-related content (see Figure 6.6). Participants choose three topics of interest on the board, and they can either scan the QR codes or click on the links to learn more about them. Afterward, they complete a brief reflection about what they learned.

When facilitating virtual workshops via Zoom, you can also offer participants choice of topic via the self-select breakout rooms feature. Here are some different ways I've seen facilitators leverage this tool:

- Name each breakout room with a different discussion topic, and let participants choose which room to join.
- Provide a numbered list of discussion topics or questions on a slide or handout, and have participants join the room that matches their topic of interest.
- Prior to the workshop, identify several individuals who would be willing to do a lightning talk or short demonstration about a specific topic. During the workshop, briefly introduce the presenters and the topics they will discuss. Then, create a breakout room for each presenter, and have participants join the room that matches the topic they are most interested in learning about. This strategy can be a great way to center other people's expertise in workshops!

Tasks

A second way to offer choices during workshops is to give participants different activity options. For example, you could let participants select tasks of interest from a menu (such as reading an article, watching a brief video, or listening to a short podcast episode about the workshop topic). Likewise, you could create a simple choice board with different activities that participants can do to demonstrate their learning; these might include doing a written exercise, recording a video, creating an audio recording, or drawing a visual to express their learning. These types of options support UDL guideline 5, "Design options for expression & communication," which encourages learners and practitioners to "use multiple media for communication (5.1)" and "address biases related to modes of expression and communication (5.4)" (CAST, 2024c). Academia tends to value and emphasize certain forms of expression (such as writing) over others; providing participants with options for how they can show what they know is a simple yet powerful way to combat this.

Additionally, you can design the workshop itself in a "Choose Your Own Adventure" (CYOA) format. I do this in my virtual "Creating Engaging Learning Opportunities with Padlet" workshop in order to better address the different levels of experience that instructors and staff may have with Padlet. Some participants may be using Padlet for the very first time, whereas others may already have experience with the tool and want to go deeper. Rather than using an approach where

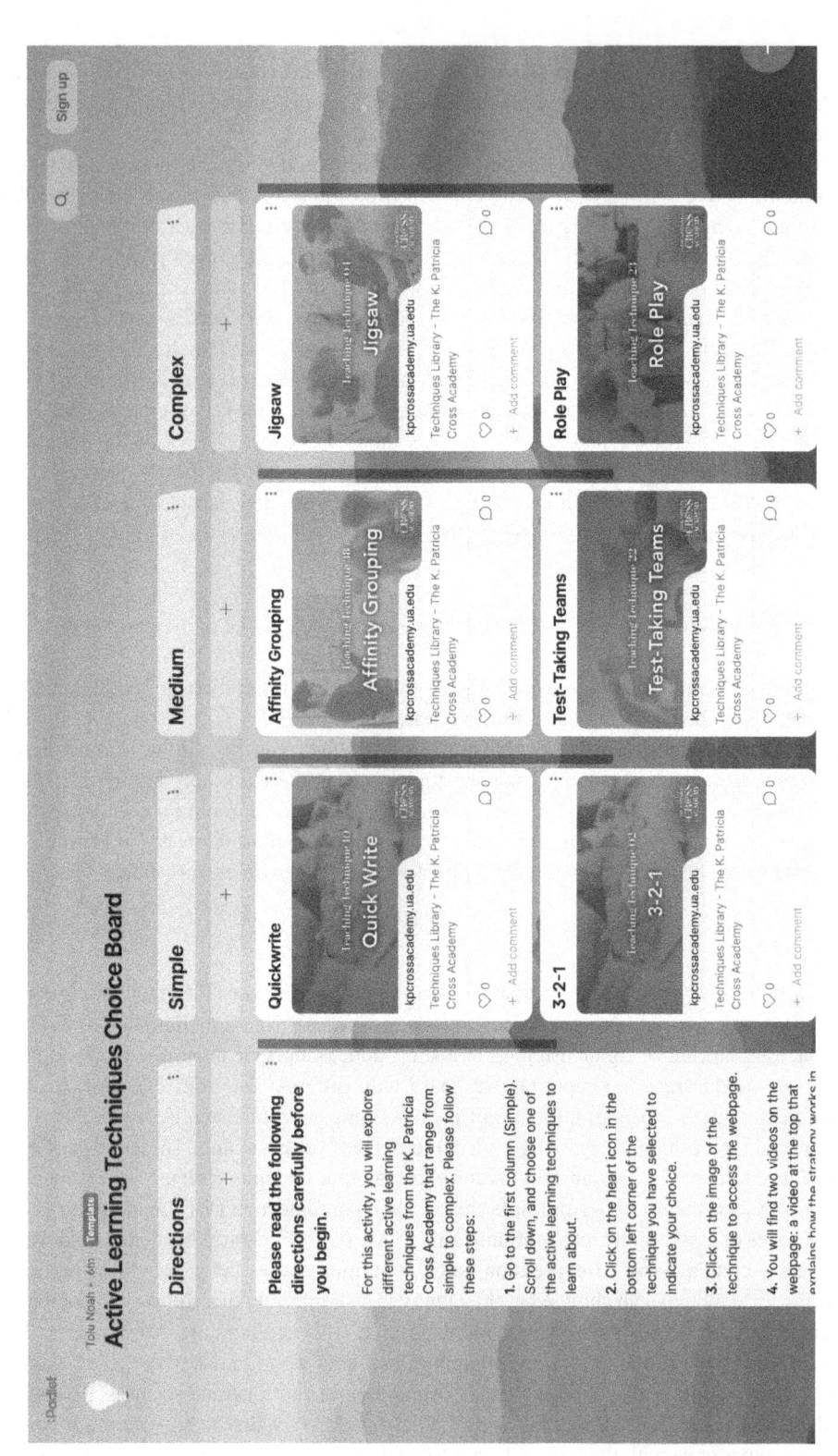

126 Designing and Facilitating Workshops with Intentionality

FIGURE 6.5 Sample Padlet Choice Board about Active Learning Techniques

QR Code Tic-Tac-Toe: Active Learning Techniques

Directions: The K. Patricia Cross Academy offers a variety of active learning techniques you can use to engage students in learning. First, choose three techniques below to learn about. Next, click on the links or scan the QR codes to explore the resources about each technique. Finally, complete the reflection box with your thoughts, takeaways, and/or application ideas.

Quickwrite	Affinity Grouping	Jigsaw
3-2-1	Test-Taking Teams	Role Play
Update Your Classmate	Note-Taking Pairs	Case Studies

Reflection

FIGURE 6.6 Sample QR Code Tic-Tac-Toe Board about Active Learning Techniques

everyone must learn the same content, I design multiple paths that offer different levels of support. This aligns with UDL guideline 5, "Design options for expression & communication," which prompts practitioners to help learners "build fluencies with graduated support for practice and performance (5.3)" (CAST, 2024c).

I start the Padlet workshop by providing a brief overview of what Padlet is and by sharing examples of the different types of boards one can create. The remainder of the workshop is facilitated in a CYOA format. I offer participants two paths: Padlet 1.0 (Padlet Basics) or Padlet 2.0 (Go Further). Padlet 1.0 is ideal for beginners. Here, I guide participants through the process of creating an account and making Padlet boards step-by-step, with ample opportunities to practice throughout. Padlet 2.0 is ideal for experienced users. Here, participants explore the newer and more advanced features of Padlet via a self-paced "game" I designed in Padlet (see Figure 6.7). The game includes multiple levels that progress from learning about simpler features of Padlet to more complex ones. At each level, participants can choose a specific feature of Padlet to learn about and try, and then they add a comment to the board describing how they might use the feature in their work. After providing a brief overview of the two paths, I invite participants to select the path they want to take and let me know their choice in the chat. Padlet 1.0 participants then remain in the main room with me, while Padlet 2.0 participants join one of two breakout rooms to complete the game (a silent room if they prefer to work on their own or a chat room if they prefer to engage in discussions with others while they work). Near the end of the workshop, the Padlet 1.0 and 2.0 participants come back together in the main room to debrief and share ways that they could incorporate Padlet into their teaching or other professional practices. I also provide all participants with access to the Padlet 2.0 game so that those who chose the Padlet 1.0 path during the workshop can still learn about other features after the session.

Tools

A third way to offer choices during workshops is to give participants options for the tools they use to complete tasks. This supports UDL guideline 5, "Design options for expression & communication," which prompts learners to "use multiple tools for construction, composition, and creativity (5.2)" (CAST, 2024c). For example, if you're having participants complete a concept map activity during your workshop, you could let them choose which tools they use to create it. Some might decide to stick with paper and pencil, whereas others might decide to use digital tools such as Google Drawings, Canva, FigJam, or Padlet Sandbox.

Additional Tips

When incorporating choice of topics, tasks, or tools into your workshops, remember that a little goes a long way. You don't need to provide dozens of options in order to provide adequate choices. In fact, research shows that providing too many choices can result in "choice overload," where people may feel more stressed, less motivated to make a decision, and less satisfied with their ultimate decision (Reutskaja et al., 2020, pp. 625–636). Providing just a few options will suffice.

Going Further

In this chapter, we explored practical ways to incorporate active learning into your workshops. However, the activities I highlighted here are just the tip of the iceberg! If you're interested in learning even more active learning techniques, check out Bowman's (2009) book, *Training from the BACK of the Room!*, and Rice's (2018) book, *Hitting Pause*. Both books offers dozens of active learning strategies for engaging learners. There are also great websites that offer a variety of active learning techniques, such as the Teaching Tools Active Learning Library and the K. Patricia Cross Academy. While some websites are geared toward the education realm, you can adapt many of the

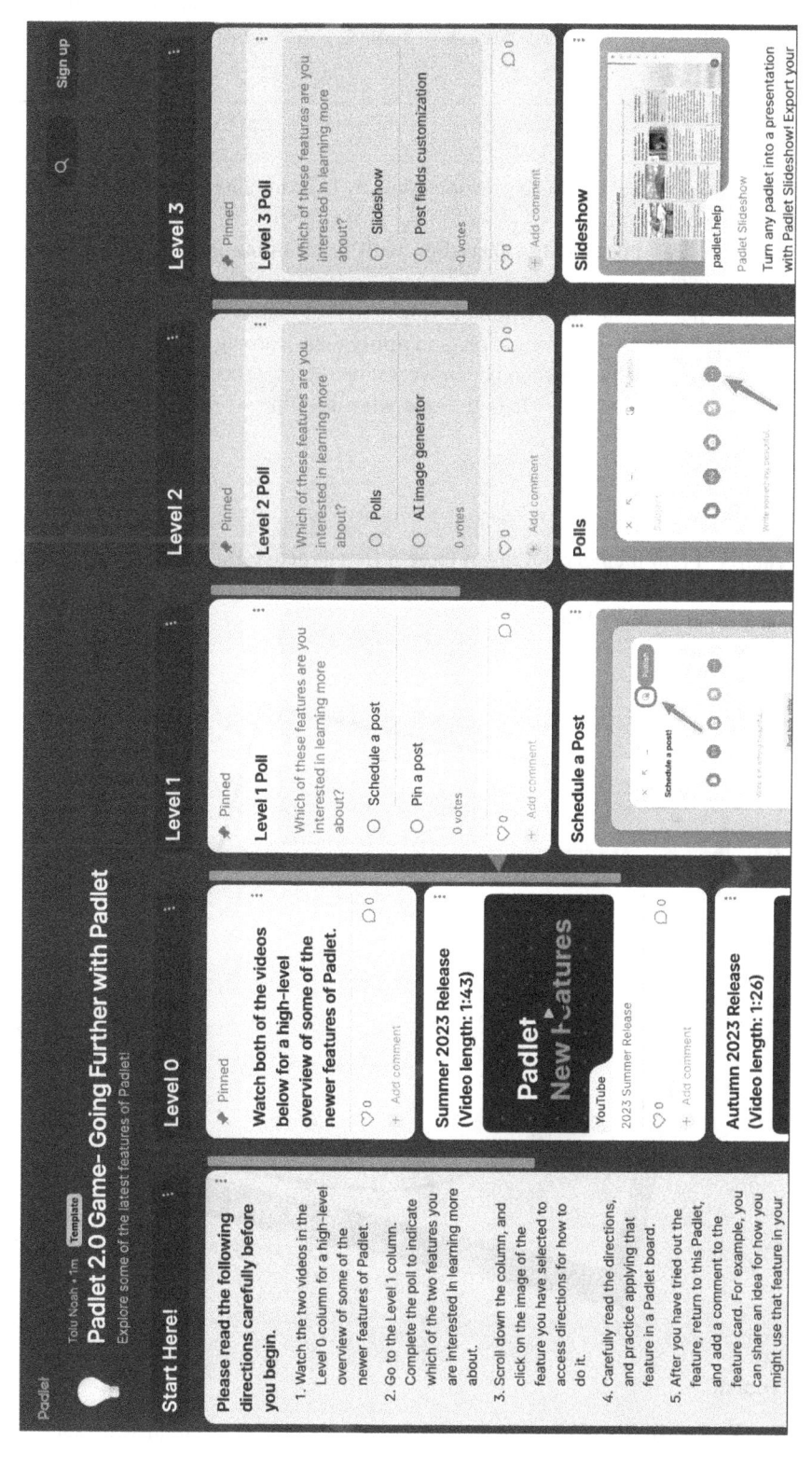

FIGURE 6.7 Padlet 2.0 Game

strategies for use within professional learning settings, too. Links to these and other active learning resources can be found in this chapter's Workshop Toolkit.

Recap

- Minimize extensive lecturing during workshops by maximizing opportunities for active participant engagement.
- Incorporate active learning activities that align with the learning goals of the workshop and engage all participants.
- Use APA format (no, not that one!) by employing activities that help participants **activate** their prior knowledge, **process** new information, and **apply** their learning.
- Consider ways to offer participants choice in workshop topics, tasks, and/or tools.
- Remember, as Terry Doyle says, "It is the one who does the work who does the learning" (StylusPub, 2012).

Sticky Note Reflection

Retrieval Practice: From memory, jot down three different active learning techniques from this chapter that you can use to help participants (a) activate their prior knowledge, (b) process new information, and (c) apply their learning.

Workshop Toolkit

Scan the QR code or visit the URL to access additional resources related to this chapter.

www.tolunoah.com/workshop-toolkits

Design Time

Review your workshop plans from a participant lens, reflecting on how much time they will spend sitting and listening versus actively engaging with the workshop topics. Consider how you can break up long periods of lecturing with active learning opportunities that help participants activate their prior knowledge, process new information, and apply their learning.

Facilitators' Lounge

Join the Facilitators' Lounge to connect with other readers and share your takeaways, strategies, and next steps!

www.tolunoah.com/facilitators-lounge/

References

Agarwal, P.K, & Bain, P.M. (2019). *Powerful teaching: Unleash the science of learning.* Jossey-Bass.
Agarwal, P.K., Roediger III, H.L., McDaniel, M.A., & McDermott, K.B. (2020). *How to use retrieval practice to improve learning.* http://pdf.retrievalpractice.org/RetrievalPracticeGuide.pdf
Angelo, T.A. (with Zakrajsek, T.D.). (2024). *Classroom assessment techniques: Formative feedback tools for college and university teachers* (3rd ed.). Jossey-Bass.

Bass, R., Eynon, B., & Gambino, L.M. (2019). *The New Learning Compact: A framework for professional learning and educational change*. Every Learner Everywhere. www.everylearnereverywhere.org/resources/the-new-learning-compact/

Bifield, J. (n.d.). *Knowledge rating scale*. EAL in the Daylight. https://ealdaylight.wordpress.com/knowledge-rating-scale/

Blachowicz, C.L.Z. (1986). Making connections: Alternatives to the vocabulary notebook. *Journal of Reading, 29*(7), 643–649. www.jstor.org/stable/40029692

Bowman, S.L. (2009). *Training from the BACK of the room! 65 ways to step aside and let them learn*. Pfeiffer.

Brown, P.C., Roediger III, H.L., & McDaniel, M.A. (2014). *Make it stick: The science of successful learning*. The Belknap Press of Harvard University Press.

Bruff, D. (2019). *Intentional tech: Principles to guide the use of educational technology in college teaching*. West Virginia University Press.

CAST. (2024a). *Design options for building knowledge*. https://udlguidelines.cast.org/representation/building-knowledge/

CAST. (2024b). *Optimize choice and autonomy*. https://udlguidelines.cast.org/engagement/interests-identities/choice-autonomy/

CAST. (2024c). *Universal Design for Learning guidelines version 3.0*. https://udlguidelines.cast.org/

Chen, A. (2020, July 16). *How to write an image description*. https://uxdesign.cc/how-to-write-an-image-description-2f30d3bf5546

Chick, N. (2013). *Metacognition*. Vanderbilt University Center for Teaching. https://derekbruff.org/vanderbilt-cft-teaching-guides-archive/metacognition/

Cilliers, F.J., & Tekian, A. (2016). Effective faculty development in an institutional context: Designing for transfer. *Journal of Graduate Medical Education, 8*(2), 145–149. https://doi.org/10.4300%2FJGME-D-15-00117.1

Clark, R.C., & Mayer, R.E. (2024). *e-Learning and the science of instruction: Proven guidelines for consumers and designers of multimedia learning* (5th ed.). Wiley.

Cougler Blom, B. (2021). *Design to engage: How to create and facilitate a great learning experience for any group*. FriesenPress.

Duffelmeyer, F.A. (1994, March). Effective anticipation guide statements for learning from expository prose. *Journal of Reading, 37*(6), 452–457. www.jstor.org/stable/40032252

Eberly Center. (n.d.). *Prior knowledge self-assessments*. Carnegie Mellon University. www.cmu.edu/teaching/assessment/priorknowledge/selfassessments.html

Eng, N. (2019). *PRESENTING: The professor's guide to powerful communication*. EDUCATIONxDESIGN.

Eyler, J.R. (2018). *How humans learn: The science and stories behind effective college teaching*. West Virginia University Press.

Eynon, B., & Iuzzini, J. (2020). *ATD teaching & learning toolkit: A research-based guide to building a culture of teaching & learning excellence*. Achieving the Dream. https://achievingthedream.org/teaching-learning-toolkit/

Facing History & Ourselves. (2009, October 19). *Anticipation guides*. www.facinghistory.org/resource-library/anticipation-guides

Freeman, S., Eddy, S.L., McDonough, M., Smith, M.K., Okoroafor, N., Jordt, H., & Wenderoth, M.P. (2014). Active learning increases student performance in science, engineering, and mathematics. *Proceedings of the National Academy of Sciences, 111*(23), 8410–8415. https://doi.org/10.1073/pnas.1319030111

Himmele, P., & Himmele, W. (2017). *Total participation techniques: Making every student an active learner* (2nd ed.). ASCD.

Kinsella, K. (2005, November). *Teaching academic vocabulary*. www.scoe.org/docs/ah/AH_kinsella2.pdf

Kuntz, A., Davis, S., & Fleming, E. (2022, May 3). *7 ways the pandemic changed faculty development*. EDUCAUSE Review. https://er.educause.edu/articles/2022/5/7-ways-the-pandemic-changed-faculty-development

Lang, J.M. (2021). *Small teaching: Everyday lessons from the science of learning* (2nd ed.). Jossey-Bass.

Lipmanowicz, H., & McCandless, K. (2013). *The surprising power of Liberating Structures: Simple rules to unleash a culture of innovation*. Liberating Structures Press.

Lovett, M.C., Bridges, M.W., DiPietro, M., Ambrose, S.A., & Norman, M.K. (2023). *How learning works: 8 research-based principles for smart teaching*. Jossey-Bass.

Noah, T. (2022, August 10). *8 ways to use QR codes in higher education classrooms*. EDUCAUSE Review. https://er.educause.edu/articles/2022/8/8-ways-to-use-qr-codes-in-higher-education-classrooms

Noah, T. (2023, March 14). *Designing virtual edtech faculty development workshops that stick: 10 guiding principles*. EDUCAUSE Review. https://er.educause.edu/articles/2023/3/designing-virtual-edtech-faculty-development-workshops-that-stick-10-guiding-principles

Oakley, B., Rogowsky, B., & Sejnowski, T.J. (2021). *Uncommon sense teaching: Practical insights in brain science to help students learn*. TarcherPerigree.

Pan, S.C., & Agarwal, P.K. (2020). *Retrieval practice and transfer of learning: Fostering students' application of knowledge*. https://pdf.retrievalpractice.org/TransferGuide.pdf

Reutskaja, E., Iyengar, S., Fasolo, B., & Misuraca, R. (2020). Cognitive and affective consequences of information and choice overload. In R. Viale (Ed.), *Routledge handbook of bounded rationality* (1st ed., pp. 625–636). Routledge.

Rice, G.T. (2018). *Hitting pause: 65 lecture breaks to refresh and reinforce learning*. Routledge.

Silverman, S. (2024, May 16). The asterisk to "active learning." *Beyond the Scope*. https://open.substack.com/pub/beyondthescope/p/the-asterisk-to-active-learning?utm_campaign=post&utm_medium=web

Steinert, Y., Mann, K., Anderson, B., Barnett, B.M., Centeno, A., Naismith, L., Prideaux, D., Spencer, J., Tullo, E., Viggiano, T., Ward, H., & Dolmans, D. (2016). A systematic review of faculty development initiatives designed to enhance teaching effectiveness: A 10-year update: BEME guide no. 40. *Medical Teacher, 38*(8), 769–786. http://dx.doi.org/10.1080/0142159X.2016.1181851

StylusPub. (2012, January 31). *The one who does the work is the one who does the learning* [Video]. YouTube. https://youtu.be/LDJU4DI13No

Sweller, J., Ayres, P., & Kalyuga, S. (2011). *Cognitive load theory*. Springer.

Talbert, R. (2017). *Flipped learning: A guide for higher education faculty*. Routledge.

Taylor, D.B., Mraz, M., Nichols, W.D., Rickelman, R.J., & Wood, K.D. (2009). Using explicit instruction to promote vocabulary learning for struggling readers. *Reading & Writing Quarterly, 25*(2–3), 205–220. https://doi.org/10.1080/10573560802683663

Thompson, M.E. (n.d.). *TQE: Thoughts, questions, and epiphanies*. Unlimited Teacher. www.unlimitedteacher.com/tqe

Urquhart, V., & Frazee, D. (2012). *Teaching reading in the content areas: If not me, then who?* (3rd ed.). ASCD.

Zakrajsek, T.D. (2010). Important skills and knowledge. In K.J. Gillespie, D.L. Robertson, & Associates (Eds.), *A guide to faculty development* (2nd ed., pp. 83–98). Jossey-Bass.

7
PROVIDE TIME AND SPACE FOR REFLECTION

Guiding Question:
How will participants reflect on their learning and determine appropriate next steps?

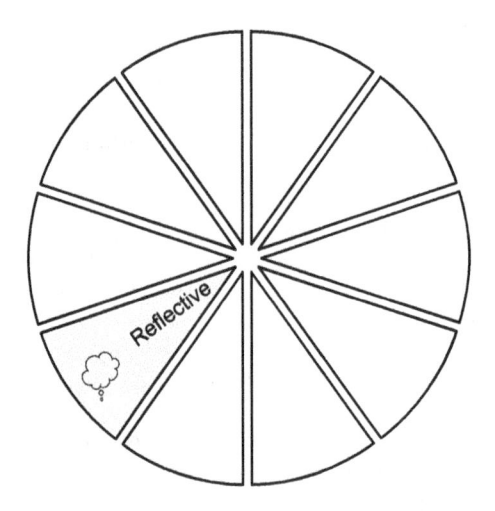

Although I haven't been to an amusement park in years, I have fond memories of trips to Disneyland with friends and family. (Living in California my entire life has definitely come with some perks!) While I can't do most rollercoasters, I have really enjoyed certain fast-speed rides such as Indiana Jones Adventure, Big Thunder Mountain Railroad, and Space Mountain. As a rider, I've noticed that there are three common stages people typically experience when going on rides. First, there is a period of anticipation when you're standing in line, waiting for it to be your turn. Once you arrive at the front of the line and take your seat, the anticipation continues to build as the ride slowly begins. Second, there is a period of exhilaration when you're in the thick of the ride, enjoying the fast speeds, sudden turns and drops, and special effects. Finally, as the ride comes to an end and you slowly re-enter the station, there is a period of reflection when you excitedly turn to your friends or family members and talk about the experience. "Oh my goodness! That was so much fun!" "That drop was intense!" "Let's get back in line and do this again!"

These three stages (anticipation, exhilaration, and reflection) also mirror what is possible within professional learning settings. Participants often experience anticipation in the time leading up to the workshop and on the day of as the session gets started. They also hopefully experience some degree of exhilaration during the workshop itself, as they are able to engage with the content and each other in meaningful ways. However, the third stage, reflection, is often either missing or cut short in workshops. Facilitators may find themselves going until the very end of the session, trying to teach one last piece of content, finish one last activity, or share some logistics without providing adequate time for participants to reflect on the learning experience. There is often no slow period of re-entry, or the re-entry period is rushed. In other words, the learning ride just suddenly ends.

While reflection time might seem like a "nice to have" in workshops, it is a critical component of any professional learning experience. Through reflection, learners can synthesize their learning and consider how they will apply it to their work. The importance of reflection is also highlighted in the New Learning Compact (NLC) principle, "Engage inquiry and reflection," which encourages educational developers to "make space for reflection, revision, and integration into broader teaching-learning practice" (Bass et al., 2019, p. 34).

Reflection also plays a critical role in the learning process. Brown et al. (2014) explain that "reflection can involve several cognitive activities that lead to stronger learning: retrieving knowledge and earlier training from memory, connecting these to new experiences, and visualizing and mentally rehearsing what you might do differently next time" (p. 27). It is through reflection that people can engage in the important work of "meaning-making" (Fink, 2013, pp. 117–118; Parker, 2018, pp. 259–260). Additionally, Universal Design for Learning (UDL) guideline 6 ("Design options for strategy development") suggests reflection as a strategy to help learners "enhance capacity for monitoring progress (6.4)" (CAST, 2024a).

In *The Art of Gathering*, Parker (2018) explains the importance of creating space during the closing of a gathering for "looking inward and turning outward" (p. 259). "Looking inward" entails participants reflecting on what occurred during the gathering and connecting with each other for the final time, whereas "turning outward" entails participants reflecting on how they will take what they learned/experienced in the gathering with them (Parker, 2018). In this chapter, we will explore practical reflection strategies you can use to help participants look inward by reflecting on their learning. We will also explore action planning exercises that can help participants turn outward by determining appropriate next steps.

Reflecting on Learning

Reflection activities can help participants process their learning, identify areas of confusion, note areas of growth, and much more. Below are several activities that can be helpful for structuring reflections. (Additional resources about these strategies are linked in this chapter's Workshop Toolkit.)

Minute Paper

The Minute Paper is a popular formative assessment technique from the education world that involves students taking a few minutes to respond to two questions (Angelo & Zakrajsek, 2024, p. 65):

"1. What was/were the most important thing(s) you learned in today's class?
2. What question(s) do you still have about that material?"

This technique could easily be adapted for use in professional learning workshops by having participants reflect on the key ideas they learned in the workshop and any lingering questions they have. Participants can submit their responses on paper or via a variety of digital tools (such as Padlet, Google Forms, Google Docs, Mural, Mentimeter, or Butter Scenes). One benefit of using Mentimeter for this purpose is that you can leverage its built-in AI features to automatically group the responses based on similar themes or create a summary of the results; this can be particularly helpful if you are facilitating a workshop for a large group, and you want to be able to quickly review some of the key themes with the group.

3-2-1 Reflection

3-2-1 is a popular reflection strategy within the education realm, where an educator creates three prompts and has students record three ideas for the first prompt, two ideas for the second prompt, and one idea for the third prompt. For example, students might record three new ideas they learned during class, two things that were interesting, and one remaining question they have (K. Patricia Cross Academy, n.d.).

The 3-2-1 reflection strategy also works well in professional learning settings. For example, if you're facilitating a workshop about an educational technology tool (such as Poll Everywhere or Hypothesis), you might invite participants to complete a 3-2-1 reflection in response to these prompts:

- 3 things I learned about [edtech tool]
- 2 ways [edtech tool] could be used for teaching and learning
- 1 feature I want to explore further

The 3-2-1 technique is incredibly versatile. You can decide what the prompts are and how many things participants should record for each one. For example, you might have participants share connections, questions, opinions, successes, challenges, next steps, application ideas, topics or resources they want to explore further, and more.

Group Anthem

Group Anthem is a simple yet powerful strategy developed by Nate Folan (Littlefield & Wise, 2021). Here, each participant shares a statement that starts with one of these three sentence starters: "I am, I believe, or I will" (Littlefield & Wise, 2021, p. 60). You could use Group Anthem as a reflection strategy at the end of a workshop by inviting participants to quickly share their statements aloud, in the chat, on sticky notes, or via a digital tool (like Mentimeter, Padlet, or Miro).

Postcard Reflection

If you're seeking a novel reflection strategy, consider using postcards (Bassot, 2023; Herring, n.d., as cited in Rice, 2018). This strategy can be particularly useful at the end of longer programs, such as an all-day workshop or a multiday institute. Simply give each participant a postcard, and invite them to complete it by addressing it to themselves and responding to a reflection question such as, "What are your key takeaways from this learning experience?" Afterward, collect the postcards, and let participants know that you will mail them to them within a few weeks or months. The postcard reflection strategy can be a great way to help participants' future selves revisit what they learned.

Learning Audit

In *Becoming a Critically Reflective Teacher*, Brookfield (2017) shares a strategy called the learning audit, where at the end of each week, students reflect on three questions:

- What do I know now that I didn't know this time last week?
- What can I do now that I couldn't do this time last week?
- What could I teach others to know or do that I couldn't teach them last week?

(p. 103)

This strategy can be adapted for use in long-term professional learning programs, such as workshop series and courses. Participants can reflect on the three learning audit questions at the end of each workshop in the series or at the end of each week in the course to see how their knowledge and skills develop over time.

Social Media Share

Social media platforms (such as Bluesky and LinkedIn) can be leveraged as reflection tools. Simply create a specific hashtag related to your program, and invite participants to share their takeaways on their platform of choice using the given hashtag. (In this book, for example, I have invited you to share your thoughts via the hashtag, #TheWorkshopWheel.) You (and participants) can then look up the hashtag to review everyone's thoughts. This strategy has the added benefit of encouraging participants to share their learning with their friends, family, and professional network so that others could potentially glean from the insights shared.

Action Planning

In addition to "looking inward" by reflecting on their learning, it's also important for participants to engage in action planning as a way of "turning outward." This can help them transfer the knowledge and skills gained in the workshop to their daily work. Cilliers and Tekian (2016) highlight the importance of goal setting in transfer, and they encourage facilitators to "keep implementation expectations realistic" by helping participants determine "small changes" they can make to their practices (Cilliers & Tekian, 2016, pp. 146–147). UDL guideline 6, "Design options for strategy development," also encourages learners to "set meaningful goals (6.1)" (CAST, 2024b). Next, we will explore practical reflection strategies that incorporate an action planning component.

Tomorrow I Will…

The "Tomorrow I will…" strategy entails participants reflecting on this question: "What one small action are you going to take to put what you've learned today into practice tomorrow?" (Monks & Shupak, 2021, p. 217). What I appreciate most about this strategy is that it conveys to participants that their actions do not need to be massive in order to be impactful. Every small step counts.

Participants can record their "Tomorrow I will…" responses on paper or share them electronically via a digital whiteboard, collaborative document, polling tool, or chat space (such as Padlet Sandbox, Google Docs, Mentimeter, Butter Scenes, or the Zoom chat). Alternatively, if the group size is not too large, you could invite each participant to quickly share their plans verbally with the whole group.

5-5-5 Action Plan

I first experienced the 5-5-5 Action Plan in a former colleague's workshop (Noah, 2023), and it has become one of my favorite action planning techniques. This simple strategy entails participants setting goals for what they want to accomplish within the next 5 minutes, 5 days, and 5 weeks. (Alternatively, you could use different time spans, such as 5 days, 5 weeks, and 5 months). I love that the 5-5-5 strategy includes a mixture of short-term and long-term goals, ranging from simple things participants can do immediately to larger things they can tackle down the line.

You could level up the 5-5-5 strategy by inviting participants to use the scheduling feature in their email to send themselves reminders of the goals they developed. For example, they could draft an email to themselves with a reminder of their 5-day goal and schedule the email to send five days from the workshop date. This process could be repeated for the other goals. This way, participants' future selves will be reminded of the goals they set and encouraged to take action if they have not yet had a chance to do so.

What? So What? Now What? Liberating Structure

With the What? So What? Now What? Liberating Structure, participants reflect on what occurred during the learning experience, what was significant about it, and what they will do as a result (Lipmanowicz & McCandless, 2013). You could adapt the prompts by having participants reflect on these questions:

1. What? What did you learn during this workshop?
2. So What? Why does this matter?
3. Now What? How will you apply what you've learned?

Wow/How/Now

In June 2023, I attended a session at the virtual Wakelet Community Week event where edtech leader, Leticia Citizen, shared how she leverages Wakelet for collaborative reflection. One strategy Leticia shared was the Wow/How/Now reflection, which she adapted from Kia Turner. Here, participants record a Wow (a "big takeaway"), a How (a "burning question"), and a Now (a "personal challenge of what you can do tomorrow with your new learning") (Wakelet, 2023). I have since used this strategy in my own professional learning workshops. For example, at the end of my "Practical Metacognitive Strategies for the College Classroom" workshop, I invite participants to post their Wow/How/Now responses on a Padlet board (see Figure 7.1). Afterward, we review the responses as a whole group.

Geometric Forms

With Geometric Forms, participants reflect on the following prompts (Responsive Classroom, 2015, pp. 22–23):

- "Something I learned that 'squares' with my thinking
- A question that is still 'circling' in my mind
- Three important 'points' I want to remember
- One new 'direction' I will go in (or action I will take)"

Provide Time and Space for Reflection 139

Metacognition Reflection: Wow/How/Now

Welcome!

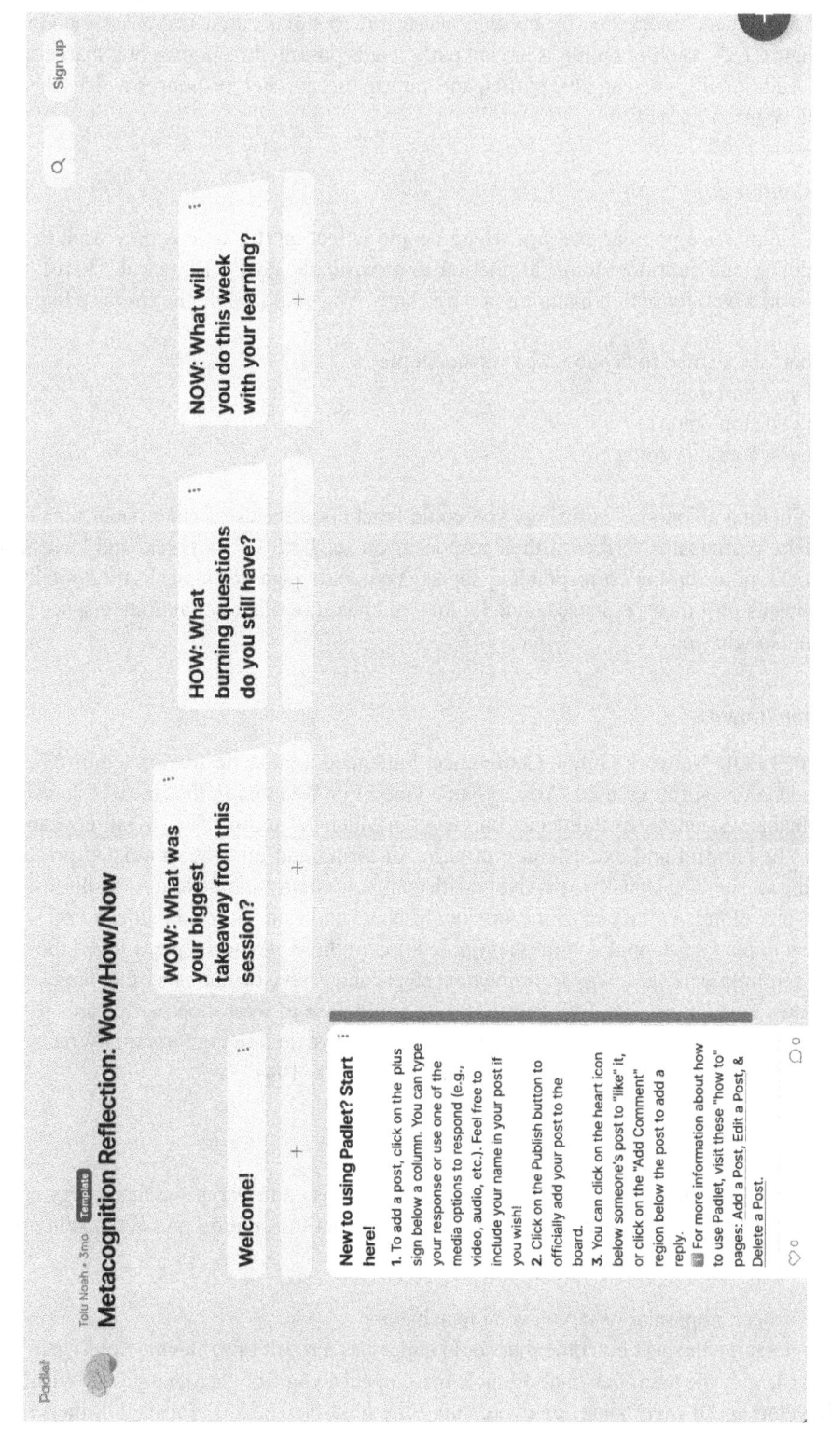

New to using Padlet? Start here!

1. To add a post, click on the plus sign below a column. You can type your response or use one of the media options to respond (e.g., video, audio, etc.). Feel free to include your name in your post if you wish!
2. Click on the Publish button to officially add your post to the board.
3. You can click on the heart icon below someone's post to "like" it, or click on the "Add Comment" region below the post to add a reply.
📝 For more information about how to use Padlet, visit these "how to" pages: Add a Post, Edit a Post, & Delete a Post.

WOW: What was your biggest takeaway from this session?

HOW: What burning questions do you still have?

NOW: What will you do this week with your learning?

FIGURE 7.1 Sample "Wow/How/Now" Padlet Board

Note: Questions adapted from Leticia Citizen and Kia Turner.

I use Geometric Forms as an exit ticket at the end of my "Maximizing Active Learning Classrooms for Student Engagement" workshop by inviting instructors to submit their responses via Google Forms (see Figure 7.2). Another option is having participants post their responses in a shared space (like Padlet). Additionally, you can give participants time to discuss their responses with each other (Responsive Classroom, 2015).

Start, Stop, Continue

Start, Stop, Continue is a popular exercise where people reflect on the actions they want to start doing, stop doing, and continue doing in relation to a particular goal (Gray et al., 2010). This strategy also works well for action planning in workshops. You could frame the exercise like this:

In light of what you learned today about [workshop topic]…
- What will you start doing?
- What will you stop doing?
- What will you continue doing?

If you are facilitating an on-site workshop, you could label three sheets of chart paper with these questions, invite participants to record their responses on separate sticky notes, and have them place their sticky notes on the corresponding sheets. You could also do this activity digitally by having participants post their responses on a digital whiteboard or other collaborative space (e.g., Padlet, Mural, Google Docs).

Personal Commitments

During the 2023 POD Network Online Conference, I attended a fantastic session led by Michael McCreary and Cait S. Kirby entitled "You're Not a Good Fit: Weaponing the 'Ideal' Educational Developer." In this session, we examined various ways in which the notion of an "ideal" educational developer can be harmful and exclusionary in terms of hiring and other work-related practices. Throughout the session, the chat box was lively with comments, and the breakout room discussions were thought-provoking. At the end of the session, Michael and Cait shared a Padlet board where they invited us to post a personal commitment in relation to the workshop topic. I loved their use of "personal commitments" as a way to frame next steps, and I have begun using that language in some of my own workshops, too. Two questions you could pose to workshop participants to help them frame their commitments are, "What are you committing to do moving forward? What action can you take right now to make that happen?" (Hughes, 2023, p. 144).

WOOP

Researcher Gabriele Oettingen (n.d.) shares how people can use a research-based strategy called WOOP (which stands for wish, outcome, obstacle, plan) to set meaningful and actionable goals. This strategy involves four steps (Oettingen, n.d.):

1. **Wish**: Identify an important wish you want to achieve.
2. **Outcome**: Imagine the best outcome that could happen as a result of achieving your wish.
3. **Obstacle**: Identify the main personal obstacle that impedes you from achieving your wish.
4. **Plan**: Develop an "if-then" plan for overcoming the obstacle (i.e., "If [obstacle], then I will [action].")

Provide Time and Space for Reflection **141**

Geometric Forms Reflection

Directions: Reflect on what you learned today about Active Learning Classrooms (ALCs) and active learning strategies by responding to the following four prompts.

Sign in to Google to save your progress. Learn more

Something I learned that "squares" with my thinking

Your answer

A question that is still "circling" in my mind

Your answer

Three important "points" I want to remember

Your answer

One new "direction" I will go in (or action I will take)

Your answer

Submit   Clear form

FIGURE 7.2 Geometric Forms Reflection in Google Forms
Note: Prompts from Responsive Classroom (2015).

You can use WOOP as an action planning strategy by inviting participants to outline their wishes, outcomes, obstacles, and plans in relation to something they hope to implement from the workshop. Since the WOOP approach encourages people to think about the obstacles they might face and how to overcome them, this strategy also aligns well with UDL guideline 6, "Design options for strategy development," which prompts learners to "anticipate and plan for challenges (6.2)" (CAST, 2024b). Oettingen's website, WOOP My Life, provides free resources about WOOP, including a WOOP Kit that offers helpful written and mental exercises. (These resources are linked in this chapter's Workshop Toolkit.)

Additional Reflection and Action Planning Ideas

Open-Ended Questions and Prompts

In addition to the more formal structures described in this chapter, open-ended questions and prompts can also work well for reflection and action planning activities. For example, you might ask participants to complete a physical or digital exit ticket where they respond to one of these prompts:

- My biggest takeaway from this workshop is _____.
- Three words that capture how I'm feeling about [workshop topic] are_____.
- One new insight I gained about [workshop topic] is _____.
- Think about the content you'll be teaching within the next 1–2 weeks. What is one new strategy you will try in order to _____?
- What would you share with a colleague who was unable to join today's workshop?
- What is one thing you will do differently as a result of what you learned today?

Individual and Corporate Reflection

When designing reflection activities, consider how to incorporate both individual and corporate reflection, where participants can reflect on their own and as a group. This practice is encouraged by UDL guideline 9, "Design options for emotional capacity," which prompts practitioners to "promote individual and collective reflection (9.3)" (CAST, 2024b). Corporate reflection can help foster relatedness (per self-determination theory), and it can tap into the power of sociality (per Eyler's, 2018, themes about human learning). Fink (2013) also highlights the importance of individual and group reflection, explaining the following:

> Some portion of the meaning-making process will always need to be done by individuals who spend time reflecting alone. But most people find that making meaning entirely by themselves is not the most effective way of accomplishing this task. When we engage in dialogue with others, the possibility of finding new and richer meanings increases dramatically. In addition, when people collaboratively search for the meaning of experiences, information, and ideas, they also create the foundation for *community*.
>
> (p. 118, emphasis in original)

This sentiment is also reflected in Parker's (2018) work, which encourages connection with the group as part of the "looking inward" process (pp. 260–261).

There are a variety of ways to fuse individual and corporate reflection in workshops. Start by inviting participants to reflect independently, and then have them share their responses with others. For example, if you're facilitating an on-site workshop, you can have participants write their reflections on sticky notes and stick them to the walls. Afterward, participants can do a mini gallery walk to read the reflections around the room. Or, you can have participants record their thoughts on an index card, collect them, and read the responses aloud. Alternatively, you could have participants discuss their responses in pairs or small groups. The 1-2-4-All Liberating Structure discussed in Chapter 5 works particularly well for this (Lipmanowicz & McCandless, 2013). If the group is small and has established a strong sense of rapport, you could do a wraparound share, where each person takes turns briefly sharing their response with the whole group (Facing History & Ourselves, 2020). Participants can also respond to reflection questions via digital tools (such as Mentimeter or Padlet), and then review the responses together.

When facilitating virtual workshops, you can invite participants to share their reflections in the chat, or share their thoughts aloud in the main room or in breakout rooms. Participants can also share their thoughts via digital tools (such as Mentimeter, Padlet, Butter Scenes, or a shared Google Doc or Slide) and then review the responses as a whole group. Additionally, participants can use analog tools to share their reflections. For example, near the end of a workshop, you might ask participants to grab a sticky note or a sheet of paper and write one word that captures how they feel. Then, you can ask participants to hold their paper up to the camera so that the screen is filled with everyone's words.

Pre-reflection Activities

While reflection activities can be used at the end of a workshop to help participants process their learning and determine their next steps, they can also be used at the beginning of a workshop to build anticipation for what's to come. With pre-reflection activities, learners reflect on their expectations for the learning experience prior to engaging in it, and then they compare their initial thoughts to their actual experiences (Falk, 1995).

Reitenauer et al.'s (2005) Hopes, Fears, Needs, and Expectations exercise is a service-learning pre-reflection activity that can be adapted for use in professional learning workshops. At the beginning of the workshop, ask participants to fold a sheet of paper into fourths and label the boxes as follows: Hopes, Fears (or Concerns), Needs, and Expectations (see Figure 7.3). (Alternatively,

Hopes	Concerns
Needs	Expectations

FIGURE 7.3 Hopes, Concerns, Needs, and Expectations Pre-reflection Activity
Note: Based on Reitenauer et al. (2005).

you could provide participants with a pre-labeled handout). Then, ask them to record their thoughts in each box. Afterward, you can have participants place their responses to the side (if the goal is to promote independent reflection), or you can incorporate group reflection by having participants share their responses in pairs, small groups, or via a collaborative online space such as Padlet. Finally, at the end of the workshop, invite participants to revisit their initial responses and compare their expectations to their actual experiences.

You can also use simple sentence starters for pre-reflection activities in your workshops. For example, you can post starters like, "I think…," "I feel…," "I believe…," "I expect…," "I predict…," or "I wonder…" on a slide or handout, and invite participants to choose one or two sentence starters to respond to. At the end of the workshop, participants can revisit their opening sentences as a post-reflection activity.

Multimodal Reflection Opportunities

In Chapter 6, we discussed the importance of supporting autonomy in learning by offering participants choices. When designing reflection and action planning activities, consider how you can offer participants multimodal response options rather than relying solely on written tasks. For example, participants could record video reflections using tools such as Padlet or Loom, or they could record audio reflections using Mote, Padlet, or Adobe Podcast. They could even create sketchnotes that capture their learning or next steps in a visual format. Offering options for reflection and action planning that extend beyond traditional written tasks supports UDL guideline 5, "Design options for expression & communication," which prompts learners and practitioners to "use multiple media for communication (5.1)" and "address biases related to modes of expression and communication (5.4)" (CAST, 2024b).

Joy and Play

Reflection activities are great places to "nurture joy and play (7.3)," as UDL guideline 7 ("Design options for welcoming interests & identities") encourages (CAST, 2024b). For example, during the 2023 POD Network Conference, Lindsey Hamilton had participants in her session do a paper plane reflection. Each participant was given a colorful sheet of paper on which to write their reflection. Afterward, they folded their sheet of paper into the shape of a paper plane, and on the count of three, they threw their paper plane across the room. Each person then picked up someone else's paper plane and read their reflection. Another adaptation of this strategy is the popular snowball toss activity, where each participant writes their reflection on a white sheet of paper, crumples it into a ball, and then tosses it across the room. Each participant then picks up a snowball to read. These activities not only incorporate individual and corporate reflection, but they do so in a fun and unexpected way that taps into the power of positive emotions (per Eyler's, 2018, themes about human learning). As participants throw their planes and snowballs across the room, it is likely to evoke a sense of exhilaration and result in plenty of smiles and laughter. Not a bad way to bring the workshop ride to a close!

Recap

- Provide adequate time and space for reflection and action planning in your workshops.
- Include opportunities for both individual and corporate reflection.
- Offer participants multimodal reflection opportunities.
- Consider how you can incorporate an element of fun or play.

Sticky Note Reflection

One Thing: What is one new reflection or action planning technique you would like to try in the future?

Workshop Toolkit

Scan the QR code or visit the URL to access additional resources related to this chapter.

www.tolunoah.com/workshop-toolkits

Design Time

Review your workshop plans and design a reflection or action planning activity if you do not already have one.

Facilitators' Lounge

Join the Facilitators' Lounge to connect with other readers and share your takeaways, strategies, and next steps!

www.tolunoah.com/facilitators-lounge/

References

Angelo, T.A. (with Zakrajsek, T.D.). (2024). *Classroom assessment techniques: Formative feedback tools for college and university teachers* (3rd ed.). Jossey-Bass.

Bass, R., Eynon, B., & Gambino, L.M. (2019). *The New Learning Compact: A framework for professional learning and educational change.* Every Learner Everywhere. www.everylearnereverywhere.org/resources/the-new-learning-compact/

Bassot, B. (2023). *The reflective practice guide: An interdisciplinary approach to critical reflection*. Routledge.

Brookfield, S.D. (2017). *Becoming a critically reflective teacher* (2nd ed.). Jossey-Bass.

Brown, P.C., Roediger III, H.L., & McDaniel, M.A. (2014). *Make it stick: The science of successful learning.* The Belknap Press of Harvard University Press.

CAST. (2024a). *Enhance capacity for monitoring progress.* https://udlguidelines.cast.org/action-expression/strategy-development/monitoring-progress/

CAST. (2024b). *Universal Design for Learning guidelines version 3.0.* https://udlguidelines.cast.org/

Cilliers, F.J., & Tekian, A. (2016). Effective faculty development in an institutional context: Designing for transfer. *Journal of Graduate Medical Education, 8*(2), 145–149. https://doi.org/10.4300%2FJGME-D-15-00117.1

Eyler, J.R. (2018). *How humans learn: The science and stories behind effective college teaching.* West Virginia University Press.

Facing History & Ourselves. (2020, August 28). *Wraparound.* www.facinghistory.org/resource-library/wraparound

Falk, D. (1995). Prereflection: A strategy for enhancing reflection. *NSEE Quarterly.* https://digitalcommons.unomaha.edu/slceeval/22/

Fink, L.D. (2013). *Creating significant learning experiences: An integrated approach to designing college courses* (2nd ed.). Jossey-Bass.

Gray, D., Brown, S., & Macanufo, J. (2010). *Gamestorming: A playbook for innovators, rulebreakers, and changemakers.* O'Reilly.

Hughes, L. (2023). *The 2-hour workshop blueprint: Design fast. Deliver strong. Without stress.* Big Charlie Press.

K. Patricia Cross Academy. (n.d.). *Teaching technique 02: 3-2-1*. https://kpcrossacademy.ua.edu/techniques/3-2-1/

Lipmanowicz, H., & McCandless, K. (2013). *The surprising power of Liberating Structures: Simple rules to unleash a culture of innovation.* Liberating Structures Press.

Littlefield, C., & Wise, W. (2021). *How to make virtual engagement easy: A practical guide for remote leaders and educators.* We and Me.

Monks, J., & Shupak, L. (2021). *Closer apart: How to design and facilitate brilliant workshops online.* Curve Creative.

Noah, T. (2023, March 14). *Designing virtual edtech faculty development workshops that stick: 10 guiding principles.* EDUCAUSE Review. https://er.educause.edu/articles/2023/3/designing-virtual-edtech-faculty-development-workshops-that-stick-10-guiding-principles

Oettingen, G. (n.d.). *How can I practice WOOP?* WOOP My Life. https://woopmylife.org/en/practice

Parker, P. (2018). *The art of gathering: How we meet and why it matters.* Riverhead Books.

Reitenauer, V.L., Spring, A., Kecskes, K., Kerrigan, S.M., Cress, C.M., & Collier, P.J. (2005). Building and maintaining community partnerships. In C.M. Cress, P.J. Collier, V.L. Reitenauer, & Associates (Eds.), *Learning through serving: A student guidebook for service-learning across the disciplines* (1st ed., pp. 17–31). Stylus Publishing.

Responsive Classroom. (2015). *Energize your meetings: 35 interactive learning structures for educators.* Center for Responsive Schools.

Rice, G.T. (2018). *Hitting pause: 65 lecture breaks to refresh and reinforce learning.* Routledge.

Wakelet. (2023, June 6). *Exploring the 5 Cs with Wakelet.* https://wakelet.com/wake/Qjbhf_TEm8ubj6LdWh1t4

8
CREATE ONGOING LEARNING OPPORTUNITIES

Guiding Question:
How will you help participants continue their learning after the workshop ends?

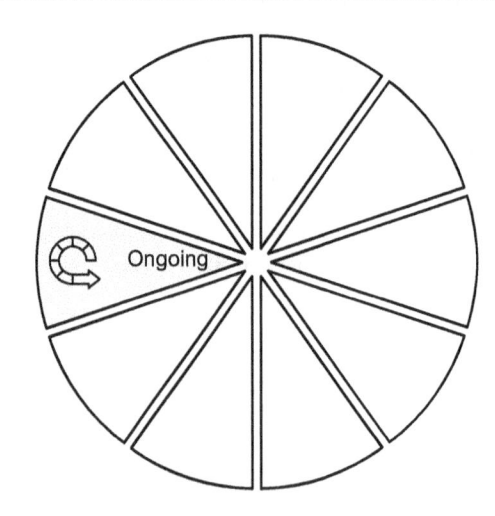

When facilitating on-site or virtual workshops, there is an understanding that everyone will gather for a set period of time for the learning experience. However, just because the workshop itself is finite doesn't mean that the learning needs to stop. In other words, if we remember that "learning is a journey, not an event" (Boller & Fletcher, 2020, p. 18), then we realize that there are numerous ways to help participants continue their learning after the workshop has ended. In this chapter, we will explore practical strategies for creating ongoing learning opportunities that can help participants review, deepen, and transfer their learning to their daily work.

Workshop Resources

One way we can extend learning beyond the scope of our workshops is by providing participants with supplementary resources. This practice supports Universal Design for Learning (UDL) guideline 3, "Design options for building knowledge," which prompts practitioners to "maximize transfer and generalization (3.4)" (CAST, 2024). By providing participants with resources they can use to review and deepen their learning, they will be more likely to implement what they learned during the workshop and perhaps even pursue specific areas of interest further. Next, we will explore six types of resources you can share with participants at the end of your workshops.

One-Pagers

One-pagers are one-page documents that summarize the key ideas, processes, and/or strategies that were addressed in the workshop. They also often include links to additional relevant resources. A key benefit of one-pagers is that they are concise, giving participants a quick, at-a-glance resource that they can revisit in the future (Noah, 2023b). You can create one-pagers using a word processing tool (such as Word, Pages, or Google Docs), a presentation tool (such as Keynote, PowerPoint, or Google Slides), or a design platform (such as Canva or Adobe Express). You can also include QR codes on your one-pagers that participants can scan to access additional information (such as related videos, audio clips, or websites) (Noah, 2023b). When designing one-pagers, be sure to keep the multimedia and digital accessibility principles discussed in Chapter 3 in mind. Also, if the document is design heavy, be sure to create an additional text-only version that will be more accessible to people using screen readers (an important practice I learned from Cait S. Kirby).

Tutorial Videos

Tutorial videos are particularly helpful for workshops that focus on helping participants develop specific skills. For example, if you're facilitating a workshop about digital accessibility, you can provide participants with short tutorial videos that demonstrate how to do specific tasks (like how to add alt text to images or create descriptive hyperlinks). Participants can watch the videos whenever they need a refresher on how to perform those tasks.

One option is to curate existing tutorial videos. YouTube can be a great place to start. When searching for tutorial videos, be sure to check that they have clear, accurate, up-to-date, and relevant content, along with accurate captions. Also, be mindful of the length of the video. Consider using a short video, selecting a specific clip, or sharing a video from a particular start time so that participants will not be overloaded with information or have to carve out a significant amount of time to watch it.

Another option is to create tutorial videos. Depending on what you're demonstrating, you could create a screen recording, a slideshow with audio or video narration, or a "talking head" video where you demo the process on camera (Costa, 2020; Noah, 2023a; Scagnoli, 2012). You could record the video using tools such as Loom, Zoom, Clips, iMovie, Padlet, or the built-in camera app on your device (Noah, 2023a). Like with curated videos, be sure that any tutorial videos you create yourself are brief and have accurate captions.

How-To Guides

How-to guides (like tutorial videos) are particularly beneficial for skills-based workshops. These guides outline the step-by-step process for completing a task, and they typically include relevant screenshots or pictures of each step. Oftentimes, creating process documentation can be a tedious and time-consuming task that involves manually typing each step, taking endless screenshots, and adding visual cues such as arrows and boxes. However, tools such as Scribe can make this process easier and faster (Noah, 2023b). Scribe captures your actions while you're completing a process on your device, and it automatically creates a how-to guide, complete with text-based directions and screenshots of each step (see Figure 8.1). (Resources about Scribe are linked in this chapter's Workshop Toolkit.)

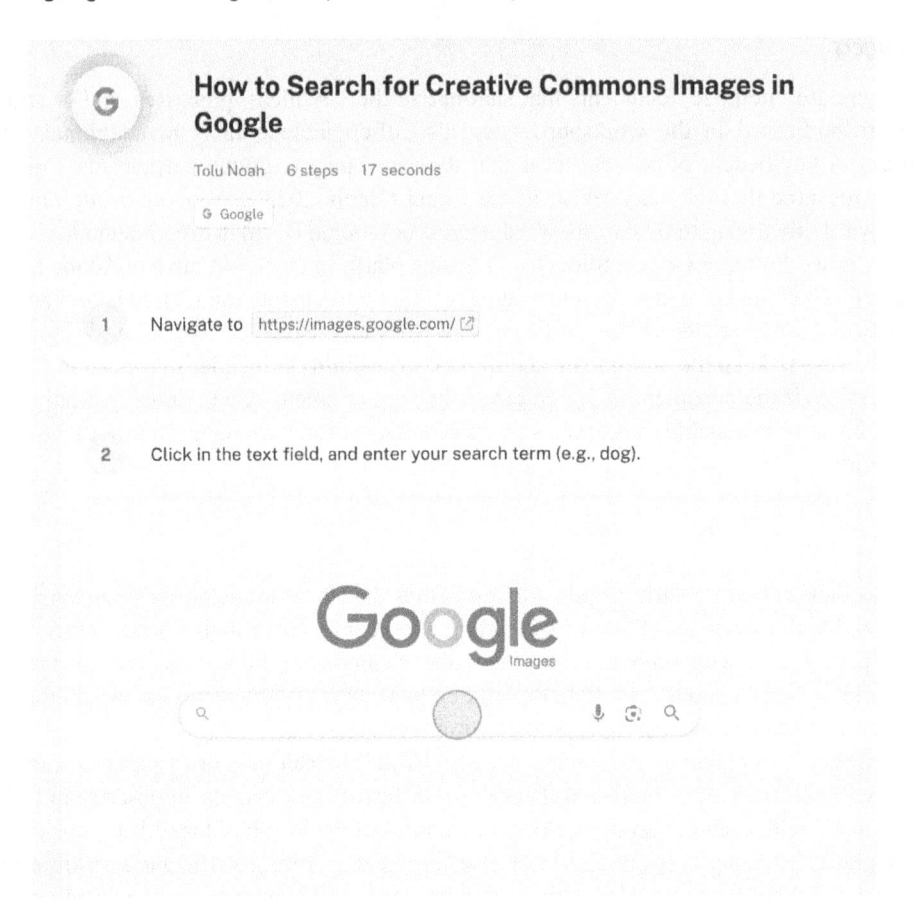

How to Search for Creative Commons Images in Google

Tolu Noah   6 steps   17 seconds

G Google

1. Navigate to https://images.google.com/

2. Click in the text field, and enter your search term (e.g., dog).

Google Images

FIGURE 8.1   Sample Scribe About How to Search for Creative Commons Images in Google

Workshop Recordings

When facilitating virtual workshops, I typically record the session so that I can send it to everyone who registered for the event afterward (Noah, 2023b). This not only provides a resource that people who attended live can review but also extends access to those who were unable to attend live. Additionally, my department has a central video portal with different channels and playlists where we can upload workshop recordings. These workshop recordings serve as "just-in-time" resources that instructors and staff can access when needed.

You might also consider turning your virtual workshop recordings into asynchronous workshops that encourage participants who are learning asynchronously to not only watch the recordings but also actively engage with them (Kirby, 2023). Tetu et al. (2024) developed a process for converting synchronous online workshops into asynchronous workshops that are intentionally designed to promote asynchronous interaction and engagement. The general process entails embedding selected video clips from the live virtual session into the workshop slides, clearing redundant information from the slides, and incorporating interactive activities that participants can complete asynchronously, such as Padlet exercises (Kirby, 2023; Tetu et al., 2024). (Further details about this process are available in this chapter's Workshop Toolkit.)

Chat Logs

For virtual workshops, the chat log can be a rich source of crowdsourced ideas and resources. Saving the chat log and sending it to participants afterward can be a helpful way to extend learning beyond the session. It can also help participants know who to reach out to should they wish to discuss a topic further.

To level up the chat log, you can use Kelly's (2024) "chat summary" technique, which involves creating a more streamlined version of the chat that participants can continue to add to after the session is over (p. 129). Here is a brief overview of how the process works (Kelly, 2022):

1. Before the workshop, prepare slides with discussion prompts that include different hashtags. For example, a slide for a workshop about metacognition might include the following prompt: "In the chat, share a strategy instructors can use to help students #monitor their learning."
2. During the workshop, ask participants to respond to the discussion prompts in the chat, ensuring that the corresponding hashtag is included in their response (e.g., #monitor). At the end of the session, save the chat.
3. After the session, clean up, organize, and summarize the chat log. (Note: The hashtags make this process easier, as you will be able to identify each time there is a shift in the topic of conversation. Also, if you decide to use AI to help generate a summary, make sure that you have participants' permission to upload their ideas to a chatbot).
4. Save the chat summary in an editable document (such as a Google Doc), and share it with participants. Encourage participants to continue adding ideas to the document.

To learn more about how to create chat summaries, check out the resources linked in this chapter's Workshop Toolkit.

Curated Collections

At the end of every workshop, I provide participants with a curated collection of related resources. The curated collection serves as a one-stop shop for participants, offering a singular space to which they can return for workshop-related materials. As a facilitator, I can also easily update the collection so that participants always have access to the latest resources.

Curated collections may include workshop slides, handouts, and activities, along with links to supplementary websites, articles, videos, podcast episodes, how-to guides, one-pagers, sample projects, recommended books, and social media pages of leaders in the field whom you recommended following. When I'm facilitating workshops internally at my university, I typically use Wakelet to create and share curated collections with instructors and staff (see Figure 8.2). When I'm facilitating workshops externally (e.g., at a conference or other speaking engagement), I typically create a dedicated webpage on my personal website (www.tolunoah.com) to share resources with participants (see Figure 8.3). Other tools you can use to create curated collections include Padlet, Bulb, Google Docs, and Google Sites.

When creating curated collections, be sure to keep the UDL principle, "Design multiple means of representation," in mind by offering resources in different formats. This can include text, video, audio, or images. For example, when curating resources for my iPad workshops, I often include both text-based directions and tutorial videos (see Figure 8.2). This way, if instructors want to review how to perform a particular task in the future, they can either read the directions or watch a video that demonstrates the process. Remember that you don't need to include every possible media type in your curated collections every single time. Rather, as we discussed in Chapter 4, consider how

152 Designing and Facilitating Workshops with Intentionality

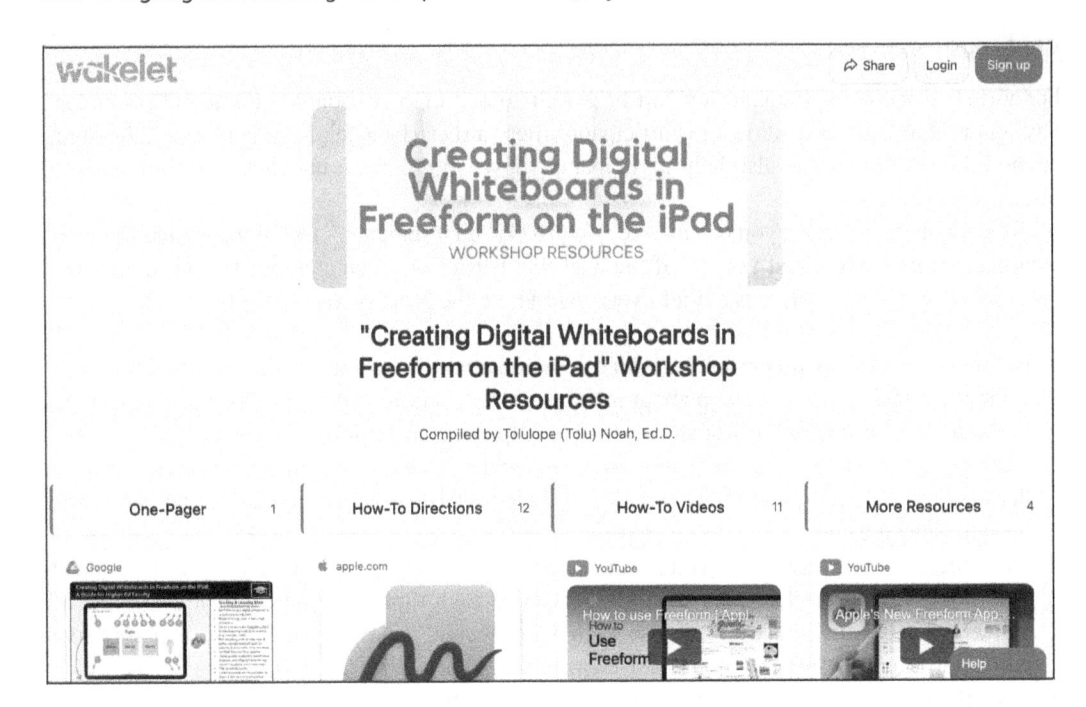

FIGURE 8.2 Sample Wakelet Collection for iPad Workshop

FIGURE 8.3 Sample Workshop Webpage
Note: Slides template on webpage from Slidesgo. Title slide photo by Surface on Unsplash (2022).

you can leverage Tobin and Behling's (2018) "plus-one approach" (pp. 134–135) by including at least one additional type of resource in the collection. Additionally, be mindful of accessibility and inclusivity with your curated collections. For example, check that any videos you link have accurate captions, and be intentional about including resources from diverse authors and creators.

Post-Workshop Communication

A second way that we can extend participants' learning after workshops is through our post-workshop communication. In my personal practice, I send a follow-up email to everyone who registered for the workshop to express gratitude for their interest/engagement and offer resources they can use to review and extend their learning (see Figure 8.4). This email typically includes the following elements:

- A **Workshop Recording** section that includes a link to the recording (if it was a virtual workshop)
- A **Retrieval Practice** section where I pose questions about the workshop content and ask participants to recall the answers from memory (This idea was inspired by one of the training tips in the book, *Make It Stick*, by Brown et al., 2014.)
  - For virtual workshops, I also include timestamped links to specific parts of the workshop recording where people can check their answers.
- A **Workshop Resources** section that includes a link to the curated collection
- A **Workshop Feedback** section that includes a link to the feedback form (for anyone who was unable to complete it during the live session)
- A **Pedagogical Consultations** section that encourages people to schedule a consultation with me
  - I also attach a copy of my pedagogical consultation menu to the email. (We will discuss this further shortly.)
- An **Upcoming Programs** section that includes links to future professional learning experiences I'll be facilitating and provides links to the registration pages
- A **Share Your Story** section that includes a link to a brief survey where people can share how they've applied their learning anytime

You could also include post-workshop activities in your follow-up emails. This is particularly useful for long-term programs (such as workshop series, institutes, and courses). For example, you might ask participants to submit artifacts throughout the series or institute that demonstrate how they're applying what they're learning to their work. Participants can share their work via a Google Drive folder, Dropbox folder, Google Forms or Qualtrics survey, Padlet board, or other tool.

Another communication strategy you can use is "boosters," which are messages you send to participants "one day, one week, and one month" after the professional learning experience has ended (Howles, 2022, pp. 318–319). Howles (2022) explains that in the first booster, she sends participants a recap of the main points from the learning experience; in the second booster, she sends a quiz that prompts participants to recall their learning; and in the third booster, she shares "an example or testimonial of how a learner successfully applied what they learned so far, or a celebration of a learner who has already implemented a part of their action plan" (p. 319). The booster strategy lends itself well to the end of long-term programs (such as workshop series, institutes, or courses).

Personalized Support

A third way to encourage ongoing learning after workshops is by offering participants opportunities to receive personalized support. The New Learning Compact (NLC) principle, "Engage inquiry and reflection," encourages educational developers to use "structures [that] will support the sustained, recursive process needed for meaningful and lasting change in practice" (Bass et al., 2019, p. 34). Furthermore, Cilliers and Tekian (2016) explain that participants should be able to "arrange opportunities for feedback (e.g., one-on-one consulting with an educational adviser,

> Hello,
>
> Thank you for registering for Tuesday's workshop, "Building Connections & Fostering a Positive Classroom Climate from Day One." This email contains links to the workshop recording and other resources.
>
> **Workshop Recording**
>
> Missed the live workshop or want to experience it again? Watch a <u>recording</u> of one of the sessions.
>
> **Retrieval Practice**
>
> If you attended one of the live sessions, try to recall the following information from memory:
>
> - According to self-determination theory, what are the three basic psychological needs? (<u>Check your answer here</u>.)
> - What are some important points to keep in mind regarding students' names? (<u>Check your answer here</u>.)
>
> **Workshop Resources**
>
> You can find all of the resources from the workshop on this <u>Wakelet page</u>.
>
> **Workshop Feedback**
>
> Please take a moment to <u>share your feedback</u> about the workshop if you have not yet had a chance to do so.
>
> **Pedagogical Consultations**
>
> I am available for one-on-one pedagogical consultations anytime! Please access the attached pedagogical consultation menu for an overview of the areas I can provide support with. To set up a time to meet, please email me at [email address].
>
> **Upcoming Programs**
>
> I will be facilitating additional learning experiences about different teaching and technology topics in the coming weeks. You can learn more about upcoming programs and register for any sessions of interest via the links below.
>
> - **February 13**: <u>Creating Engaging Learning Opportunities with Padlet</u>
> - **March 6**: <u>Metacognitive Strategies for the College Classroom</u>
>
> **Share Your Story!**
>
> How have you used what you've learned in this workshop (or previous programs) in your teaching or other professional practices? I'd love to hear from you and highlight the awesome work you're doing! Please share your story via this <u>brief survey</u>.
>
> I hope to see you soon in a future workshop or consultation!
>
> Best,
>
> Tolu

FIGURE 8.4 Sample Workshop Follow-Up Email

face-to-face or online; direct observation of teaching; feedback from students; and/or advice from a peer, mentor, or supervisor)" (p. 146). This can help participants transfer what they learned in the workshop to their specific context and support them in continuing to build competence over time (per self-determination theory). Two related strategies I use to offer participants personalized support are pedagogical consultations and support menus.

Pedagogical Consultations

Theory

Consultations are a popular strategy that centers for teaching and learning use to provide instructors with personalized support (Wright, 2023). These consultations typically "involve a one-on-one meeting, often, but not exclusively, around a teaching issue (e.g., syllabus design, challenges to authority, student course feedback)" (Wright, 2023, p. 107). Eynon et al. (2023) note that consultations can offer "sustained support" as faculty transfer what they are learning about effective teaching to their practices (p. 26). Consultations can also be an important source of "just-in-time" support (Robertson, 2010, p. 45).

Research on consultations demonstrates that consultants may take on different roles in their meetings with instructors. Brinko (1991) highlights five consultation styles drawn from the research literature (pp. 42–46):

- **Product**: The instructor identifies an instructional problem and solution and then seeks the support of the consultant in developing the solution.
- **Prescription**: The consultant diagnoses the instructional problem the instructor is facing and tells them how to solve it.
- **Collaborative/Process**: The consultant works with the instructor to discuss the instructional challenge and possible solutions.
- **Affiliative**: The consultant helps the instructor navigate personal matters that may be impacting their professional work.
- **Confrontational**: The consultant challenges the instructor's "attitudes and assumptions" that may be contributing to the issue.

Brinko notes that consultants often use a variety of styles depending on the instructor's needs, level of experience, and other factors. In other words, "consultant behavior is greatly influenced by client behavior, and, in turn, client behavior is greatly influenced by consultant behavior" (Brinko, 1991, p. 47).

Little and Palmer (2011) encourage the use of a three-part consultation model that focuses on listening, questioning, and acting. The first part of the process ("deep listening") involves the educational developer "listening attentively and with empathy" to the instructor and paraphrasing what they are saying along the way in order to ensure that they understand them (Little & Palmer, 2011, pp. 105–107). The second part of the process ("asking powerful questions") involves the educational developer asking clarifying and probing questions that prompt the instructor to reflect and consider new ideas (Little & Palmer, 2011, pp. 107–109). This may include questions such as "What would you like to see happen?" or "What other options can you think of?" (Little & Palmer, 2011, pp. 108–109). The final part of the process ("prompting action") involves the educational developer encouraging the instructor to identify a next step or goal that they want to work toward and to consider how they will assess progress toward the goal (Little & Palmer, 2011, pp. 109–111).

Together, this three-part model of listening, questioning, and acting keeps the consultation focused on the instructor, and it fosters a more collaborative space for discussing teaching and learning topics.

Practice

When facilitating internal workshops for instructors at my university, I always include an invitation to schedule pedagogical consultations with me at the end of every workshop and in every follow-up email. The consultations are meant to serve as a natural extension of the workshop, helping instructors transfer what they learned to their work. I inform instructors that consultations can be used for anything that would be helpful to them: discussing questions and ideas, practicing skills together, planning ways to implement what they learned in their teaching or other professional work, obtaining feedback about their work, and more.

Pedagogical consultations are instructor-driven and non-evaluative. Each meeting typically lasts 30–60 minutes, and instructors are welcome to schedule as many meetings as they would like. Moreover, consultations don't always have to be in relation to a particular workshop; rather, I am available year-round to discuss any teaching or technology-related matters.

During consultations, I listen actively and ask questions so that the instructor feels heard, and so that I can gain a better understanding of their goals and needs. Furthermore, I aim to position myself as an educational thought partner rather than as an expert who can solve the instructional challenges they're facing. Through dialogue, we work together to unearth new understandings and instructional possibilities, and I often learn just as much from these conversations as I hope the instructors do.

In a blog post entitled "A Philosophy of Faculty Development," Derek Bruff describes his personal approach to consultations. His closing remarks resonate with me and capture how I, too, seek to engage with instructors. Bruff (2022) writes:

> When I am working with faculty, I think a lot about scaffolding. Where are they coming from, in terms of their teaching practices and beliefs about learning? Where do they want to go and how can I help them identify those directions? What options do they have and which ones do they want to try? My goal isn't to change everything about their teaching, it's to help them decide to take two or three next steps in their development as a teacher.

Support Menus

One thing I've discovered in my work as an educational developer is that instructors may not always be aware of the different ways I can provide support. Neal and Peed-Neal (2009) explain that "in consulting work, you must be explicit about your availability, the extent to which you can be a resource for your client, and the kinds of resources that you can provide" (p. 22). Inspired by the coaching menus I saw K-12 instructional coaches and educational technology coaches sharing on social media, I designed a pedagogical consultation menu that highlights different ways I can partner with instructors at my university (see Figure 8.5). The pedagogical consultation menu aims to make things more transparent for instructors and hopefully expand their notion of how I can help while also clarifying boundaries about the areas in which I can provide support.

Create Ongoing Learning Opportunities 157

Teaching and Technology Talks with Tolu
PEDAGOGICAL CONSULTATION MENU

TECH TUTORIALS
Learn how to use iPads and other edtech tools (e.g., Padlet, Wakelet, etc.) for instruction.

LECTURE PLANNING
Co-plan an upcoming lecture that incorporates relevant instructional technology tools.

ENGAGEMENT STRATEGIES
Explore different student engagement strategies and active learning techniques.

ASSIGNMENT DESIGN
Revamp a current course assignment, or design a new assignment together.

SYLLABUS SUPPORT
Review your syllabus, and discuss ways to make it more inclusive.

ASSESSMENT TECHNIQUES
Explore strategies for assessing student learning.

UDL SUPPORT
Discuss how to incorporate Universal Design for Learning principles into your instruction.

TEACHING REFLECTIONS
Reflect on a recent teaching experience together.

CELEBRATIONS AND CHALLENGES
Celebrate a teaching success, or brainstorm possible solutions to a teaching challenge.

SPOT CHAT
Reflect on your SPOT data together (or have Tolu review your data and pull out relevant comments).

PROFESSIONAL GROWTH
Discuss ways to continue growing and developing as an educator.

OTHER SUPPORT
Need support with another teaching or technology-related topic that is not on this menu? Let's chat!

Consultations are non-evaluative and available throughout the year. Email Tolu at [email address] to share the details of your request and schedule a time to chat!

FIGURE 8.5 Pedagogical Consultation Menu

My current iteration of the pedagogical consultation menu includes 12 avenues of support:

- **Tech Tutorials**: Learn how to use iPads and other edtech tools (e.g., Padlet, Wakelet, etc.) for instruction.
- **Lecture Planning**: Co-plan an upcoming lecture that incorporates relevant instructional technology tools.
- **Engagement Strategies**: Explore different student engagement strategies and active learning techniques.
- **Assignment Design**: Revamp a current course assignment, or design a new assignment together.
- **Syllabus Support**: Review your syllabus, and discuss ways to make it more inclusive.
- **Assessment Techniques**: Explore strategies for assessing student learning.
- **UDL Support**: Discuss how to incorporate Universal Design for Learning principles into your instruction.
- **Teaching Reflections**: Reflect on a recent teaching experience together.
- **Celebrations and Challenges**: Celebrate a teaching success, or brainstorm possible solutions to a teaching challenge.
- **SPOT Chat**: Reflect on your SPOT data together (or have me review your data and pull out relevant comments.) (SPOT stands for "Student Perceptions of Teaching," and it's the end-of-term student evaluation system that's used at my university.)
- **Professional Growth**: Discuss ways to continue growing and developing as an educator.
- **Other Support**: Need support with another teaching or technology-related topic that is not on this menu? Let's chat!

The bottom of the pedagogical consultation menu includes a reminder that consultations are non-evaluative and available throughout the year. I also include my email address and a QR code, which, when scanned, automatically creates a new email with my email address pre-populated. This makes it easier for instructors to get in touch with me and schedule a time to meet. I attach my pedagogical consultation menu to every workshop follow-up email so that participants are reminded of the different ways they can seek support beyond the workshop.

Additional Ideas

If you're interested in exploring even more ways to extend learning after professional learning events, check out Fenning's (2024) book, *39 Ways to Make Training Stick*. Some of his ideas lend themselves well to short-term programs (such as workshops), whereas others may work well following long-term programs (such as workshop series, courses, institutes, and book clubs). A few ideas include:

- **Collaborative Online Boards** (Fenning, 2024, pp. 140–142): Create a collaborative online space (such as a Padlet board) with sections labeled "Key Takeaways," "Questions," "Challenges Faced," and "Success Stories." Share the board with participants at the end of your program, and invite them to add posts and comments anytime.
- **Virtual Hangouts** (Fenning, 2024): Schedule at least one informal virtual meeting a month or so after the program has ended where participants can ask questions, share their experiences, and dive deeper into topics of interest.

- **Digital Badges and Certifications** (Fenning, 2024): Design digital badges or certificates that participants can earn for submitting examples of how they have applied their learning to their work. (I use this approach in my "Classroom Assessment Techniques" workshop series, where instructors can earn a certificate for submitting evidence of implementing at least one formative assessment technique from each workshop in their teaching.)

Recap

- Provide participants with resources they can use to review and extend their learning.
- Send a follow-up email after each workshop with links to resources and additional learning opportunities.
- Offer ways for participants to obtain ongoing personalized support.

Sticky Note Reflection

Sentence Starters: Complete the following sentence starters by describing one thing you currently do to help participants continue their learning after workshops and one thing you would like to try.

- Currently, I…
- I want to try…

Workshop Toolkit

Scan the QR code or visit the URL to access additional resources related to this chapter.

www.tolunoah.com/workshop-toolkits

Design Time

Review your workshop plans. Create a resource that you can share with participants or develop a post-workshop communication or personalized support plan.

Facilitators' Lounge

Join the Facilitators' Lounge to connect with other readers and share your takeaways, strategies, and next steps!

www.tolunoah.com/facilitators-lounge/

References

Bass, R., Eynon, B., & Gambino, L.M. (2019). *The New Learning Compact: A framework for professional learning and educational change*. Every Learner Everywhere. www.everylearnereverywhere.org/resources/the-new-learning-compact/

Boller, S., & Fletcher, L. (2020). *Design thinking for training and development: Creating learning journeys that get results*. ATD Press.

Brinko, K.T. (1991). The interactions of teaching improvement. *New Directions for Teaching and Learning, 1991*(48), 39–49. https://doi.org/10.1002/tl.37219914805

Brown, P.C., Roediger III, H.L., & McDaniel, M.A. (2014). *Make it stick: The science of successful learning*. The Belknap Press of Harvard University Press.

Bruff, D. (2022, October 7). *A philosophy of faculty development*. Agile Learning. https://derekbruff.org/?p=3903

CAST. (2024). *Universal Design for Learning guidelines version 3.0*. https://udlguidelines.cast.org/

Cilliers, F.J., & Tekian, A. (2016). Effective faculty development in an institutional context: Designing for transfer. *Journal of Graduate Medical Education, 8*(2), 145–149. https://doi.org/10.4300%2FJGME-D-15-00117.1

Costa, K. (2020). *99 tips for creating simple and sustainable educational videos: A guide for online teachers and flipped classes*. Routledge.

Eynon, B., Iuzzini, J., Keith, H.R., Loepp, E., & Weber, N. (2023, January 17). *Teaching, learning, equity and change: Realizing the promise of professional learning*. Every Learner Everywhere. www.everylearnereverywhere.org/resources/teaching-learning-equity-and-change-realizing-the-promise-of-professional-learning/

Fenning, C. (2024). *39 ways to make training stick: What to do after trainees leave the room*. Alignment Group.

Howles, D.L. (2022). *Next level virtual training: Advance your facilitation*. ATD Press.

Kelly, K. (2022). *How to turn a Zoom chat into a useful summary*. http://tiny.cc/zoom-chat-summary

Kelly, K. (2024). *Making college courses flexible: Supporting student success across multiple learning modalities*. Routledge.

Kirby, C.K. (2023, August 28). *Developing a better way to share recorded workshops*. https://caitlinkirby.wordpress.com/2023/08/28/developing-a-better-way-to-share-recorded-workshops/

Little, D., & Palmer, M.S. (2011). A coaching-based framework for individual consultations. *To Improve the Academy, 29*, 102–115. http://dx.doi.org/10.3998/tia.17063888.0029.012

Neal, E., & Peed-Neal, I. (2009). Experiential lessons in the practice of faculty development. *To Improve the Academy, 27*, 14–31. http://dx.doi.org/10.3998/tia.17063888.0027.006

Noah, T. (2023a, February 13). *Microlectures 101: What, why, & how?* Faculty Focus. www.facultyfocus.com/articles/online-education/online-course-delivery-and-instruction/microlectures-101-what-why-how/

Noah, T. (2023b, March 14). *Designing virtual edtech faculty development workshops that stick: 10 guiding principles*. EDUCAUSE Review. https://er.educause.edu/articles/2023/3/designing-virtual-edtech-faculty-development-workshops-that-stick-10-guiding-principles

Robertson, D.L. (2010). Establishing an educational development program. In K.J. Gillespie, D.L. Robertson, & Associates (Eds.), *A guide to faculty development* (2nd ed., pp. 35–52). Jossey-Bass.

Scagnoli, N. (2012, November 1). *7 things you should know about microlectures*. EDUCAUSE. https://library.educause.edu/resources/2012/11/7-things-you-should-know-about-microlectures

Surface. (2022, March 31). *A woman sitting on the floor, using a laptop* [Photograph]. Unsplash. https://unsplash.com/photos/a-woman-sitting-on-the-floor-using-a-laptop-ddcLX7Iis44

Tetu, I.C., Kelly, S., Fu, J., Kirby, C.K., Schopieray, S., & Thomas, S. (2024). Developing asynchronous workshop models for professional development. *Communication Design Quarterly, 12*(1), 37–43. https://cdq.sigdoc.org/wp-content/uploads/2024/04/CDQ-12.1.pdf

Tobin, T.J., & Behling, K.T. (2018). *Reach everyone, teach everyone: Universal Design for Learning in higher education*. West Virginia University Press.

Wright, M.C. (2023). *Centers for teaching and learning: The new landscape in higher education*. Johns Hopkins University Press.

9
BE RESPONSIVE

Guiding Question:
How can you be responsive to participants before, during, and after the workshop?

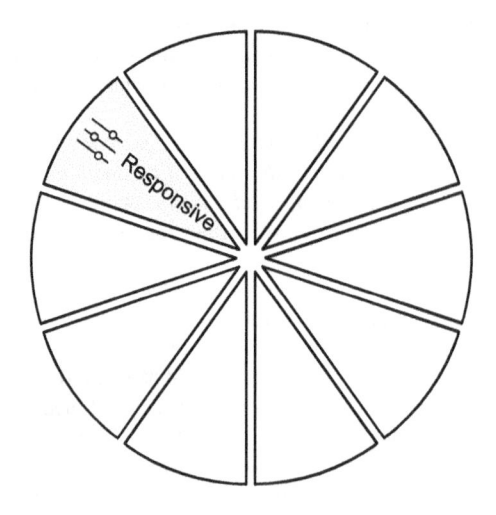

In Chapter 1, we discussed the importance of using a learner-centered approach to workshop design that begins with learning about participants and their context so that we can create relevant professional learning experiences. Starting our planning process with learners in mind is a key way that we can be responsive to them prior to the workshop. In Chapter 4, we explored how to use pre-workshop communication to solicit questions from participants and learn about their goals for attending so that we can adjust our workshop plans accordingly. This, too, is a critical way that we can be responsive to learners prior to the workshop. Participants may also reach out on their own before the workshop to ask questions and seek additional information. Responding to their inquiries in a kind and timely manner is yet another way that we can be responsive and set a caring and positive tone.

However, being responsive is important not only in the planning and preparation stages of a workshop but also during and after the live event. As we engage with participants during workshops, we need to check in with them and adjust our plans in the moment based on their needs and interests. Additionally, after workshops, we need to consider changes we can make to ensure that future offerings are responsive to participants. In this chapter, we will explore practical strategies for being responsive to participants during and after workshops so that we can continue to iterate and design more meaningful and impactful professional learning experiences.

DOI: 10.4324/9781003482963-10

Responsiveness During Workshops

Conduct Formative Assessments

A key way that we can be responsive to participants during workshops is by checking their understanding throughout the session. In Chapter 2, we discussed the important role formative assessments play in the development of a Macro Workshop Plan, and in Chapters 5–7, we explored practical collaborative, active learning, and reflection activities, many of which work well as formative assessment tools. If you're interested in exploring even more assessment strategies, check out Angelo and Zakrajsek's (2024) book, *Classroom Assessment Techniques*. It describes over 50 formative assessment techniques, many of which can be adapted for use in workshops (Angelo & Zakrajsek, 2024).

By pausing at strategic points throughout the workshop to check in with participants and assess their understanding, we can glean valuable information about their knowledge, skills, beliefs, and attitudes. This can help us make important adjustments in the moment, such as reviewing concepts/skills that participants are confused about or struggling with, or taking things to the next level if participants are ready to dive deeper. As we discussed in Chapter 3, learning how to be flexible and adapt on the spot is a critical facilitation skill. It requires constantly monitoring where participants are and what they need, and allowing that information to shape our decisions about how to proceed.

Invite Questions

Providing space for participants to ask questions during workshops is another way that we can be responsive to their needs. Questions tap into the natural curiosity of participants and create space for wonder. They also unearth different perspectives and possibilities that can help push the conversation deeper.

Be sure to explicitly invite questions and provide a clear way for participants to ask. In virtual sessions, you might invite participants to raise their virtual hand or post their questions in the chat or Q&A window. In on-site sessions, you might invite participants to raise their hand or create a backchannel space (like a Google Doc or Padlet board) where they can anonymously post their questions throughout the session. Polling tools (such as Mentimeter, Slido, and Poll Everywhere) and other tools (such as the Q&A feature in Google Slides) can also be used to anonymously collect questions from participants in any modality. Additionally, you can include multiple Q&A slides in your slide deck as a visual cue to pause and check in with participants about their questions throughout the session.

Another strategy you can use to solicit questions is a parking lot. This is a popular facilitation and teaching strategy where, throughout the session, participants write any questions that are not pertinent to the current topic on sticky notes and then place them on a sheet of chart paper in the room that is labeled "Parking Lot." This strategy can also be done digitally, using tools such as Padlet Sandbox, Miro, FigJam, or an editable Google Slide or Doc. At the end of the session, the facilitator visits the parking lot and addresses the questions placed there. (Alternatively, you could incorporate multiple pause points into the workshop where you check the parking lot so that you can address questions in a more timely fashion.) One of the benefits of the parking lot approach is that because participants jot down their questions in the moment, they don't have to try to remember them until the end of the session. This strategy also allows the facilitator to hold questions that are not pertinent to the current topic until a more strategic time, while still showing participants that their inquiries matter.

One caveat to keep in mind with respect to participants' questions is that it's important to consider the nature of their request. At times, participants may ask questions that are beyond the scope of the session, highly specific to their personal situation, or time consuming to address in the moment. In cases such as these, it may be best to invite them to schedule a one-on-one consultation after the workshop rather than addressing the question with the entire group.

There may also be times when participants ask questions that you don't know the answer to. These are pivotal moments where we, as facilitators, can model vulnerability by admitting that we don't know and either working with the group to find the answer or offering to research the issue after the session and then following up. For example, in my iPad workshops, instructors often ask if it's possible to perform specific tasks within whichever app we're using. If the task is one that I haven't tried before, I'll admit that I'm unsure and then invite them to tinker along with me so that we can figure it out together.

Participants' questions can also be valuable in strengthening and revising the workshop. For example, during a past QR codes workshop, an instructor asked me a question about accessibility that I was unsure of. I admitted I didn't know and said I would look into it. Immediately after the session, I spent some time researching the topic and came across some excellent resources about important accessibility considerations when using QR codes. I also re-discovered a company called NaviLens, which has created accessible QR code technology for blind and low-vision users. Not only was I able to send a follow-up email to the instructor with these additional resources, but my own understanding of the topic grew as well. As a result, I revised my QR codes workshop by adding a new section about accessibility so that future participants would be better equipped to create accessible QR code experiences.

Provide Feedback to Participants

As participants engage in activities during workshops, they need to receive feedback so that they know how they're doing and can adjust accordingly. Wiggins and McTighe (2005) explain that "learning is maximized when cycles of *perform-feedback-revise-perform*" are part of the learning process (p. 154, emphasis in original), and Steinert et al. (2016) highlight "opportunities for feedback and reflection" as critical components of effective faculty development programs (p. 777). The importance of feedback is also reflected in Universal Design for Learning (UDL) guideline 8, "Design options for sustaining effort & persistence," which prompts practitioners to "offer action-oriented feedback (8.5)." Additionally, guideline 6, "Design options for strategy development," prompts practitioners to "enhance capacity for monitoring progress (6.4)" (CAST, 2024).

When providing feedback, it's important to address what learners are doing well along with what can be improved. Cavanagh (2016) refers to this as "progress feedback" and "discrepancy feedback" (pp. 131–132). This feedback can be provided in multiple forms, including facilitator-provided feedback (where you offer feedback to learners through verbal or written comments) and self-assessment (where learners evaluate their own work using guiding questions, checklists, or rubrics). Participants can also provide feedback to each other. For example, they can engage in a Paired Teach-Back, where they pair up, take turns explaining concepts or modeling skills learned during the workshop, and provide feedback to each other (Bowman, 2009). Additionally, participants can do peer review and coaching activities using structured protocols. Examples of peer-based protocols include the following:

- **Tuning Protocol: Examining Adult Work** (based on Joseph McDonald and David Allen's Tuning Protocol; Center for Leadership & Educational Equity [CLEE], n.d.-b): A learner shares their work with the group and provides background information about the context and their

goals. The group then asks clarifying questions. Afterward, the group silently examines and annotates the work, and they think about the feedback they want to provide the presenter. The group then has a discussion about the work's strengths and areas for growth, with a particular focus on how the work aligns or contrasts with the goals the presenter initially shared. During this conversation, the presenter simply listens. Afterward, the presenter shares what they gleaned from the conversation, and then the whole group debriefs the experience. This protocol can also be replicated in virtual workshops via breakout rooms.
- **Feedback Carousel** (CLEE, n.d.-a): Participants post a sample of their work on the wall, along with a sheet of chart paper that is divided into four quadrants: "clarifying questions," "probing questions," "recommendations," and "resources." Then, participants go around the room and examine the work on the walls. As they do so, they record their feedback on sticky notes and stick them to the corresponding sections of each chart paper. This activity can also be done in a digital format by creating a collaborative Google Slide deck or a Padlet Sandbox where each person has a dedicated slide/card to paste or link their work. Participants can then use the text or sticky note features of the platform to share their feedback as they visit each slide/card.
- **Troika Consulting Liberating Structure** (Lipmanowicz & McCandless, 2013, pp. 194–196): Participants form groups of three and engage in three rounds of coaching. In each round, one person takes on the role of the "client" while the other two people are "consultants." The client begins by asking for help about a particular issue, and the consultants ask questions to ensure that they understand the issue. Then, the consultants discuss ideas while the client listens. Afterward, the client shares what they gleaned from the conversation. The process repeats with a new client for each round so that each person in the group receives feedback. This protocol can also be replicated in virtual workshops via breakout rooms.

These protocols could work well in a variety of workshops. For example, if you're facilitating a workshop for instructors about how to design transparent assignments, you could ask participants to bring a copy of an existing course assignment to the session. Participants could then use one of the protocols to provide feedback to each other about how they could make their assignments more transparent.

Regardless of the feedback methods used, it's important to be mindful of how the feedback is provided to learners. According to self-determination theory, the type of feedback learners receive can impact their sense of competence (Ryan & Deci, 2020). Consider how to promote a growth mindset that conveys to participants that they can continue to improve with practice. Fink suggests providing "FIDeLity feedback," which stands for feedback that is frequent, immediate, discriminating (i.e., it clarifies the difference between work that does and does not meet the expectations), and loving (i.e., it is given with kindness and care) (Fink, n.d., p. 14; Fink, 2013, pp. 105–107). Additionally, Wind notes that effective feedback has four qualities: constructive (it explains how to strengthen the work), specific (it refers to particular examples), justified (it explains the rationale for the suggested changes), and kind (it is conveyed in a supportive and encouraging way) (Eduflow, 2021; Wind, 2020).

Obtain In-The-Moment Feedback About Workshop Activities

In addition to ensuring that participants have ways to obtain feedback during the session, we can also be responsive by providing space for them to share in-the-moment feedback about the workshop activities. One popular framework for this is "Plus/Delta" (Gray et al., 2010). Following a workshop activity, display a physical or digital two-column chart where the left column is labeled with a plus sign (+), and the right column is labeled with the delta symbol (Δ). Then, ask participants to share what they liked about the activity, and record their responses in the left column. Afterward, ask them what they would change about the activity, and record their responses in the right column. Gray et al. (2010) note that "Plus/Delta" can be used with "any activity, idea, work product, or action" (p. 246), making it a versatile feedback mechanism for workshops.

Another helpful framework for obtaining in-the-moment feedback from participants is "I Like, I Wish, I Wonder," which is a popular adaptation of the "I Like, I Wish" and the "I Like, I Wish, What If" feedback protocols developed at Stanford University (d.school, 2018; Hyper Island, n.d.; Stanford Online, 2014). Following a workshop activity, pause and invite participants to share what they liked about it, what they wish, and what they wonder. Participants can share their responses verbally, record them on sticky notes, or post them in a shared digital space (such as Mural, Miro, FigJam, or Padlet Sandbox). For example, during my "Helping Faculty Design Engaging Microlectures" workshop at the 2023 POD Network Online Conference, I shared a microlecture planning template with participants and then gave them a few minutes to independently explore the template and record what they liked, what they wished, and what they wondered about it on a Padlet board. Afterward, we reviewed the responses as a group. This activity allowed me to address participants' questions and suggestions about the planning template immediately, and it offered me helpful feedback that I could use to modify the template for the future. "I Like, I Wish, I Wonder" and "Plus/Delta" can also be used as peer-based feedback protocols, and they can be used at the end of a workshop to obtain participants' feedback about their overall learning experience.

Engage in In-The-Moment Reflection

Good facilitation requires the ability to be both on the ground and in the air simultaneously. What I mean by this is that facilitators need to be in the moment with participants while concurrently maintaining a bird's-eye view of the entire learning experience. This requires constant reflection in the moment about what is occurring so that you can adjust accordingly. One simple practice that I've found helpful in my personal facilitation work is keeping a mini notepad and pen near me when I'm facilitating a workshop. On this notepad, I jot down notes about tweaks I need to make either during or after the session in order to improve the learning experience. Sometimes, the note is as simple as "Shorten time for _____ activity," "Increase time for ____ discussion," or "Replace original discussion question with this question: _____." By reflecting in the moment, I can not only be more responsive to participants during the live session but also generate a list of concrete changes I can make after the session to improve it for the future.

Responsiveness After Workshops

Obtain Feedback About the Overall Learning Experience

Soliciting feedback from participants about their overall experience in the workshop is a critical way that we can be responsive to them after the workshop ends. In my personal practice, I typically solicit feedback informally (through a closing reflection activity) and formally (through an end-of-workshop feedback survey). (Refer to Chapters 2, 3, and 7 for more information). Together, these tools provide valuable insight into what participants learned during the workshop and what their learning experience was like. After every workshop, I set aside time to carefully review the feedback survey data. (I typically review the reflection responses with participants during the live workshop.) As I review the feedback survey data, I reflect on the trends and constructive comments participants shared and note changes for the future.

If you're facilitating a workshop series or a multiday institute, you can incorporate discussion of the feedback survey data into each session in order to make it clear to learners that you're listening and adjusting accordingly (Kirkpatrick & Kirkpatrick, 2016). Kirkpatrick and Kirkpatrick (2016) describe their approach as follows:

> After each of the five sessions of our online certification program, we gather data. At the beginning of each session, the feedback from the previous session, as well as any related questions, are debriefed. Participants often comment that they are so pleased to be heard and proud when they see us implement one of their suggestions. This feedback also provides an opportunity to fully explain when we are unable to implement certain suggestions, so participants know they were considered.
>
> *(pp. 153–154)*

As we discussed in Chapter 2, while feedback surveys are helpful, they should ideally be part of a more robust evaluation plan that examines the greater impact of the professional learning experience. If your workshop evaluation plan incorporates implementation data, be sure to schedule time to gather and review that data. For example, you might send out a delayed survey to learn about participants' implementation of the workshop content, set up observations, or provide an avenue for learners to submit artifacts that demonstrate how they've applied what they've learned to their work. Regardless of the methods chosen, be sure to use the data you collect to shape future programming decisions.

Review the Chat Log

For virtual workshops, one of the most valuable artifacts of learning is the chat log. After facilitating virtual workshops, I take some time to review the chat log to gain deeper insight into what was happening during the learning experience and catch things I might have missed in the moment. As I review the chat log, I note any key themes, questions, or issues I might need to address in the future. I also gather resources participants shared (such as links to related articles or websites) so that I can add them to the curated resource collection.

Follow Up

Following up with participants regarding any specific needs or requests they shared during the workshop is another important way that we can be responsive. If a participant asked a question that you were unsure of, expressed interest in meeting with you to discuss a specific topic further, or had challenges during the session that would benefit from one-on-one support, you can proactively send them a personal email after the session to provide a response or schedule a time to meet. This simple act conveys a message of care and that you mean what you say when you tell them, "I'll look into that!" or "Let's meet afterward to discuss that."

Make Changes the Second Time Around

Because I typically facilitate virtual workshops twice a day (once in the morning and again in the afternoon), a key way that I'm responsive to learners is by making revisions during the time between the two sessions. Sometimes, I notice challenges or questions participants had during the first session that I can proactively address during the second session. Other times, I realize that there are small tweaks I need to make to the timing or format of an activity, the content addressed, or the phrasing of my questions. Still other times, I simply think of a more effective, efficient, or engaging way to do something. Whatever the case may be, I can use the time between the two sessions to make any necessary changes so that the learning experience is even better for participants the second time around.

For on-site workshops (which I typically facilitate once per day), I take time after the session to review the in-the-moment reflection notes I jotted down on my mini notepad. Then, I open the workshop slide deck and add comments to specific slides where changes are needed. This way, the next time I'm preparing to facilitate the on-site workshop, I have clear and specific notes about what I need to tweak.

Administer Critical Incident Questionnaires

Brookfield (2017) shares how instructors can use a strategy called the Critical Incident Questionnaire (CIQ) to obtain anonymous student feedback at the end of each week. The CIQ consists of the following five questions:

- At what moment in class this week did you feel most engaged with what was happening?
- At what moment in class this week were you most distanced from what was happening?
- What action that anyone (teacher or student) took this week did you find most affirming or helpful?
- What action that anyone took this week did you find most puzzling or confusing?
- What about the class this week surprised you the most?

(Brookfield, 2017, p. 108)

You can adapt the CIQ for use in long-term programs, such as workshop series, institutes, and courses, by changing the terminology in the questions to better fit your program and participants. You can then use the feedback you receive at the end of each session or week to determine what is working well, what could be improved, and if there are any issues that need to be addressed.

Send End-of-Semester Surveys

One technique I use to obtain delayed feedback from participants about their professional learning experiences is an end-of-semester survey. I learned about this technique from Rudy Leon via the POD Network Listserv (personal communication, October 13, 2023), and I have adapted her prompts into questions that I use in the survey (along with some of my own original questions). The first section of the survey lists the programs I facilitated that term, and the remainder of the survey includes the following questions for participants to respond to:

- What do you remember learning in these professional learning programs?
- What have you implemented in your teaching or other professional practices?
- What results (if any) have you seen based on the changes made?
- What are you still confused about or grappling with?
- Which teaching and/or technology topics would you like to explore in the future?
- Which days and times work well for professional learning programs?
- Is there anything else you would like to share?

The feedback I receive from the end-of-semester survey helps me gain insight into what has resonated with participants long term and how they have applied their learning. It also helps me identify potential topics for future professional learning programs so that I can continue to be responsive to participants' needs.

Recap

- Be responsive to participants before the workshop by using a learner-centered design approach, sending pre-workshop communication, and responding to participants' inquiries in a kind and timely fashion.
- Be responsive to participants during the workshop by conducting formative assessments, inviting participants to ask questions, providing feedback, obtaining in-the-moment feedback about workshop activities, and engaging in in-the-moment reflection.
- Be responsive to participants after the workshop by obtaining feedback about the overall learning experience, reviewing the chat log, following up with participants, making changes the second time around, administering CIQs, and/or sending end-of-semester surveys.

Sticky Note Reflection

Rating Scale: On a scale of 1–5 (with 1 being "not responsive" and 5 being "very responsive"), how would you rate your level of responsiveness to participants *before* workshops? *During* workshops? *After* workshops? Jot down your ratings and rationales below.

Workshop Toolkit

Scan the QR code or visit the URL to access additional resources related to this chapter.

www.tolunoah.com/workshop-toolkits

Design Time

Review your workshop plans. Consider how you can be more responsive to participants, and craft any tools or activities you might need for this purpose.

Facilitators' Lounge

Join the Facilitators' Lounge to connect with other readers and share your takeaways, strategies, and next steps!

www.tolunoah.com/facilitators-lounge/

References

Angelo, T.A. (with Zakrajsek, T.D.). (2024). *Classroom assessment techniques: Formative feedback tools for college and university teachers* (3rd ed.). Jossey-Bass.

Bowman, S.L. (2009). *Training from the BACK of the room! 65 ways to step aside and let them learn.* Pfeiffer.

Brookfield, S.D. (2017). *Becoming a critically reflective teacher* (2nd ed.). Jossey-Bass.

CAST. (2024). *Universal Design for Learning guidelines version 3.0.* https://udlguidelines.cast.org/

Cavanagh, S.R. (2016). *The spark of learning: Energizing the college classroom with the science of emotion.* West Virginia University Press.

Center for Leadership & Educational Equity. (n.d.-a). *Feedback carousel.* www.clee.org/resources/feedback-carousel/

Center for Leadership & Educational Equity. (n.d.-b). *Tuning protocol: Examining adult work.* www.clee.org/resources/tuning-protocol-examining-adult-work/

d.school. (2018). *Design thinking bootleg.* https://static1.squarespace.com/static/57c6b79629687fde090a0fdd/t/5b19b2f2aa4a99e99b26b6bb/1528410876119/dschool_bootleg_deck_2018_final_sm+%282%29.pdf

Eduflow. (2021, October 28). *What makes feedback good?* [Video]. YouTube. https://youtu.be/Tly6J0H00gY?feature=shared

Fink, L.D. (n.d.). *A self-directed guide to designing courses for significant learning.* https://intentionalcollegeteaching.org/wp-content/uploads/2022/07/GuidetoCourseDesignAug05.pdf

Fink, L.D. (2013). *Creating significant learning experiences: An integrated approach to designing college courses* (2nd ed.). Jossey-Bass.

Gray, D., Brown, S., & Macanufo, J. (2010). *Gamestorming: A playbook for innovators, rulebreakers, and changemakers.* O'Reilly.

Hyper Island. (n.d.). *I like, I wish, I wonder.* SessionLab. www.sessionlab.com/methods/i-like-i-wish-i-wonder

Kirkpatrick, J.D., & Kirkpatrick, W.K. (2016). *Kirkpatrick' four levels of training evaluation.* ATD Press.

Lipmanowicz, H., & McCandless, K. (2013). *The surprising power of Liberating Structures: Simple rules to unleash a culture of innovation.* Liberating Structures Press.

Ryan, R.M., & Deci, E.L. (2000). Self-determination theory and the facilitation of intrinsic motivation, social development, and well-being. *American Psychologist, 55*(1), 68–78. https://doi.org/10.1037/0003-066X.55.1.68

Stanford Online. (2014, November 11). *Stanford webinar: Design thinking and the art of critique – I like/I wish* [Video]. YouTube. https://youtu.be/QkWM2--3TQo?feature=shared

Steinert, Y., Mann, K., Anderson, B., Barnett, B.M., Centeno, A., Naismith, L., Prideaux, D., Spencer, J., Tullo, E., Viggiano, T., Ward, H., & Dolmans, D. (2016). A systematic review of faculty development initiatives designed to enhance teaching effectiveness: A 10-year update: BEME guide no. 40. *Medical Teacher, 38*(8), 769–786. http://dx.doi.org/10.1080/0142159X.2016.1181851

Wiggins, G., & McTighe, J. (2005). *Understanding by design* (2nd ed.). ASCD.

Wind, D.K. (2020, August 18). *Encourage better peer feedback with our guide to feedback rubrics.* Eduflow. www.eduflow.com/blog/encourage-better-peer-feedback-with-our-guide-to-feedback-rubrics

10
OWN YOUR DISTINCTIVE STYLE

Guiding Question:
How will you bring who you are to your workshop design and facilitation approach?

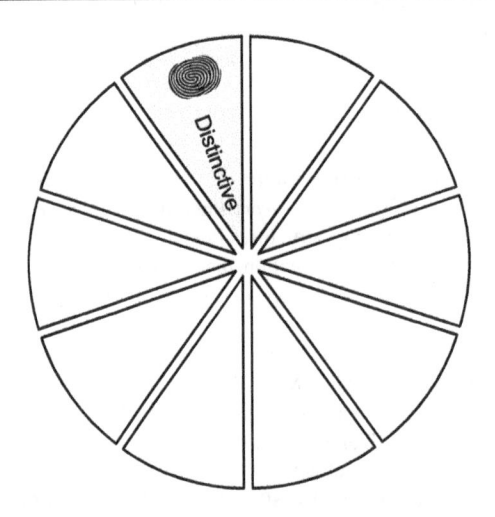

In his bestselling book, *The Courage to Teach*, Palmer (2017) emphasizes the importance of educators understanding who they are as that will impact how they teach. He captures this sentiment with the powerful line, "We teach who we are," and he explains that "good teaching requires self-knowledge" (Palmer, 2017, pp. 2–3). While Palmer's work is primarily geared toward those who teach in traditional settings (such as classrooms), his words also ring true for those who teach in other settings (such as workshops). As designers and facilitators of professional learning, our identities also shape our approaches. We cannot separate who we are from what we do, and each of us has a distinctive fingerprint that marks our unique approach to workshop design and facilitation.

While this book has offered a plethora of strategies and ideas that will hopefully be of use to you, ultimately, what you choose to do has to align with your personal values and style. As we've discussed throughout this book, there is no one "right" way to design and facilitate workshops, and whichever methods you choose to adopt should feel in sync with who you are.

As facilitators, there are multiple personal factors that may shape our professional learning approaches. For example, Bell et al. (2023) note that "our particular and unique personalities, family backgrounds, life histories, and educational training (to name a few) impact both *who we are* and *how we appear* in a classroom or workshop" (p. 409, emphasis in original). In their article, "Identity, Intersectionality, and Educational Development," Little et al. (2019) encourage educational developers to use an intersectional lens as they consider how different aspects of their personal identity (e.g., race, gender, age, religion, sexuality, socioeconomic status, etc.) "intersect" and influence their work

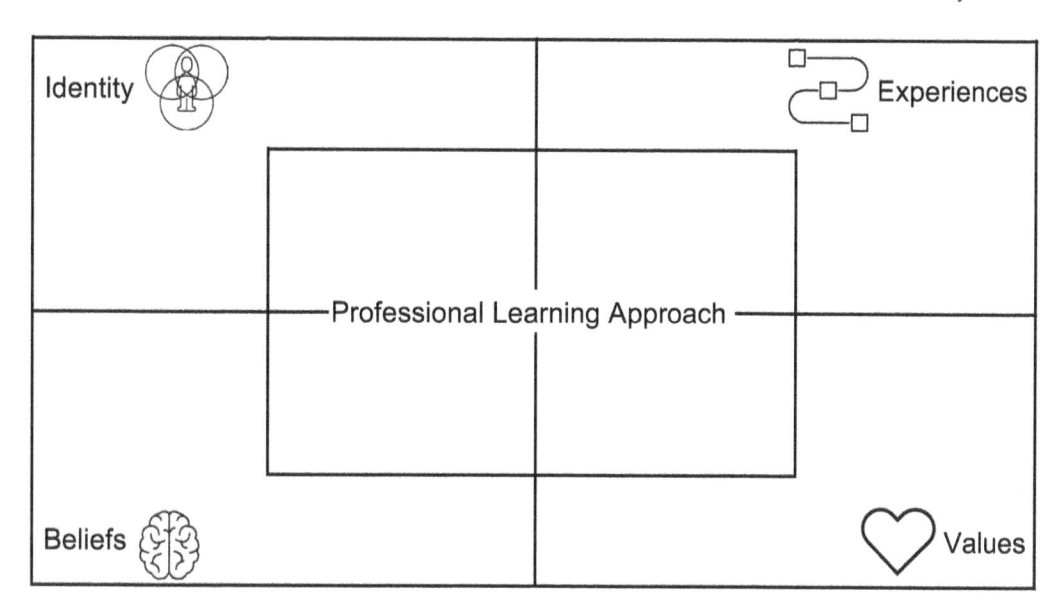

FIGURE 10.1 Facilitator Map

in different ways (pp. 12–13). The authors explain that "intersectionality helps us critically evaluate how aspects of our identities come into play in ways that may help, hinder, or complicate our work as we interact with others" (Little et al., 2019, p. 14). Their article (which is linked in this chapter's Workshop Toolkit) offers helpful guiding questions and scenarios to reflect on.

As you consider how who you are shapes what you do, it can be helpful to reflect on four key areas:

- **Identity**: What are the most salient parts of your identity, and how do they shape your professional learning approach?
- **Experiences**: How have your prior experiences shaped your professional learning approach?
- **Beliefs**: What are your beliefs about professional learning?
- **Values**: What is important to you when designing and facilitating professional learning experiences?

Figure 10.1 depicts these four areas in the form of a Facilitator Map. In the four corners of the map, you can list specific examples of your personal identity markers, experiences, beliefs, and values that are core to who you are. In the overlapping rectangle in the center of the map, you can list how these factors shape your professional learning approach. (There is an editable copy of the Facilitator Map in this chapter's Workshop Toolkit.)

When I reflect on the defining identity markers, beliefs, values, and experiences that make me who I am, there are several core aspects that rise to the surface. I am the daughter of Nigerian immigrants, and I was born and raised in the United States. I am Christian, young, and introverted. I believe that professional learning experiences should be relevant, purposeful, structured, inclusive, connective, active, reflective, ongoing, responsive, and distinctive (basically, everything we've explored so far in this book). I value learning, integrity, equity, care, creativity, and practicality. I have known since 4th grade that I wanted to be an educator, and that dream became a reality at the age of 20, when I started my career as a K-12 teacher. The dream continued to expand when I transitioned to higher education and became a teacher education professor. Throughout my career, I have had opportunities to facilitate various forms of professional learning for teachers and professors in different settings (including K-12, higher education, and corporate edtech).

These factors not only make me unique as an individual, but they also influence how I approach my professional learning work. For example, as a Black woman of Nigerian heritage who has a unique name, I am incredibly intentional about learning, using, and correctly pronouncing workshop participants' names. I know on a deeply personal level how it feels to have people not make the effort, and I never want anyone in my sessions to ever feel that way. As an introvert, I always consider how I can incorporate activities that will allow *all* participants to contribute to the conversation (not just those who are extroverted or feel comfortable raising their hands to speak in front of the group). As a former K-12 teacher and college professor, my educator lens significantly shapes my professional learning approach. I believe that the science of learning and pedagogy can be applied to the design and facilitation of workshops in order to create more meaningful, impactful, and engaging professional learning experiences. To me, facilitation is a form of teaching, and I can't separate who I am as an educator from who I am as a facilitator.

However, at this point in the book, I think you've heard enough from me, so I'd like to pass the mic.

In this chapter, you will hear from seven fantastic individuals who facilitate professional learning in various higher education contexts. Interviewing these facilitators was such a joy, and I'm excited to share some snippets from our conversation that demonstrate how who they are shapes what they do. During our conversations, many of the facilitators mentioned specific frameworks, methodologies, tools, and influential authors and/or works that they have found useful. While detailed descriptions of these topics are beyond the scope of this book, you can find links to related resources (along with links to the personal websites of many of the facilitators) in this chapter's Workshop Toolkit, should you wish to learn more.

Karen Costa

Karen Costa is an author, adjunct professor, and faculty development facilitator at 100 Faculty. Her journey as a professional learning facilitator began in 2006 when she was an assistant director of enrollment at a community college, where her role entailed training others about academic advising. She was concurrently teaching a first-year experience course at the college, and she found that her teaching and facilitation work overlapped in many ways. Karen explained:

> From the get go, I went into my facilitation work thinking about the same things I was thinking about in the classroom with my college students. How do people learn? How do our brains work? How do our bodies work in learning situations? How can we teach and learn most effectively? …I was always very much as focused on engaging adult learners/professional learners as I was on engaging my students.

As Karen taught and facilitated professional learning at the college, she also sought to learn as much as she could about the latest research on teaching and learning, and she applied what she was learning to both roles. Over the years, Karen also began writing about her teaching ideas, which led to invitations to facilitate professional learning externally. After publishing her first book, *99 Tips for Creating Simple and Sustainable Educational Videos*, the facilitation requests increased, marking a significant "turning point" in her facilitation journey.

Since 2019, Karen has been offering 100% virtual professional learning for faculty and staff in higher education and for professionals in other organizations. Her decision to pursue fully virtual professional learning was influenced by several factors. First, in 2019, Karen was diagnosed with a chronic illness that made travel difficult. The COVID-19 pandemic and her deep care about climate change have also influenced her decision. Additionally, Karen recognizes that virtual professional learning can reduce barriers for people who would otherwise be unable to participate. Since making the decision to go fully virtual, Karen has come to own and celebrate her skills as a virtual facilitator, even though this means declining requests to facilitate on-site. She commented:

> I think it's important that we recognize that we can't be everything to everyone, and to focus on doing our part with our unique skills and limitations. To be a voice that virtual facilitation can be as good, if not sometimes better, than on-site is really important. …I feel really strongly that that's my bag, that's my focus, and I'm happy about that.

Karen's professional learning approach is also shaped by her attention-deficit/hyperactivity disorder (ADHD), and she leverages a "strengths-based, challenge-aware model of ADHD" that recognizes both its benefits and limitations. A strength she noted is that her ADHD influences her decision to facilitate professional learning about a wide range of topics (such as trauma-aware teaching, climate action pedagogy, and facilitation strategies), as she finds the variety energizing. It also shapes Karen's facilitation style, which she describes as being "very energetic." She often receives positive feedback from participants who feel "energized," "engaged," and like time has flown by in her sessions. On the other hand, Karen's ADHD and chronic illness also mean that facilitation can be "exhausting." As such, she sets clear boundaries for herself about how frequently she will facilitate, sticking to one facilitation per week so that she can maintain her energy, protect her voice, and avoid burnout.

Three words that capture Karen's values are "holistic," "communal," and "invitational."

- Holistic: "I show up as a whole person, not just as a facilitator, and I create space for my learners to show up as [whole people], not just as workers, learners, or clients."
- Communal: "The communal piece for me is a non-hierarchical approach to facilitation. What that looks like in my sessions is that I am recognizing and using my expertise while I am decentering myself in the learning experience and trying to instead center the community that we are in that moment."
- Invitational: "I share what I know is true, what has worked for me, and what I've learned from the literature and from my community. I offer it to people, and I invite [them] to engage with it. I trust people to make their own decisions and to do what is best for them."

One way Karen's values shape her facilitation approach is through her intentional use of the Zoom chat. She explained, "I feel like the Zoom chat is a really democratizing space where we can have that holistic, communal energy." Karen includes explicit and repeated invitations for participants to share their thoughts in the chat so that everyone can learn from each other. Another way that Karen's values shape her facilitation approach is in the language she uses during sessions. She avoids using the word "should"; instead, she uses the word "could." This practice is shaped by her experience in recovery programs. At the time of our conversation, Karen was 7½ years sober, and she learned in recovery to avoid giving advice or telling people what they should do. A key phrase from her past recovery days that she brings into her facilitation work is, "Take what you need and leave the rest," and she emphasizes the importance of "inviting instead of imposing" things on learners.

Karen believes that good professional learning workshops acknowledge learners, invite them to engage, and provide them with opportunities to share what they know about the topic before the facilitator explains what they know. In terms of the qualities of a good facilitator, Karen believes that confidence is key. She elaborates:

> Confidence, for me, is not cockiness. …To me, the most confident people are the humble, quiet people who don't need to always be showing off. …I think being quiet and decentering yourself and encouraging your learners to share what they know [is] confidence because you're saying, "I am confident in who I am as a facilitator and an educator to not feel like I have to prove anything to anybody, and to turn it over and open it up to my learners."

Karen also notes that good facilitators own their role as leaders by "holding space" and taking responsibility for managing any challenging or inappropriate dynamics that may arise. Additionally, good facilitators "do it scared," meaning that they acknowledge their fears, anxieties, or nerves and "then still go out and do [their] good facilitation work."

When designing new workshops, Karen begins the process in an "analog" fashion by drawing a mind map where she brainstorms and organizes ideas. She then transfers these ideas to Google Slides and builds out the session there. Karen uses a clean and minimal slide design with limited text, and she puts most of the content and links in the speaker notes section so that when she shares the slide deck with participants, the speaker notes can serve as "resource guides" for them.

In terms of structure, Karen's workshops begin with a welcome, followed by an invitation for participants to introduce themselves. She includes multiple activities throughout the session, and she constantly monitors the chat to check in with participants and draw out the ideas and questions shared there. Additionally, Karen believes in the importance of modeling, and she often leverages a technique that she calls "pulling back the curtain" (an ode to *The Wizard of Oz*). Here, she will do an activity with participants and then pause and ask, "What did I just do?" so that participants can reflect on what she did, why she did it, and how they could apply a similar strategy to their own work.

There are several key frameworks that inform Karen's facilitation approach. One is the Community of Inquiry (CoI) framework (Garrison et al., 2000), which prompts her to consider how she is connecting with learners, how learners are connecting with content, and how learners are connecting with each other. Additionally, Michelle Pacansky-Brock's (n.d.) work on humanized online teaching, Laura Rendón's (n.d.) validation theory, and adrienne maree brown's (2017, 2019) work on "emergent strategy" and "pleasure activism" have been influential in Karen's work. For example, drawing on brown's "small is all" principle, Karen encourages participants in her workshops to "play the game of small" if they feel overwhelmed, by determining the smallest action they can take to act upon what they have learned and then build from there. Karen also uses a "strengths-based model" of facilitation that acknowledges and builds upon people's strengths and expertise instead of a "prescriptive model" that is rooted in telling participants what to do.

Three closing thoughts Karen shared are:

- "Design a facilitation style and system that works for you."
- "Prioritize accessibility."
- "Take care of yourself so that you can continue to show up and take care of your learners."

Norman Eng

Norman Eng is the founder and president of EDUCATIONxDESIGN, Inc., and a lecturer in the School of Education at Brooklyn College in New York. While he does not consider himself to be a professional learning facilitator, workshops are one of the many "avenues" he uses to help professors learn how to "teach more effectively." Other avenues are his blog, online courses, and books (which include *Teaching College* and *PRESENTING*).

Norman's professional background has shaped his approach to workshops in important ways. He began his career as a marketing executive before becoming a K-12 teacher and then a college professor. As such, he believes it is critical to understand the group with which you are working. Norman stated, "The biggest insight I gained from marketing, K-12 teaching, and college teaching is this: the more you understand your target audience, the better you can design meaningful learning experiences."

When designing workshops, Norman focuses on the experience that learners will have. He commented, "I've always said that the most important role that we as teachers and trainers have is being architects of learning experiences." Norman draws important parallels between user experience (UX) in the business realm and learner experience (LX), explaining:

> User experience is defined as the sum total of experiences that customers have with your company, your product, or your service. …It's no different with workshops or with teaching in general. There is a user experience there too, except I refer to it (and I'm not the one who created this) as the learner experience. Are you making it easy for your audience to grasp your point? Are you understanding their biggest challenges, their frustrations, the obstacles that they have to overcome in order to change? Do you provide simple, focused, and actionable next steps?

Norman believes that the most important characteristic of a good workshop is that it is a "meaningful learning experience." This serves as an umbrella term for other important workshop characteristics, such as being "collaborative," "focused," "engaging," and "actionable." In terms of facilitator qualities, Norman believes that a good facilitator has "an unrelenting focus on the learner experience." This requires the facilitator to consider each element of the workshop from the learner's perspective. Additionally, Norman believes that good facilitators keep things simple by considering if they have "distilled [the] workshop to its essence."

When Norman is invited to do a workshop for a university, he begins by asking questions about who the participants are and the challenges they're facing. Sometimes, he will also send a pre-workshop survey to participants several weeks before the workshop so that he can use their responses to shape the session. Norman will then "boil [the workshop] into a one-sentence presentation plan that incorporates the what, the how, and the why" of the session. This sentence answers three important questions:

- "What's the goal of the workshop?"
- "How will attendees reach that goal?"
- "Why is this workshop beneficial to them?"

For example, Norman crafted the following one-sentence presentation plan for a faculty workshop about student motivation: "By the end of this workshop, attendees will be able to develop more meaningful assignments (what) by incorporating autonomy, mastery, and purpose (how) so that students will be more motivated to learn (why)." The one-sentence presentation plan serves as the filter for what goes into the workshop and what stays out. Norman elaborated, "Everything that I design or plan for this workshop…has to align with this one-sentence presentation plan. …That's the skeleton that I can build my whole presentation around." Norman uses the same strategy in his college courses, referring to it as a "one-sentence lesson plan" instead.

When preparing workshops, Norman creates a script of what he plans to say, and if he will be using slides, he makes them last as "support" for his ideas. He practices the script many times in many different places, such as during his subway commute and while exercising. This helps him to fully internalize what he plans to say so that he can "focus on being present" during the workshop and adjust based on how participants are responding. Norman explained, "There's this 'withitness' that you have to have when you're in the moment to be an effective presenter or teacher, and it's hard to have that withitness when you're focused on what you have to say."

Because Norman facilitates professional learning about instruction (i.e., how to teach), he explicitly tells participants in his workshops to pay attention to *how* he is facilitating the session. During workshops, Norman uses active learning strategies that give participants the opportunity to apply what they are learning. For example, during the student motivation workshop, he gave faculty time to revise one of their course assignments so that it incorporated the motivational principles of autonomy, mastery, and purpose. Norman also designs every workshop with these three motivational principles in mind by considering how he can give participants opportunities to exercise autonomy, develop mastery, and engage in purposeful tasks. Additionally, he typically provides participants with a graphic organizer or worksheet to guide their work during the session.

Three closing thoughts Norman shared are:

- Skip the introductory content about yourself, and instead, "jump right into the thing that you need to teach or train."
- "Don't save your best stuff for last. …Put your most impactful thing at the very beginning. Lead with your best stuff."
- "If you can end your presentation 5 minutes early, [participants will] love you."

Tasha Souza

Tasha Souza is the faculty recruitment and retention coordinator and a professor of communication at Sacramento State University. Her journey as a professional learning facilitator began when she took a training and development course as an undergraduate student. In this course, Tasha learned how to conduct needs assessments, and she collaborated with her peers to create and implement training for a client. Tasha was also working as a tutor at the time, and she had the opportunity to develop a workshop for other students about public speaking. Through these experiences, Tasha realized her love for "developing creative learning opportunities."

Currently, Tasha's favorite topic to facilitate workshops about is microresistance. In these workshops, she helps participants understand that in regard to microaggressions, everyone can "observe one, experience one, and commit one all in the same day." Tasha helps "empower [participants] to behave differently in the presence of microaggressions, whether they perpetrated or they observed, so that they can be a better ally." She commented, "I love workshops where I feel like people can leave with practical skills, and it makes a difference not just in their personal lives, but hopefully, makes other people's lives around them better."

Tasha's upbringing has shaped her professional learning work in important ways. She grew up "very low income" and experienced housing and food insecurity, yet people often assumed that she was well off with "tennis lessons and parents at home" because of her white privilege. Tasha explained, "I saw how it felt to have my identity disregarded but also the privilege in that there were all these assumptions." Additionally, because of the financial challenges her family faced, Tasha's mother often had renters stay with them to help make ends meet. The renters were often "international students or recent immigrants," and Tasha witnessed how negatively they were treated in society. These experiences have shaped how Tasha approaches participants in her workshops and the topics she addresses. She explained, "I always think about where people are and try not to assume where they've come from, and how what I offer can hopefully be useful toward more equity and social justice in the world."

Three core values that shape Tasha's professional learning approach are "communication," "relationships," and "integrity." In workshops, she incorporates interactive activities that promote belonging and relationship building, and she aims to foster "a space where everyone feels like they can contribute." In terms of integrity, Tasha remarked, "I choose to do the work that aligns with my values," and she declines opportunities that do not.

Tasha believes that a good workshop begins with a needs assessment so that it can be designed in a way that meets participants' needs. She also believes that good workshops are "interactive," "engaging," "practical," "thought provoking," and leave people "feeling inspired to do better in the future." In terms of facilitator qualities, Tasha believes that a good facilitator is "responsive," "enthusiastic," "engaging," and "flexible." Additionally, she believes that a good facilitator operates with "compassion and humility," is "warm and inviting," and can "read the room well."

When designing workshops, Tasha begins by conducting a needs assessment, and then she leverages backward design to determine the workshop goals, formative assessments, and activities. She emphasizes the importance of "alignment, clarity, and transparency" in determining what should or should not be included in the workshop. To help her manage her time, Tasha likes to plan workshops "to the minute," and she builds in cushion time where she knows what she can "drop or condense" in the moment if needed.

When facilitating workshops, Tasha arrives early, and she greets each participant personally. She starts the session with an icebreaker activity to help participants connect with each other. As she facilitates the session, Tasha aims to talk for no more than 10–12 minutes at a time, and she includes interactive activities throughout, such as discussions, sorting activities, role-playing, reflections, and HMOYs (which are "How many of you...?" questions). Tasha also enjoys using debriefing frameworks that she learned about in graduate school, such as EDIT (experience, describe, infer, transfer) and the Four Fs (facts, feelings, findings, future). (These frameworks are attributed to Anita Covert [adapted] and Roger Greenaway, respectively [Gray, 1991; University of Edinburgh, 2018].)

Three closing thoughts Tasha shared are:

- "Assess needs as much as you can and design according to those needs."
- "Create spaces where people can stretch their comfort zones."
- "Be open to always learning about how to be a better facilitator and also [learning] from your participants."

Courtney Plotts

Courtney Plotts is a faculty developer and founder of the company, NeuroCulture, where she facilitates professional learning about cultural responsiveness. Her journey as a professional learning facilitator was shaped by some not-so-great experiences as a participant in professional development workshops when she was a K-12 teacher. Courtney explained, "I was always excited about learning, but I always felt like [professional development] was very patronizing. There was a hierarchy to it, and it was more about the presenter than it was about the people." She explained that it often felt like the facilitator was trying to sell programs and products or offer strategies that could not be readily implemented without jumping through additional hoops. These negative experiences led Courtney to pursue opportunities to train other teachers at her school, and she has continued to facilitate professional learning in her higher education and independent consulting roles ever since.

Two values that shape Courtney's professional learning approach are her "love for people" and her desire to "meet people where they are." She explained, "If you love your content more than you love people, it usually doesn't work out well." These values are evident in the various ways in which Courtney prioritizes connection with participants. Before workshops, she sends a series of pre-workshop emails to participants to prepare them for the experience. Some of these emails include questions to get to know participants, others include information about herself, and still others include fun elements such as "mini contests." Courtney also sends an email that clarifies the scope of the session so that participants have a better sense of what to expect. During workshops, Courtney is intentional about connecting with participants on a personal basis. In smaller on-site sessions, she walks around the room before the start of the workshop and introduces herself to each participant or shares a compliment. She also uses a set of laminated badges to let participants know that they are seen and valued and to add an element of fun to the workshop. For example, while participants are engaged in small group discussions, she will walk around the room and drop badges on participants' tables that celebrate things she is noticing, such as critical thinking, divergent thinking, and vulnerability (e.g., through the sharing of personal stories). Every participant receives a badge by the end of the session.

To Courtney, the qualities of a good facilitator include "patience," "a heart for people," "thick skin," "conflict resolution" skills, and the ability to "separate you as a person from the feedback you receive." She feels that good facilitators need to be adept at a variety of instructional techniques, and she models different techniques in her work so that faculty not only learn about the strategies she is teaching but also learn from how those strategies are implemented.

Courtney believes that good professional learning workshops prioritize "relationship building," the production of a "tangible product," and active learning. As such, Courtney follows an 80/20 rule in her workshops, where faculty are actively doing something 80% of the time, and she speaks 20% of the time. She commented that the time gathered with faculty is "such a precious time, so in that time, I really want to make sure that they're connecting with each other." Courtney also employs "simple fixes" and "plug-and-play" strategies that faculty can immediately use. She empathizes with faculty, noting the heavy expectations they have, along with the fatigue and limited bandwidth they are experiencing because of the COVID-19 pandemic. Courtney explained, "I try to be very careful about what I ask faculty to do and how I ask faculty to do it." For example, in regard to the topic of representation, faculty often feel overwhelmed at the prospect of designing culturally relevant learning experiences and materials given the great diversity of students in their classrooms. A "simple fix" that faculty can apply to their case study activities is giving students the freedom to fill in the demographic information themselves rather than pre-populating that information. Courtney explained that this small tweak allows students to complete the case study with information that is more relevant to them, and it allows for richer conversations among students. It also requires little to no time on the part of faculty to implement.

One unique aspect of Courtney's facilitation approach is that she has developed an app for use in her workshops. (She also offers a physical workbook for participants who prefer the information in a different format.) The app can be accessed on any device, and it provides participants with the workshop materials and activities, along with a running chat where they can anonymously post their comments and questions throughout the session. The app provides Courtney with valuable data that she can use to make her multiday workshops more responsive to participants. For example, at the end of the first day of a workshop, she reviews the data and uses it to adjust her plans for the next day, based on participants' interests and needs.

Three closing thoughts Courtney shared are:

- "You can't do it all, so don't try."
- "The more your participants are doing, the more valuable your workshop is."
- "Whatever makes your faculty's life easier, do that."

Lindsay Masland

Lindsay Masland is the executive director of the Center for Excellence in Teaching and Learning for Student Success at Appalachian State University. Her interest in facilitating learning experiences began when she was a child; at the age of 10, she created a summer camp for other kids in her neighborhood, complete with "developmentally appropriate" activities geared toward kids of different ages. This interest in facilitating learning experiences continued as an adult. In graduate school, Lindsay did a guest lecture in one of her mentor's courses, and the positive feedback she received motivated her to pursue teaching. During her second year as a faculty member, Lindsay joined a faculty learning community about Universal Design for Learning (UDL) through which she met the faculty developers at her university. They later invited her to lead her first official professional learning workshop about UDL, and opportunities to facilitate continued from there. Today, Lindsay often facilitates workshops that challenge participants to consider the nuances, ethical implications, and research basis of different topics. She commented, "I tend to find myself facilitating workshops on controversial topics or things where I feel like everybody is in favor of this new idea, and I have concerns."

When it comes to Lindsay's personal identity, she recognizes the various ways in which her positionality as a white person with tenure who is "coded as a woman" and holds a leadership position has afforded her power and privilege. She directly addresses this in her workshops by sharing how her personal context and values impact her pedagogical choices and by inviting participants to reflect on these factors, too. Lindsay noted:

> A big piece of the workshop starts out with values and context, helping people to get really clear on that for themselves and understanding that every single person's set of values and context is going to be different. Identical pedagogical choices are going to mean different things coming out of different people.

One prior experience that has influenced Lindsay's professional learning approach was her participation in the POD Network's 2020 book club series, which focused on Saad's (2020) book, *Me and White Supremacy*. Lindsay volunteered to help co-facilitate one of the reading groups, and all of the facilitators used a discussion approach that Saad recommends in the book, which is called The Circle Way. Lindsay found this to be a "powerful" way to structure discussions, and she has continued to incorporate the approach (or elements thereof) into her design of learning experiences ever since.

Lindsay's professional learning approach is shaped by three "threshold concepts." One is values-based decision making. Her guiding values are "joy & ease," "belongingness," "intentionality/alignment," and "liberation." Adapting Parker's (2018) popular phrase, "Make purpose your bouncer" (p. 32), Lindsay makes her values her bouncer, and she designs learning experiences that align with them. Two other threshold concepts that Lindsay draws on from her scholarly background are structural equations modeling and self-determination theory (SDT). Lindsay explained:

> Structural equations modeling helps me to continue to think about all of the various contextual factors that interact to explain any outcome. Although I'm never using any actual math or statistics in planning a learning experience, I am thinking of it in terms of "What are all the relevant things that are interacting here to produce some outcome?" Some of these things I have no control over because people are just bringing [them] to the table, and some of these things are actually manipulable.

In terms of SDT, Lindsay aims to "maximize" competence, autonomy, and relatedness in her workshops. To maximize competence, she helps participants identify what they already know/can do and how they can build upon that foundation. To maximize autonomy, she supports participants in "making choices that align to what [they] care about." To maximize relatedness, she incorporates activities that help foster a sense of community so that participants know they have support and are not alone.

Lindsay believes that good workshops are designed with "intentionality" and "thoughtfulness," meaning that there is a clear rationale for the choices that are made, and this rationale is also evident to participants. She also believes that workshops should be designed with UDL by offering participants "multiple ways to enter, multiple ways to do whatever it is we're doing, and multiple ways to leave." Lindsay believes that good facilitators have a deep understanding of who they are (including their context and values) and that they operate in ways that "respect" that. She notes that there are many effective ways to facilitate and that it is important for people to do so in a way that feels authentic to them rather than trying to imitate others.

When designing workshops, Lindsay draws on backward design by thinking about the end goal, which, for her, is often an "emotional," "worldview," or skills-based goal. She then considers the "constraints" of the situation, such as the modality and number of attendees. Afterward, she determines what will occur during the session. In terms of the workshop structure, Lindsay draws on her background as a performing artist by leveraging a "narrative arc" with a clear beginning, middle, and end. During the opening, she typically begins by telling a story that helps participants connect with the topic personally and communally. She then poses a "wicked problem" to frame the session, and she often shares relevant research related to the issue. During the middle portion of the workshop, Lindsay helps participants explore different ways that they can think about the topic, and she offers various options for engagement (such as discussions, brainstorms, and "multistage collaborative slides" where each task builds upon the previous one). Lindsay ends her workshops by linking the ideas participants generated with the opening story, inviting participants to generate a commitment or next steps, and closing with an "inspirational note." A throughline in her design and facilitation of learning experiences is her consideration of participants' feelings and emotions. Lindsay remarked:

> To me, the function of a workshop is to make people feel good and to make people feel good in a wide range of ways: to make people feel good because they realize they're not alone, [or] to make people feel good because now they have an idea or a tip that's going to solve a problem they have or that's going to move them further in the direction of their values.

Three closing thoughts Lindsay shared are:

- "Get super clear on what this is for. …Why is it worth it to gather?"
- "Once you know why we are gathering, you need to know who is gathering, and that means both who you are as the person who might be bringing the gathering together and [who] the other people who are going to experience the gathering with you [are]."

- "Think of learning experiences as experiences. ...What kind of experience might you like to give to people, and what experience are they saying they might like to have?"

Todd Zakrajsek

Todd Zakrajsek is an associate professor at the University of North Carolina School of Medicine and director of four Lilly Conferences on evidence-based teaching and learning. His journey as a professional learning facilitator began unexpectedly in the early 1990s when he was an assistant professor at Southern Oregon State College. Todd started feeling bored with teaching, so he reached out to two colleagues to see if they would be interested in grabbing lunch to talk about teaching. The lunch went well, and afterward, they decided to do it again, this time inviting any other faculty who were interested in talking about teaching and learning. To their surprise, 19 people came (which at the time, was approximately 10% of the faculty at the school). By the end of lunch, faculty were already inquiring about the next meeting, and the meetings continued every month for the remainder of the year. Eventually, Todd was able to obtain leadership support to start a center dedicated to helping faculty with their teaching. He went on to lead faculty development efforts at multiple universities.

Topic-wise, Todd has always enjoyed facilitating workshops about student engagement, motivation, active learning, and teaching tips. In recent years, he has become increasingly passionate about neurodivergence and individual struggles in gaining an education, topics on which he has been facilitating workshops. Todd elaborated:

> Higher education is really built for fast-talking, risk-taking extroverts who have resources. ... The question becomes, what happens with the individuals who are on the autism spectrum, people who [have] ADHD, people with any number of other learning challenges, mobility issues, or students who just need a few extra seconds to think before they are able to respond in class?

Todd has a personal connection to this topic, as he learned later in life that he has ADHD. One way this impacts his work is that he is easily distracted, so he has developed helpful strategies to keep track of things. For example, when he facilitates on-site workshops, he uses the physical space to help him remain grounded when he goes off on a related tangent to emphasize a point. Todd will begin explaining his first point in one part of the room, then walk a few feet to a different spot to explain the unscheduled supplemental point, and so on. When he is ready to return to the main point, he will walk back through those areas, quickly recapping each point and following the mental breadcrumbs back to the original point. Todd also uses this movement strategy to help participants follow key ideas in his sessions. For example, when explaining two different concepts, he will stand in one spot whenever explaining aspects of the first concept and another spot when explaining aspects of the second concept. Before long, participants are able to predict what he is going to talk about based on where he is located in the room.

One of Todd's core values is that "everybody deserves an opportunity to work for what they desire." He also values honesty and integrity. A concrete way this appears in his professional learning work is in his willingness to share when he makes mistakes. Todd explained, "Personally, I think it's great modeling to admit when mistakes happen and learn from those mistakes. That's a growth-minded approach."

Todd believes that good workshops are "grounded" in the scholarly and experiential work of others and give credit for whatever shaped that content (whether it is a published work or word-of-mouth from a colleague). He also believes that good workshops model sound practices, "have utility," and meet participants' needs. In terms of facilitator characteristics, Todd believes that good facilitators have strong knowledge of the topic they're addressing, are "open-minded" to different approaches, give credit where it's due, admit their mistakes, convey energy that propels people to action, and "believe in the ultimate potential of each individual."

In terms of his personal facilitation approach, Todd describes himself as a "storytelling lecturer" who mixes a variety of active learning strategies into his sessions. He uses stories to help participants connect with the content, and then activities to model teaching strategies and help participants experience the content. Todd also explicitly addresses struggles in his sessions. As a first-generation college student who almost dropped out because of poor grades his first semester, Todd empathizes with the struggles others face. In fact, one of his favorite paraphrased quotes (often attributed to Ian Maclaren) is, "Everyone is fighting a battle you know nothing about, so you should be kind." One way Todd addresses struggles in his workshops is by modeling vulnerability about his own struggles so that he can help others who are struggling "see through a growth mindset." He also provides time for participants to discuss their struggles. For example, he does a card-passing activity where each participant anonymously writes a teaching or learning challenge they are facing on an index card, and then they exchange cards multiple times so that no one knows whose card they have. Participants then engage in discussions and develop potential solutions to the challenges on the cards.

Three closing thoughts Todd shared are:

- "Make sure that as a facilitator, you're authentic and kind to those you're working with."
- "Carve out your area of expertise as a facilitator just as faculty have areas of expertise within their discipline."
- "The strategies you're using to facilitate learning should complement the content you're teaching."

Maha Bali

Maha Bali is a professor of practice at the American University in Cairo (AUC). She has had a strong interest in education since she was a child, and she began working at the Center for Learning and Teaching at AUC when she was 23 years old. Maha enjoys facilitating professional learning about "anything that allows people to interact with each other and delve into socio-emotional aspects of identity or self." She also enjoys facilitating deep conversations about social justice. In fact, even when she is asked to do workshops about other topics (such as artificial intelligence), she incorporates activities that leverage a socio-emotional and/or social justice lens. For example, in workshops about AI, she checks in with participants to get a sense of their attitudes toward AI, and if she demonstrates a specific tool, she tries to help participants see how biases can appear in the output.

One aspect of Maha's identity that shapes her professional learning work is her upbringing. Maha explained, "I'm a very culturally hybrid person. I'm 100% Egyptian in terms of parentage, but my education and my upbringing were part British, part American, [and] part Egyptian." Maha also grew up in Kuwait (which is a very diverse nation), and she works at a multicultural university that includes people from Europe, North America, Australia, and several Arab countries. As a result, Maha feels comfortable and adept at working in multicultural spaces. Her work in higher education extends globally as well, and she has co-developed a variety of novel professional learning experiences that connect people around the world. These include Virtually Connecting (which increases access to conferences for people who cannot attend on-site) and MYFest (a three-month virtual professional learning experience). Additionally, Maha has co-developed a framework called Intentionally Equitable Hospitality (IEH) which unpacks how facilitators can leverage their power as hosts to create more equitable learning experiences.

Three of Maha's core values are "care," "equity," and "the love of learning," and these values are evident in her beliefs about the qualities of a good facilitator and a good workshop. In terms of facilitator qualities, Maha believes that good facilitators care about participants' experiences and are attentive to what is happening during the session. Drawing on adrienne maree brown's (2017) concept of "intentional adaptation" and Priya Parker's (2018) concept of "generous authority," Maha also believes that good facilitators are willing to adapt based on people's needs and leverage their power to "step in to make sure that the least powerful voices are getting heard." In terms of workshop characteristics, Maha believes that good workshops offer "multiple pathways for engagement or at least a variety of pathways for engagement." Multiple pathways offer participants choices for how to engage in the moment (such as inviting participants in virtual sessions to share their thoughts in the chat or unmute). By contrast, a variety of engagement means that the workshop includes different types of activities (such as an independent activity followed by a breakout room activity). Maha also believes that good workshops are "warm," "recognize the expertise and experience of the people in the room," and include time for participants to reflect on their learning.

When designing workshops, Maha draws upon the IEH framework. She emphasizes the importance of pre-planning, which entails educating oneself about marginalized groups. Maha notes that pre-planning is not just something one does before preparing to facilitate a particular workshop. "This is a thing you do as a lifestyle, as in, read books by more people of color, read books by more indigenous people," and "build relationships." As she designs workshops, Maha also tries to find ways to involve learners in the process and "make it participatory." Additionally, she proactively designs workshops "in ways that predict the possibility of difference among the participants," such as by offering multiple pathways for engagement or including a variety of activities.

When facilitating workshops, Maha takes care to build a sense of community with learners. She does warm-up activities, checks in with participants about how they are feeling, incorporates frequent opportunities for participation, and invites participants' feedback. Maha also welcomes participants as they are by "making sure people know that it's okay to come in whatever form they want to come, so not feeling like they have to turn their camera on or not feeling like if their child shows up on camera, that it's a disaster." She believes it's important to "make it as permissive as possible for people to show up as they are, and not to feel like they have to do something extra in order to feel like they belong."

Three closing thoughts Maha shared are:

- "Make it participatory from the start, and in a gradual way."
- "Be responsive to the needs of the audience and be willing to adapt."
- "Make it as accessible and equitable as possible."

Recap

- Consider how your identity, experiences, beliefs, and values shape your professional learning approach.
- Own who you are as a workshop designer and facilitator, and use techniques that feel authentic to and congruent with who you are. Don't try to be someone you're not.

Sticky Note Reflection

Text Rendering Experience (revised by Angela Breidenstein; Center for Leadership & Educational Equity, n.d.): Jot down a sentence, a phrase, and a word from this chapter that you found particularly meaningful, insightful, or powerful.

Workshop Toolkit

Scan the QR code or visit the URL to access additional resources related to this chapter.

www.tolunoah.com/workshop-toolkits

Design Time

Create a Facilitator Map that outlines how your identity, experiences, beliefs, and values shape your professional learning approach. You can access a blank template in the Workshop Toolkit.

Facilitators' Lounge

Join the Facilitators' Lounge to connect with other readers and share your takeaways, strategies, and next steps!

www.tolunoah.com/facilitators-lounge/

References

Bell, L.A., Goodman, D.J., & Varghese, R. (2023). Critical self-knowledge for social justice educators. In M. Adams, L.A. Bell, D.J. Goodman, & D. Shlasko (with R.R. Briggs & R. Pacheco) (Eds.), *Teaching for diversity and social justice* (4th ed., pp. 409–432). Routledge.
brown, a.m. (2017). *Emergent strategy: Shaping change, changing worlds.* AK Press.
brown, a.m. (2019). *Pleasure activism: The politics of feeling good.* AK Press.
Center for Leadership & Educational Equity. (n.d.). *Text rendering experience.* www.clee.org/resources/text-rendering-experience/
Garrison, D.R., Anderson, T., & Archer, W. (2000). Critical inquiry in a text-based environment: Computer conferencing in higher education. *The Internet and Higher Education, 2*(2–3), 87–105. https://doi.org/10.1016/S1096-7516(00)00016-6
Gray, P.L. (1991). The R3A3 processing system for experiential learning in the classroom. *Basic Communication Course Annual, 3*, Article 16. http://ecommons.udayton.edu/bcca/vol3/iss1/16
Little, D., Green, D.A., & Felten, P. (2019). Identity, intersectionality, and educational development. *New Directions for Teaching and Learning, 2019*(158), 11–23. https://doi.org/10.1002/tl.20335
Pacansky-Brock, M. (n.d.). *Humanizing.* https://brocansky.com/humanizing
Palmer, P.J. (2017). *The courage to teach: Exploring the inner landscape of a teacher's life* (3rd ed.). Wiley.
Parker, P. (2018). *The art of gathering: How we meet and why it matters.* Riverhead Books.
Rendón, L. (n.d.). *Validation theory.* www.laurarendon.net/validation-theory/
Saad, L.F. (2020). *Me and white supremacy: Combat racism, change the world, and become a good ancestor.* Sourcebooks.
University of Edinburgh. (2018, November 5). *The four F's of active reviewing.* www.ed.ac.uk/reflection/reflectors-toolkit/reflecting-on-experience/four-f

11
OPTIMIZE YOUR WORKFLOW

Guiding Question:
What are some tips that can help streamline, enhance,
and maximize your workshop workflow?

In Chapters 1–10 of this book, we explored ten key principles that are important to consider when designing and facilitating workshops. There are also many granular details that go into creating a smooth on-site or virtual professional learning experience. For example, facilitators need to consider how they will organize workshop materials and manage other important preparation tasks. Additionally, there are unique considerations for facilitating virtual workshops. In this chapter, we will explore 20 practical tips for enhancing your workshop workflow. The first ten tips focus on time management, organization, and design strategies for any modality, and the remaining ten tips focus on virtual facilitation. (Related resources are linked in this chapter's Workshop Toolkit.)

Time Management, Organization, and Design Tips

Tip 1: Protect Your Time

Finding time to prepare for workshops can be tricky, especially nowadays, when our calendars can fill up quickly with meeting requests. One time management strategy that I've found helpful is time blocking, which entails blocking off time on your calendar to focus on specific tasks (Scroggs, n.d.). On my calendar, I block off:

- The time of each workshop
- Prep time immediately before each workshop (where I focus on setting up the session)
- Follow-up time immediately after each workshop (where I focus on completing closing tasks)
- Design time in the weeks leading up to each workshop (where I focus on planning the session and creating materials)
- Rehearsal time on the days leading up to each workshop (where I focus on rehearsing the session and making any final changes)

By intentionally blocking off time on my calendar, I can ensure that I'm able to dedicate adequate time to planning, facilitating, and wrapping up each workshop.

Tip 2: Develop a System for Managing Workshop Projects

If your role entails facilitating multiple professional learning programs at a time, it can be helpful to have a system for managing and keeping track of the status of each one. I use a Kanban board for this purpose. This project management technique, developed by David Anderson, is often used in organizations to manage the workflow for team projects (Rehkopf, n.d.). Jim Benson and Tonianne DeMaria have also adapted the technique for use in personal planning (Personal Kanban, n.d.; Rehkopf, n.d.).

A Kanban board is a physical or digital board with multiple columns, each of which is labeled with a different status (e.g., "To Do," "In Progress," "Done") (Rehkopf, n.d.). In the first column, you place the specific tasks you need to complete on separate cards or sticky notes, and as you work on the tasks, you move them around to their respective columns until they are completed.

At the beginning of each semester, I use Microsoft Planner to create a Kanban board for managing all of the professional learning programs I'll be facilitating that term (see Figure 11.1). For each workshop, I typically create three task cards: one for designing the workshop, one for facilitating the workshop, and one for completing follow-up tasks. Each task card also includes subtasks. For example, the task card for designing the workshop includes subtasks such as "Plan session," "Make slides & handouts," "Create feedback form," and so on. I assign due dates to the cards so that I will receive email reminders as things come due.

There are plenty of other analog and digital tools you can use to create a Kanban board. For example, you can draw a Kanban board on a whiteboard or a large sheet of paper and use sticky notes as the task cards (Rehkopf, n.d.). Or, you can use other digital tools such as Padlet, Trello, or Todoist.

Tip 3: Capture Ideas on the Go

When designing a new workshop or series, it can be helpful to have a system for capturing ideas on the go, as new ideas will often strike when you least expect them. I typically create a dedicated workshop note in the Notes app on my iPhone where I can type or dictate ideas as they come to me. The note is also helpful for saving any workshop-related resources I come across, such as articles, videos, websites, or podcast episodes that I want to take a closer look at once I'm ready to plan the session. I also use the Voice Memos app on my Apple Watch and iPhone to record voice notes when I'm out and about. By using the apps on my mobile devices to capture ideas on the go, I not only reduce the chance of forgetting the ideas but also avoid the "blank page" phenomenon (or, in the case of workshops, the blank slide phenomenon) because I have been collecting ideas and resources over time that I can use in planning the session.

Tip 4: Leverage Slide Timers to Manage Pacing

As we discussed in Chapter 3, when planning workshops, it's important to be mindful of pacing and timing. One practice I've found helpful is embedding countdown timers from YouTube on my slides (see Figure 11.2). For example, if participants will be doing an independent activity, working on a collaborative task, or taking a formal break, I typically include a timer that lets them know how much time they have. This not only helps me manage the pacing of the workshop but also enables participants to self-monitor their time. While the timers are useful tools, I always remain flexible in my approach by shortening or extending the time as needed during the live session in response to participants' needs.

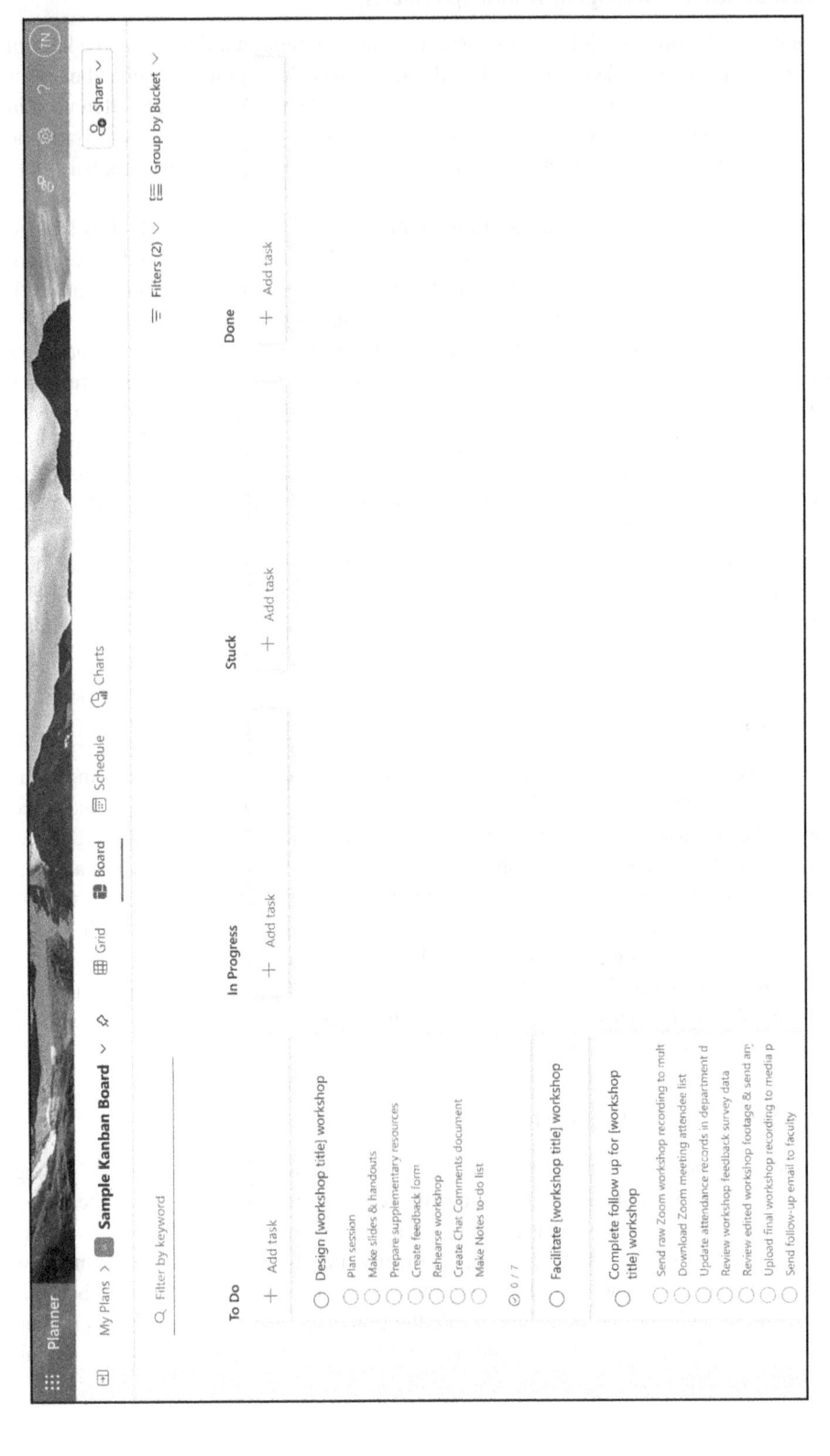

FIGURE 11.1 Sample Kanban Board in Microsoft Planner

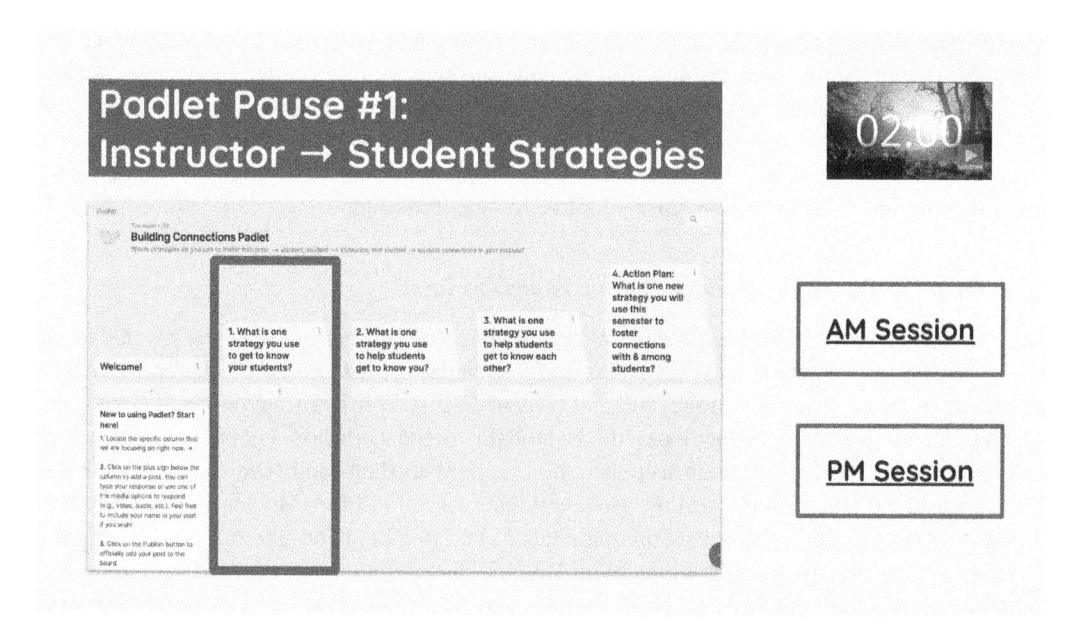

FIGURE 11.2 Sample Workshop Slide with Countdown Timer
Note: Slides template from Slidesgo. YouTube timer from Gentle Acoustic Guitar channel.

Tip 5: Use QR Codes and Shortened Links for Easy Access

If your workshop involves participants completing digital activities, examining online resources, or accessing digital handouts, consider how you can provide quick access to the materials via QR codes and shortened links. QR codes allow participants to simply scan the code with their mobile device to access the material, and shortened links provide a less cumbersome way for participants to manually enter URLs on their device. You can easily create QR codes and shortened links using tools like Bitly and Padlet TA. When using QR codes, be sure to keep accessibility in mind. For example, QR codes should be an appropriate size with good color contrast, and they should always be accompanied by a link so that participants have multiple ways to access the content (Lamyman, 2022).

I often use QR codes and shortened links on my slides and other workshop materials to provide participants with quick access to polls, handouts, websites, videos, feedback forms, and more. I have also used them in external workshops and conferences to give participants quick access to my social media platforms should they wish to stay in touch after the session.

Tip 6: Rehearse, Rehearse, Rehearse!

Prior to facilitating a workshop, it's important to set aside time to rehearse it. This not only helps you internalize the session but also helps you determine if the session flows well, if the content and activities are complete, and if there are any changes you need to make in order to strengthen the session. Rehearsing is also an important way to demonstrate respect for participants' time by ensuring that what you have planned can actually be accomplished within the allotted time.

When rehearsing workshops, I open my slides, grab a notepad and a pen, and use the stopwatch on my iPhone to time how long each section takes as I talk through it. I jot down these times on my notepad, along with notes about any tweaks I need to make to improve the session. After rehearsing the entire workshop, I add up the minutes to get the overall time. I aim for the workshop rehearsal time to be slightly shorter than the actual workshop time because things often take longer during the live session due to transitions between activities and other factors. If my overall rehearsal time is the same length as the workshop or longer, I revisit my workshop plans and make adjustments. This may entail cutting some of the content and activities, adjusting the timing for specific parts, and/or determining what I can skip during the live session if needed.

Tip 7: Create To-Do Lists to Manage Specific Workshop Tasks

Once you have rehearsed and finalized the workshop, it can be helpful to outline the specific tasks you need to do to facilitate it. I use the Notes app to create to-do lists because I can easily access the lists on my iPhone and MacBook, and add content or check off items anytime and anywhere. The type of to-do list I create varies based on the modality of the workshop. For on-site workshops, my to-do list typically has two main sections: "Before the Workshop" and "Day of the Workshop" (see Figure 11.3). The "before" section lists everything I need to print, buy, or assemble for the workshop. The "day of" section lists the materials I need to take, notes about how to configure the room, tech-related tasks (such as enabling Do Not Disturb on my devices and setting up the microphone), personal prep tasks (such as creating a name tag for myself and using the restroom before the session begins), and clean-up tasks (such as removing chart paper from the walls and resetting the room to its original configuration).

For virtual workshops, my to-do list primarily focuses on the technical tasks I need to complete on the day of the workshop (see Figure 11.4). This list is typically organized into three sections: "Before Joining Zoom," "During Zoom Session," and "After Zoom Session." The "before" section lists tasks I need to do to get my devices and physical workspace ready, the "during" section lists tasks I need to complete when starting the Zoom session, and the "after" section lists tasks I need to do to "reset" my devices and/or workspace once the workshop has ended. (Editable versions of my to-do lists are linked in this chapter's Workshop Toolkit.)

Tip 8: Organize Workshop Materials

It's helpful to develop a system for organizing workshop materials. This is especially true for on-site workshops, which typically involve many physical items, such as chart paper, sticky notes, and handouts. A strategy I use to organize on-site workshop materials is to place items in labeled baggies and folders so that I know exactly where everything is and can quickly grab what I need and set it up on the day of the workshop. For example, I always have an extra large "Staples" baggie that contains office supplies (such as pens, pencils, index cards, sticky notes, scissors, clear tape, painter's tape, duct tape, binder clips, colorful markers, whiteboard markers, black Sharpies, dot stickers, glue sticks, and a mini stapler). I also have a "Sign-In" folder with the materials for the sign-in table (such as the welcome sign, sign-in sheets, name tags, and name tents). Additionally, I prepare a "Facilitator" folder with all of my personal items (e.g., printed copies of the workshop slides, handouts, and registration list). If the workshop involves a small group activity with many moving parts (such as a card sort), I organize the card sort envelopes and table signs in advance and place them in a "Card Sort" baggie so that I can quickly set up the activity on the day of the session. Also, if participants will be using multiple handouts or physical objects during the session, I prepare a folder and mini baggie for each participant with all of the resources they need (see Figure 11.5). This not only expedites the process of setting up the room but also saves valuable time during the session which would otherwise be spent distributing materials.

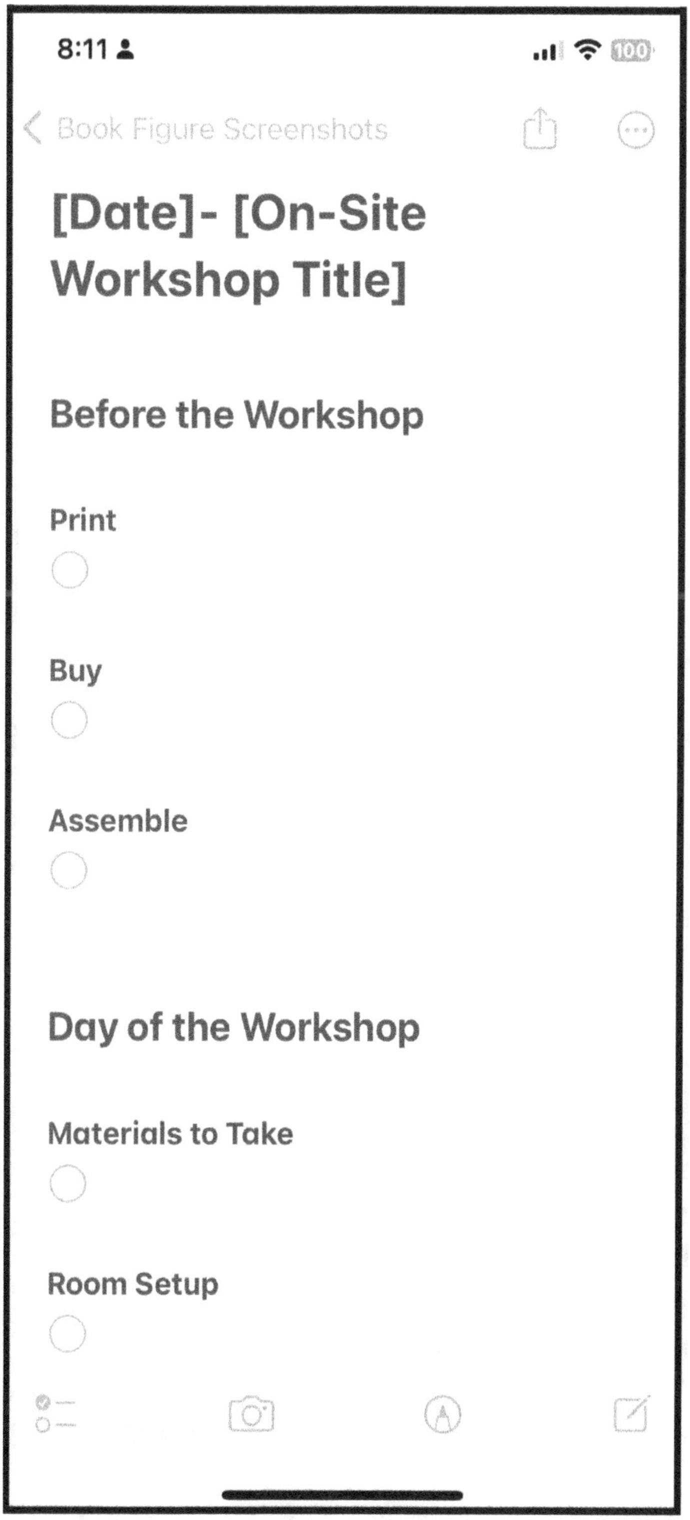

FIGURE 11.3 Screenshot of Blank Notes To-Do List Template for On-Site Workshops

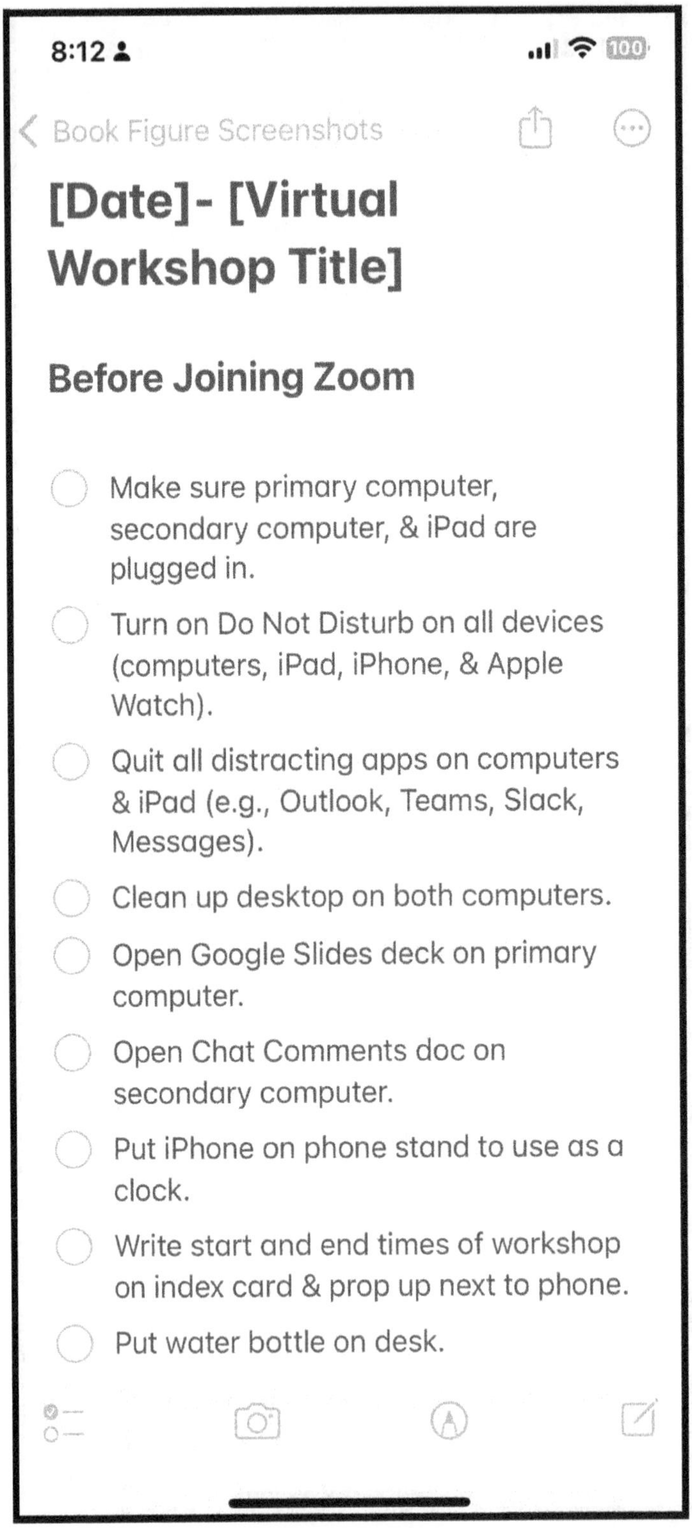
8:12
Book Figure Screenshots
[Date]- [Virtual Workshop Title]
Before Joining Zoom
Make sure primary computer, secondary computer, & iPad are plugged in.
Turn on Do Not Disturb on all devices (computers, iPad, iPhone, & Apple Watch).
Quit all distracting apps on computers & iPad (e.g., Outlook, Teams, Slack, Messages).
Clean up desktop on both computers.
Open Google Slides deck on primary computer.
Open Chat Comments doc on secondary computer.
Put iPhone on phone stand to use as a clock.
Write start and end times of workshop on index card & prop up next to phone.
Put water bottle on desk.

FIGURE 11.4 Screenshot of Sample Notes To-Do List Template for Virtual Workshops

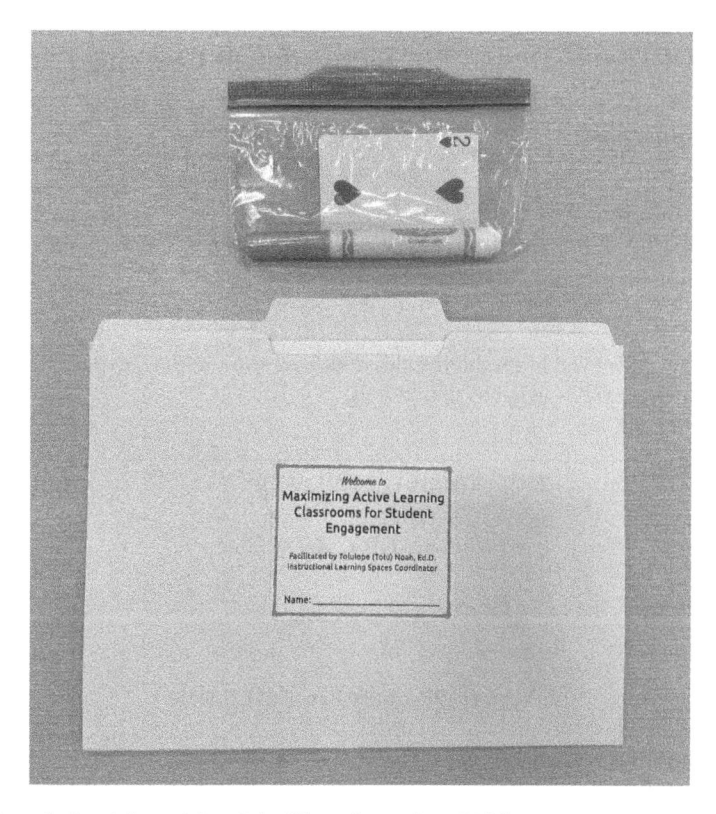

FIGURE 11.5 Sample Participant Materials (Photo by author, 2023)

While virtual workshops are typically easier to manage in terms of physical materials (due to the reliance on digital resources), organization matters here, too. When preparing virtual workshops, I organize the slides, handouts, and related resources in clearly labeled folders in Google Drive and confirm that the sharing permissions are set appropriately for each file. I typically offer multiple ways for participants to access the workshop materials by including both QR codes and shortened links on my slides. Additionally, I always prepare a Chat Comments document that includes everything I need to post in the chat, such as the welcome message, discussion questions, directions, summaries of steps, and links to online activities and resources (see Figure 11.6). The Chat Comments document streamlines the process for sharing resources with participants because everything I need to post in the chat is in one place.

Tip 9: Run a Tech Check

Prior to facilitating a workshop, be sure to run a tech check so that you can troubleshoot any issues in advance. For on-site workshops, I typically visit the room where the workshop will be held a few days prior to the session. I bring my laptop, presentation remote, a portable voice amplifier or lavalier microphone (depending on the room), and any other technology I plan to use for the session. Then, I do a dry run of the session, making sure the microphone works, the slides appear clearly on the screen with good color contrast, and any audio or video elements play smoothly.

For virtual workshops, I always log into Zoom early (typically 30-45 minutes prior to the session) so that I can set up the room, ensure everything is working properly, and be ready to

"Using QR Codes to Design Engaging Student Learning Experiences" **Chat Comments Doc** **[Workshop Date]**
BEFORE WORKSHOP BEGINS **"Welcome" Slide** Welcome to this session! We will begin shortly. Please introduce yourself in the chat by sharing your name, role, department, & why you joined this session.
DURING WORKSHOP **"What are QR Codes?" Slide** Share one place where you have seen QR codes being used. **"Why are QR Codes Beneficial?" Slide** Which of these six benefits is resonating with you the most? **"Try This!" Slide** Creating QR Codes in Google Chrome **"To Recap…" Slide** Which QR code-creation tool are you most interested in using in the future? **"Menti Poll: QR Code Action Plan" Slide** Closing Menti Poll
END OF WORKSHOP **"Workshop Wakelet" Slide** Workshop Wakelet **"Feedback Form" Slide** Feedback Form

FIGURE 11.6 Sample Chat Comments Document

greet participants upon arrival. My typical tech check tasks (try saying that three times fast!) include sharing my screen and clicking through my slides to ensure that all of the elements are working. I also perform an audio check, a video check, and download backup copies of my slides and handouts in other formats (such as PDF). Additionally, I confirm that my Zoom settings are properly configured for the session. For instance, I will disable annotation if I'm not planning to use it so that participants cannot accidentally mark up the screen. There are also some account-level Zoom settings that apply to all of my meetings. For example, my account is set to automatically mute participants when they join a meeting and automatically save the chat log to my computer when I end the session.

Tip 10: Be Mindful and Intentional About Your Use of Generative Artificial Intelligence

With the proliferation of generative AI tools such as ChatGPT and Adobe Firefly, facilitators are finding new ways to incorporate AI into their workshop workflow. For example, Hughes (2024) shares how facilitators can use AI to generate images, discussion questions, case studies, frameworks to structure the session, and creative titles for the session.

Facilitators might also find AI helpful for tasks such as the following:

- Generating possible prompts for a needs assessment survey or workshop feedback form
  - You could even ask it to align the feedback form with a particular evaluation model such as the New World Kirkpatrick Model (Kirkpatrick & Kirkpatrick, 2016).
- Obtaining feedback about workshop activities and how to improve them
  - You might ask it to help identify potential barriers participants might face with a particular activity and how you can use Universal Design for Learning (UDL) to address those barriers.
- Generating alt text for the images used in workshop materials
  - Be sure to check and revise the output to ensure that it's accurate, complete, and conveys the key information in the image.
- Creating workshop to-do lists to manage tasks
  - AI tools such as GoblinTools' Magic To-Do can be particularly useful for this purpose.

Although AI can be helpful for these and other tasks, it's important to be mindful of the ethical implications of these tools, such as the negative impact of AI on the environment and human labor (Tan & Cabato, 2023; Verma & Tan, 2024). (In discussions with instructors, I often frame the potential benefits and drawbacks of these tools in terms of the "light" and "shadows" of AI). While it may be tempting to offload every task to AI in the name of speed and efficiency, being intentional and thoughtful about when, how, why, and how often we use these tools is critical. For instance, Trust (n.d.) encourages her students to avoid using AI-generated media if there is similar existing media available due to ethical concerns regarding intellectual property and energy consumption (Appel et al., 2023; Heikkilä, 2023). Likewise, when designing workshop slides and other materials, you might consider minimizing the use of AI-generated images if there are similar existing photos you can use instead. Additionally, you might consider reserving the use of AI for more time-consuming tasks (such as generating case studies for a workshop if no other materials exist) rather than using AI for every workshop planning and preparation task. Regardless of what you decide, keeping both the light and shadows in mind is key as we continue navigating this ever-evolving terrain.

Virtual Facilitation Tips

Tip 11: Set Up Your Workspace

When facilitating virtual workshops, taking the time to set up your workspace beforehand can ensure a smoother facilitation experience. Typically, I facilitate workshops solo, so I use multiple devices to help me manage different aspects of the workshop. Figure 11.7 shows what my personal desk setup looks like.

On my desk, I have my primary computer on a laptop stand. This is the Zoom host, and I use it to share my screen during the workshop. To the right of my primary computer is a water bottle (to keep myself hydrated) and a notepad (to jot down notes to myself during the workshop). To the left of my primary computer is an iPad on a stand, where I display notes that I want to be able to refer to during the session. Directly below my iPad is my iPhone on a stand, along with an index card that lists the start and end time of the workshop so that I can easily monitor the time. Additionally, if my internet suddenly cuts out, I can use my phone as a mobile hotspot. To the left of my iPad and iPhone is my secondary computer. On this computer, I display two things: my Chat Comments document and the Zoom session. That's right: I join every Zoom session from two different computers, but on my secondary computer, the audio is disconnected in order to avoid feedback. The secondary computer is assigned the role of co-host, and it helps in several ways. First, I can easily ensure that participants are seeing what they should be seeing on their screen without having to ask them. Second, I can easily copy and paste content from the Chat Comments document into the chat. Third, the secondary computer aids with troubleshooting; if participants are doing an independent activity and someone needs personalized support, I can easily join a breakout room with them from my secondary computer while my primary computer remains in the main room. Or, if a participant asks a question I don't know the answer to, I can quickly search for the answer on my secondary computer.

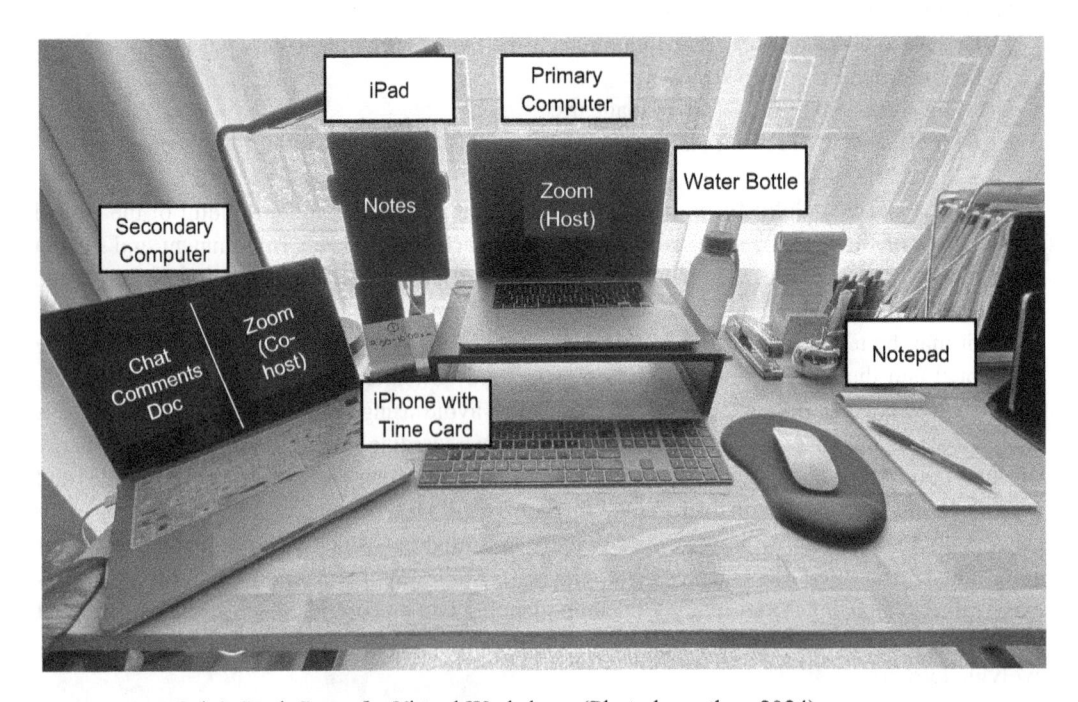

FIGURE 11.7 Tolu's Desk Setup for Virtual Workshops (Photo by author, 2024)

My personal desk setup is one way to organize a workspace, but it's not the only option. You will need to consider what will work best for you based on the technology resources you have available, the size of your physical workspace, your budget, and your preferences. Some facilitators facilitate solely from their laptops, while others have an additional monitor or multiple monitors. I also know of some prominent facilitators who have much more advanced workspace setups, complete with special lighting, cameras, microphones, streaming software, and gadgets (like a teleprompter)! While these extras can be nice, remember that you don't need to have all the bells and whistles to create a meaningful virtual workshop experience.

Tip 12: Pin Your Tabs

If you're facilitating a virtual workshop where you will be navigating between multiple online resources (such as a Google Slide deck, a Padlet board, and an article), consider opening the tabs ahead of time and pinning them. When you pin a tab, it makes it smaller by only displaying the icon, which can reduce the amount of clutter at the top of your web browser window. It also hides the X on the tab so that you can't accidentally close it. In most web browsers, you can pin a tab by simply right clicking on it and selecting the "Pin" or "Pin tab" option.

Tip 13: Use an Inviting Background

When facilitating virtual workshops, we must consider not only what is in front of us (i.e., our workspace) but also what is behind us (i.e., our background). Your background is one of the main things participants will see when they look at your video feed during the session, so be sure to keep it clean, organized, and free of distractions. As Howles (2022) explains, "a busy, cluttered, bright, moving, or odd background can call attention to itself and distract learners away from where they should be focused" (p. 126).

Your background can also serve as an organic way of connecting with participants. For example, during the onset of the COVID-19 pandemic when everyone was working from home, I started collecting houseplants, which I used to create a makeshift "wall" separating the part of my living room that became my home office from the rest of my living room (see Figure 11.8). This plant wall has served as the real background for all my virtual workshops ever since, and it has sparked fun, informal conversations with participants in the opening minutes of my workshops prior to the official start. Whether you use your real background or a virtual background, consider how you can include a personalized element that provides insight into who you are and helps participants connect with you on a personal level.

Tip 14: Be Mindful of Lighting and Clothing

The clothing we wear and the lighting we use when facilitating virtual workshops can impact how well participants can see us. Be sure that you are well-lit from the front by either sitting near a window (for natural light) or using another light source (such as a ring light). Also, consider how your clothing will appear on screen. Howles (2022) suggests wearing solid colors (such as blue, green, or brown), avoiding stripes and "busy" patterns, and wearing colors that contrast with your background so that you stand out (p. 139).

FIGURE 11.8 Tolu's Plant Wall Background (Photo by author, 2022)

Tip 15: Help Learners Get Acclimated

Just as facilitators need to prepare to facilitate in the virtual setting, participants need to prepare to learn in the virtual setting. A key aspect of this is being comfortable navigating the platform and using its various features (e.g., knowing how to mute/unmute, turn the camera on/off, send reactions, etc.). To aid with this, some facilitators display a slide at the beginning of their workshop that includes a labeled screenshot of the virtual platform controls and what they do. Others prepare a tip sheet that they send to participants before the session as part of their pre-workshop communication.

In addition to helping participants become comfortable with the platform, it can be helpful to share some virtual meeting norms so that participants understand how they can engage and help minimize distractions. You could share these norms with participants prior to the workshop via your pre-workshop communication, and/or review the norms during the "roadmap" part of the live session. My typical virtual meeting norms include the following:

- Please keep your mic muted in order to reduce background noise.
- Share your thoughts and questions in the chat.
- Feel free to turn on your camera if you wish.
- Use the reactions button to share your feelings and the raise hand button if you would like to unmute.
- Click on the CC button if you would like to view the automated captions.

Tip 16: Use "Conversation Cuts"

Glenn Fajardo developed the Conversation Cuts technique to guide participants' attention during virtual gatherings (Ozenc & Fajardo, 2021). This technique involves suggesting when participants could switch their view in the virtual platform. For example, if you will be doing a whole-group discussion, you might invite participants to switch to gallery view so that they can see everyone. Then, if you will be explaining a concept or modeling skill, you might invite them to switch to speaker view so that your video feed takes up the majority of the screen.

Tip 17: Leverage the Power of the Chat

In virtual workshops, the chat serves as a pivotal space for the active processing and sharing of information. Intentionally leverage the chat by posing questions for participants to respond to; inviting them to share ideas, questions, and resources; and checking the chat regularly for ideas that you can pull into the conversation. For example, you can use the popular waterfall chat strategy where you pose a question to the group, ask them to type their response in the chat but not submit it yet (i.e., they should not press the return or enter key), and then have everyone submit their response at the same time on the count of three.

When used well, the chat can be one of the most powerful learning spaces in virtual workshops because it:

- Combats the "sage-on-the-stage" mindset, where participants are simply expected to listen to the facilitator
- Encourages active participant engagement
- Offers a space where a variety of learning activities can take place, such as written discussions, brainstorms, quizzes, and polls

- Allows for multidirectional learning
- Provides a way for the facilitator to monitor participants' thinking and assess their understanding
- Allows for crowdsourcing of ideas and resources related to the workshop topic
- Provides a way for quieter participants to contribute to the conversation
- Offers an avenue for participants to reflect on what they are learning throughout the session
- Allows participants to ask questions and seek input from others
- Creates the "buzz," or energy that is often present when people gather physically in a space
- Provides a way for the facilitator to "take the temperature of the room" and adjust as needed
- Fosters connection, a sense of community, and support as participants share their experiences and suggestions with each other
- Provides a space where facilitators and participants can affirm and encourage each other
- Helps spark new ideas and possibilities
- Reminds participants that they are not alone

In sum, the chat is a critical space where the *work* in virtual workshops takes place.

As you leverage the chat in your virtual workshops, be mindful of participants' preferences, and invite them to do what works best for them. For example, some participants may find a lively chat distracting. Remind them that they can close the chat window and disable chat previews if they wish.

You might also consider replicating the chat in your on-site workshops by creating a backchannel chat. Tools such as Google Docs, Padlet, Slack, Discord, and Microsoft Teams can be useful for this.

Tip 18: Use Breakout Rooms Intentionally

When using breakout rooms in virtual workshops, be sure to do so in a purposeful and intentional way that aligns with the goals of the session. Keep these guiding principles in mind:

- **No Surprises**: Avoid springing breakout rooms on participants during the workshop, as this can result in people feeling caught off guard and perhaps even deciding to leave the workshop altogether. Instead, inform participants *ahead of time* if you plan to use breakout rooms so that they can be mentally and physically prepared. Whenever I plan to use breakout rooms in a virtual workshop, I mention this in this workshop description so that participants know what to expect before they even register for the session. I also include reminders in the confirmation and reminder emails. The simple inclusion of this detail in your workshop registration materials can help "prime" participants for the breakout room experience.
- **Be Purposeful**: Our use of breakout rooms should be intentional and aligned with the goals and purpose of the session. Breakout rooms can work well in workshops focused on brainstorming ideas, sharing personal experiences, problem solving, providing feedback, community-building, and the like. Ask yourself if the activity you're planning would truly benefit from small-group collaboration, or if it's better suited to a whole-group discussion or a chat discussion in the main room. Also, be sure to avoid overusing breakout room activities in a given session, as participants can tire of this quickly.
- **Ease Into It**: Consider how to ease participants into breakout rooms by doing low-stakes activities beforehand that allow them to get comfortable with each other. For example, you might do polling activities, chat discussions, digital whiteboard activities, and/or discussions as a whole group before transitioning into breakout rooms. Or, you might scaffold the breakout room activity itself by having participants do an activity where they only communicate via the chat, followed by an activity where they communicate via audio or video (if possible).

- **Clarity Matters**: Provide clear instructions for the breakout room activity so that participants know what to do. For example, you can prepare a Google Doc with the discussion questions or a Google Slide deck with a designated slide for each group where they can access the directions and complete their work. Padlet and Padlet Sandbox also have a breakout links feature that allows you to create a board or card deck with separate sections for each group. You can then share a specialized breakout link with each group, where they will only be able to access the posts of their group members.
- **Timing Matters**: Be sure that the time you allocate to the breakout room activity fits the task. If you give participants 15 minutes to discuss a question or do an activity that they could easily complete in 5 minutes, they will not feel like their time is being used well.
- **Provide Options**: When using breakout rooms, allow participants to choose their own adventure and opt out if desired. There are many reasons why people either cannot or do not want to engage in breakout rooms. Perhaps they're joining the workshop from a setting that is not conducive to discussions or the timing of the workshop overlaps with their meal break. Maybe they just don't have the bandwidth to engage with others that day, or they need more time to process the information independently. Regardless of the rationale, it can be helpful to design breakout room activities with these possibilities in mind. For example, if you're creating automatic breakout rooms, you can let participants know that they are welcome to decline joining a room and remain in the main room instead. Or, you can create self-select breakout rooms based on different modes of communication, like this:
  - Room 1: Video discussion
  - Room 2: Audio-only discussion
  - Room 3: Chat-only discussion
  - Room 4: Quiet room (No discussion)

This simple tweak gives participants more autonomy in *how* they engage in breakout rooms, and it may also lessen the common occurrence of people leaving the session altogether when breakout rooms are announced.

Tip 19: Seek Facilitation Support

If you are part of a professional learning team, it can be helpful to leverage your colleagues' support in facilitating virtual workshops. This way, you can focus on facilitating the workshop content and activities while your partner helps manage all other aspects (such as assisting with technical issues, monitoring the chat, responding to participants' questions, muting participants when there is background noise, and so on). Howles (2022) refers to the latter role as a "producer" (p. 109). Having a producer can help reduce the facilitation load for the primary facilitator while ensuring that participants receive timely and targeted support.

Tip 20: Get Creative

As you facilitate virtual workshops, consider how you can add fun, variety, and novelty to the session and prevent things from becoming stale. Here are some ideas:

- Mix times when you are screen sharing with times that you are not (Littlefield & Wise, 2021). For example, you might stop screen sharing during discussions or during the beginning and ending portions of the workshop when participants are doing connection and reflection activities. By being more intentional about when you share your screen and when you don't, you can add

variety to the session while leveraging the screen real estate in purposeful ways that promote connection among participants.
- Incorporate podcast clips into your workshops to bring in other voices, perspectives, and experiences. Tools such as Headliner make it easy to select a specific podcast clip, complete with captions you can edit for accuracy. In keeping with UDL principles, be sure to also provide a transcript of the podcast clip so that participants have multiple ways to access the content.
- Use a tablet and stylus (such as an iPad and Apple Pencil) to do live annotation of your slides or other documents. Leanne Hughes often does this via the Notability app on her iPad (IABC Queensland, 2022), whereas Penny Pullan uses the pen feature in PowerPoint (Jones, 2020).
- Use the live video feature in Keynote or the cameo feature in PowerPoint to add live video of yourself to your slides (Mulvihill, 2021, 2022).
- Send participants physical objects via mail that they will use during the live workshop. For example, I once participated in a virtual session where each participant was sent a mini LEGO set in advance, which we used for an activity.
- "Blend analog with digital" by using physical objects to facilitate your workshop instead of using slides (Littlefield & Wise, 2021, p. 225). Leanne Hughes often holds up sheets of paper that contain key words, phrases, or questions related to the workshop topic (IABC Queensland, 2022). Chad Littlefield frequently uses physical props, quote cards, image cards, and signs in his virtual sessions. He elaborates:

> Oftentimes, when I'm laying out my agenda for a workshop, it'll actually be a series of objects placed in a particular order on my desk. Each object will represent either a story I'm going to share, an activity we're going to do, a question I want the group to answer in the chat, or a point I'm trying to make. When I do that, I don't actually look at a screen or use PowerPoint slides. This method of introducing my learners to several different analog items that exist "off camera" for them creates a curiosity gap. People start to wonder what's coming next.
> *(Littlefield & Wise, 2021, p. 225)*

(Note: If planning to use analog objects to facilitate a virtual workshop, be sure to keep accessibility in mind by providing verbal descriptions of whatever items you're using so that learners who are blind, have low vision, or are participating in the workshop while in transit don't miss out. Also, consider providing a summary of the key details from the workshop in an additional format [such as a handout] so that participants have another option for reviewing the main points.)

Recap

- Develop systems for managing workshop tasks and materials.
- Rehearse each workshop and do a tech check to ensure a smoother facilitation experience.
- When facilitating virtual workshops, be intentional about how you set up your space and support learners.
- Consider how you can leverage novel tools and approaches to enhance your workshop workflow and create more engaging learning experiences.

Sticky Note Reflection

Gain & Give: What is one new tip you gained from this chapter? What is one helpful tip from your personal practice that you would like to give (i.e., add to this chapter)?

Workshop Toolkit

Scan the QR code or visit the URL to access additional resources related to this chapter.

www.tolunoah.com/workshop-toolkits

Design Time

Make a list of what you would like to start, stop, and continue doing in order to optimize your workshop workflow.

Facilitators' Lounge

Join the Facilitators' Lounge to connect with other readers and share your takeaways, strategies, and next steps!

www.tolunoah.com/facilitators-lounge/

References

Appel, G., Neelbauer, J., & Schweidel, D.A. (2023, April 7). Generative AI has an intellectual property problem. *Harvard Business Review*. https://hbr.org/2023/04/generative-ai-has-an-intellectual-property-problem

Heikkilä, M. (2023, December 1). Making an image with generative AI uses as much energy as charging your phone. *MIT Technology Review*. www.technologyreview.com/2023/12/01/1084189/making-an-image-with-generative-ai-uses-as-much-energy-as-charging-your-phone/

Howles, D.L. (2022). *Next level virtual training: Advance your facilitation.* ATD Press.

Hughes, L. (Host). (2024, January 21). 5 workshop hacks using ChatGPT with Leanne Hughes (No. 242) [Audio podcast episode]. In *First Time Facilitator*. www.firsttimefacilitator.com/podcast/five-workshop-hacks-using-chatgpt-leanne-hughes

IABC Queensland. (2022, February 13). IABC Qld presents delivering virtual events that pop! with Leanne Hughes [Video]. YouTube. https://youtu.be/cvVVBwrYGGk?feature=shared

Jones, A. (2020, April 9). PI-Q webinar: Virtual meetings, real engagement with Penny Pullan (Public) [Video]. YouTube. https://youtu.be/fj7BnuOuY7c?feature=shared

Kirkpatrick, J.D., & Kirkpatrick, W.K. (2016). *Kirkpatrick' four levels of training evaluation.* ATD Press.

Lamyman, J. (2022, August 8). *Accessibility and QR codes.* Tetra Logical. https://tetralogical.com/blog/2022/08/08/accessibility-and-qr-codes/

Littlefield, C., & Wise, W. (2021). *How to make virtual engagement easy: A practical guide for remote leaders and educators.* We and Me.

Mulvihill, C. (2021, October 6). Add live video to Keynote presentations (Demo) [Video]. YouTube. www.youtube.com/live/j8uL_i5NiYA?feature=shared

Mulvihill, C. (2022, December 22). Using cameo in PowerPoint (Add your camera into slides) [Video]. YouTube. www.youtube.com/watch?v=E-BzgP4Ipbg

Ozenc, K., & Fajardo, G. (2021). *Rituals for virtual meetings: Creative ways to engage people and strengthen relationships.* Wiley.

Personal Kanban. (n.d.). *Why and how to personal kanban.* www.personalkanban.com/personal-kanban-101

Rehkopf, M. (n.d.). *What is a kanban board?* Atlassian. www.atlassian.com/agile/kanban/boards

Scroggs, L. (n.d.). *Time blocking.* Todoist. https://todoist.com/productivity-methods/time-blocking

Tan, R., & Cabato, R. (2023, August 28). Behind the AI boom, an army of overseas workers in 'digital sweatshops.' *The Washington Post*. www.washingtonpost.com/world/2023/08/28/scale-ai-remotasks-philippines-artificial-intelligence/

Trust, T. (n.d.). *AI syllabus policy statement.* https://docs.google.com/document/d/1caSLk2JM40K4tdQHlLRwftYVGM6k8z0ZA2J12SwLhtU/edit?tab=t.0

Verma, P., & Tan, S. (2024, September 18). A bottle of water per email: The hidden environmental costs of using AI chatbots. *The Washington Post*. www.washingtonpost.com/technology/2024/09/18/energy-ai-use-electricity-water-data-centers/

12
CONTINUE GROWING AS A FACILITATOR

Guiding Question:
How will you engage in ongoing reflection on your practices and continue to hone your craft as a facilitator over time?

If we want to be effective at designing and facilitating meaningful professional learning experiences, we must be lifelong learners. Howles (2022) aptly captures this sentiment, stating, "As learning professionals who develop others, we should also be developing ourselves. In this way, we walk our talk" (p. 296). Being a lifelong learner requires ongoing introspection, as we reflect on our facilitation practices and set goals for the future.

In *Becoming a Critically Reflective Teacher*, Brookfield (2017) shares four important lenses through which educators and "practitioners in staff development and training" can reflect on their practices and grow over time (p. x). These lenses are as follows:

- **Students' Eyes:** "Researching students' perceptions of our actions and words alerts us to problems and mistakes that otherwise we might miss. It also tells us what's working and why." (Brookfield, 2017, p. 99)
- **Colleagues' Perceptions**: "Inviting colleagues to watch what we do or engaging in critical conversations with them helps us to notice aspects of our practice that are usually hidden from us." (Brookfield, 2017, p. 8)
- **Personal Experience**: "Our own experiences as learners provide important clues to the kinds of classroom dynamics that hinder or further the ability to learn" (Brookfield, 2017, p. 8)
- **Theory and Research**: "Reading educational literature can help us investigate the hunches, instincts, and tacit knowledge that shape our pedagogy. It can suggest different possibilities for practice as well as help us understand better what we already do and think" (Brookfield, 2017, p. 171).

These four lenses serve as the organizing framework for the first part of this chapter, with a specific focus on how you can use them within the context of professional learning to continuously reflect on your facilitation practices. The second part of this chapter offers additional strategies you can use to continue learning, growing, and evolving over time, and it discusses the importance of celebrating success and setting goals along the way. This chapter also highlights dozens of concrete resources that can aid you in your journey. (You can find links to the resources in this chapter's Workshop Toolkit.)

Participants' Eyes

Brookfield (2017) explains that "awareness of how students are experiencing learning" is essential for doing "good work" (p. 99). Within the context of professional learning, our "students" are the participants, or learners, in our workshops. Thus, one of the most important ways that we can continue growing as facilitators is by looking through participants' eyes to gain a better sense of how they're experiencing our workshops and what we can do to improve that learning experience.

In Chapter 7, we discussed the importance of providing opportunities for participants to reflect on their learning, and in Chapter 9, we explored the value of reviewing participant feedback and other artifacts of learning in order to be responsive to their needs. By carefully reviewing participants' reflections, feedback, and other learning data, we can gain important insight into their learning experiences and perceptions. As you review these sources of information, take note of the comments participants make. What are they learning? What are they confused about or grappling with? What do they appreciate about your facilitation approach? What are they finding challenging? What suggestions do they offer? What overarching themes or trends are you noticing? By carefully reflecting on these types of questions, you can glean helpful information about how participants are experiencing your workshops so that you can adapt your approach and improve future learning experiences.

Colleagues' Perceptions

A second way that we can reflect on our practices and grow as facilitators is by inviting our colleagues' input through peer observation, co-facilitation, and discussion.

Peer Observation

Invite a trusted colleague to observe your workshops and provide feedback. The observations can be informal or formal. For informal observations, you could simply ask a colleague to sit in on some workshops, and schedule time afterward to debrief what worked well and what could be improved. For formal observations, you could ask your colleague to use a structured observation protocol to provide feedback about your approach. One classroom observation protocol that can be adapted for workshop observations is the Protocol for Advancing Inclusive Teaching Efforts (PAITE), developed by Tracie Addy and colleagues (Addy et al., 2023). With this protocol, the observer uses different codes to note the occurrence of various inclusive teaching practices, and the coded data are used to produce a chart that highlights the frequency of each inclusive practice. Afterward, the observer has a follow-up conversation with the instructor to discuss the data.

Some of the codes and descriptions in the current iteration of the PAITE protocol include the following (Addy et al., 2023, p. 83):

- NAME (Student Names): The instructor calls on students by their names during class.
- DIVEX (Diverse Examples): The instructor provides examples that present a diversity of people, situations, perspectives, or ideas.
- ACTIVE (Active Learning): The instructor uses active learning strategies which involve students engaging with the material and thinking about what they are doing.
- REL (Relationship Building): The instructor allows time for informal student-to-student or student-to-instructor conversation for relationship building.
- EXCL (Address Exclusionary or Other Oppressive Acts): The instructor acknowledges and addresses exclusionary or oppressive acts if they occur during class.

- AFFIRM (Verbal Affirmations): Instructor uses words of encouragement and praise that validate students' contributions.
- CHOICE (Student Choice): The instructor offers students the opportunity to choose between different activities or options.

All of these inclusive practices are also essential in the realm of professional learning. Facilitators should use participants' names, offer diverse examples, use active learning strategies, foster relationships with and among participants, address exclusionary behavior, affirm participants, offer choices, and more. As such, you could adapt the language of the PAITE protocol to focus on facilitators and participants, and invite a colleague to use the protocol to observe you so that you can receive feedback about your use of inclusive practices in workshops. (Links to resources about the PAITE protocol can be found in this chapter's Workshop Toolkit.)

Co-Facilitation

By co-facilitating workshops, you not only share the facilitation load but also have the opportunity to reflect on your practices with another facilitator. This approach is similar to the team-teaching approach Brookfield (2017) discusses in his book. As you facilitate workshops with a partner, you will likely use different methods, notice different things, and respond in different ways to what's happening. This means that you can not only learn from how your partner facilitates but also engage in more nuanced discussions of the experience afterward that draw on multiple perspectives.

When co-facilitating workshops, communication is key. The Center for Research on Learning and Teaching at the University of Michigan (2024) has developed a helpful workshop pre-facilitation questionnaire that includes important questions for co-facilitators to discuss as they prepare to facilitate workshops. Examples of questions include "How would you describe your facilitation or presentation style?" and "How do you feel about your co-facilitator jumping in to add an additional point when you are talking?" (Center for Research on Learning and Teaching, 2024). You can find a link to the questionnaire in the Workshop Toolkit at the end of this chapter.

Discussion

Engaging in synchronous or asynchronous discussions with others can also help you reflect on your practices. For example, you might have a trusted friend in the field you can call to talk about your facilitation experiences and obtain their input. Alternatively, you might join an online listserv or community where you can seek input from other facilitators. (Access this chapter's Workshop Toolkit for links to popular facilitation communities.)

Personal Experience

A third way that we can reflect on our practices and grow as facilitators is through personal experience. Brookfield (2017) equates this with "becoming a student" (p. 8), where you participate in learning opportunities and reflect on what those experiences are like. Two examples of learning opportunities that Brookfield highlights are professional development workshops and conference attendance, both of which are directly applicable to professional learning facilitators. That is, as we engage as learners in workshops and conference sessions led by other facilitators, we can gain valuable insight into what helps and hinders learning.

In my work, personal experience as a participant in other people's workshops has been one of the most pivotal and valuable forms of continued professional learning and growth for me. Whenever I attend other people's sessions, I always pay attention not only to the content of the workshop (i.e., the what) but also to the way the workshop is designed and facilitated (i.e., the how). Conducting these informal observations of other facilitators not only helps me learn new approaches and techniques but also prompts me to reflect on my own facilitation practices.

As you attend workshops and conference sessions led by other facilitators, be intentional about observing their facilitation techniques. Below are some general questions you might want to take note of throughout the learning experience:

- **Beginning of Workshop**
  - How does the facilitator leverage the time prior to the official start of the workshop?
  - How does the facilitator welcome participants into the learning space?
  - What types of opening activities or other strategies do they use to launch the session?
  - How do they convey the purpose and goals of the workshop?

- **Middle of Workshop**
  - How do they structure the workshop?
  - How much time does the facilitator spend talking to participants versus having them engage in active learning activities?
  - What types of active learning activities do they use? How well do these activities align with the goals of the workshop?
  - How does the facilitator organize activities?
  - How do they invite participants' voices into the conversation and provide ways for participants to connect with each other?
  - What is the facilitator's tone and demeanor like? How do they build rapport with participants?
  - What do you notice in terms of participants' engagement and reactions? What factors appear to be influencing this?
  - How does the facilitator make the workshop relevant and responsive to participants' needs and interests?
  - What do you notice in terms of the pacing of the workshop? Are things going too fast, too slow, or just right?
  - How are the facilitators' slides, handouts, and/or other instructional materials designed? How does the design of these materials help or hinder learning?
  - Which voices and perspectives are included in and excluded from the workshop content?
  - How is technology used to engage participants?
  - How does the facilitator offer participants choices in their learning?

- **End of Workshop**
  - How does the facilitator wrap up the session?
  - What opportunities for reflection and/or action planning are provided?
  - What types of resources does the facilitator offer to help participants continue their learning?

- **After the Workshop**
  - How did you feel as a participant in the workshop? What factors influenced this?
  - How welcoming, inclusive, and accessible was the learning experience?
  - What worked well? What could be improved?
  - What new facilitation techniques did you notice?

- What did you like about the facilitation of the workshop that you would like to adopt in your own practices? What did you not like about the facilitation of the workshop that you would like to avoid in your own practices?

Theory and Research

A fourth way that we can reflect on our practices and grow as facilitators is by exploring the literature. Brookfield (2017) explains that "reading educational theory, philosophy, and research can provide new and provocative ways of seeing our actions" (p. 171). As professional learning facilitators, it's important for us to stay updated on the latest research in the science of learning, technology, and other areas so that we can continuously improve our design of learning experiences. Luckily, many books, journals, and other sources can help us reflect on and refine our practices.

Books

Confession: I am a self-professed nerd who can't get enough of reading books about teaching and learning. While this obsession is driven by my intrinsic love for education, it also helps me to be a more effective facilitator. First, reading books about teaching and learning helps me to better support instructors in their work and ensure that the strategies I'm sharing with them are relevant, timely, and supported by the literature. Additionally, many of the teaching and learning books I read include research on the science of learning that is applicable to learners of all ages, along with practical strategies that I can adapt for the professional learning context. Some helpful teaching and learning books include the following:

- *How Humans Learn* by Joshua R. Eyler
- *Make It Stick* by Peter C. Brown, Henry L. Roediger III, and Mark A. McDaniel
- *How Learning Works* by Marsha C. Lovett, Michael W. Bridges, Michele DiPietro, Susan A. Ambrose, and Marie K. Norman
- *Small Teaching* by James M. Lang
- *Classroom Assessment Techniques* by Thomas A. Angelo with Todd D. Zakrajsek
- *Design for Learning* by Jenae Cohn and Michael Greer
- *Hitting Pause* by Gail Taylor Rice

Another book that I consider to be a must-read for professional learning facilitators is *Teaching for Diversity and Social Justice*, edited by Maurianne Adams, Lee Anne Bell, Diane J. Goodman, and Davey Shlasko, with Rachel R. Briggs and Romina Pacheco (2023). Whether your role specifically entails facilitating workshops about equity, diversity, and inclusion, or you simply seek to deepen your own understanding of these topics so that you can create more inclusive and equitable learning experiences, *Teaching for Diversity and Social Justice* offers a wealth of insightful research and practical guidance. Part one of the book helps readers build a solid foundation in key concepts such as justice, oppression, and power. It also offers practical strategies for designing and facilitating learning experiences about social justice topics. Part two focuses on specific "isms" in society (such as racism, sexism, classism, and ableism), offering a detailed examination of the history of each ism and how it manifests itself in society, along with concrete workshop ideas, activities, and resources for teaching others about each ism. I have found *Teaching for Diversity and Social Justice* to be a critical resource in my lifelong journey toward becoming a more informed, inclusive, and equitable facilitator and educator.

As an educational developer, I also enjoy reading books that offer greater insight into the field of educational development, the roles of centers for teaching and learning (CTLs), and the different types of professional learning programs offered at other higher education institutions. A few books that have been helpful in this regard include the following:

- *Centers for Teaching and Learning* by Mary C. Wright
- *A Guide to Faculty Development* (edited by Kay J. Gillespie, Douglas L. Robertson, and associates)
- *Taking Flight* by Laura Cruz, Michele A. Parker, Brian Smentkowski, and Marina Smitherman

There are also great books that focus on the art of facilitation and the design of instructional materials. Some of these books include a blend of theory and practice, whereas others are written more as practical guides that draw on the author's lived experiences. Some helpful facilitation and design books are:

- *The Art of Gathering* by Priya Parker
- *Design to Engage* by Beth Cougler Blom
- *The PD Book* by Elena Aguilar and Lori Cohen
- *Training from the BACK of the Room!* by Sharon L. Bowman
- *The 2-Hour Workshop Blueprint* by Leanne Hughes
- *PRESENTING* by Norman Eng
- *The Surprising Power of Liberating Structures* by Henri Lipmanowicz and Keith McCandless
- *The Discussion Book* by Stephen D. Brookfield and Stephen Preskill
- *Energize Your Meetings!* by Responsive Classroom
- *e-Learning and the Science of Instruction* by Ruth Colvin Clark and Richard E. Mayer

Additionally, the Association for Talent Development (ATD) Press publishes numerous books on the topics of facilitation, training, learning design, and instructional design, written by professionals from various industries. One such book is *Next Level Virtual Training* by Diana L. Howles, which offers helpful insight into how to design and facilitate effective virtual programs.

Newsletters

Reading newsletters written by other educational developers has also helped me think more critically about my practices. These newsletters often incorporate a unique blend of theory and practice, exploring relevant research about a topic while infusing the author's lived experiences.

One newsletter that has really been stretching my thinking lately is Sarah Silverman's (n.d.), *Beyond the Scope*. In each post, she focuses on a teaching and learning topic typically addressed in faculty development workshops, unpacking the nuances of the topic and diving deeper into its potential implications. Reading Sarah's newsletter has not only helped me engage in more critical reflection on my own practices but also pushed me to consider how I can embed more nuanced discussions of popular teaching and learning topics into my workshops and other programs.

Another newsletter that I enjoy is the Engaged Learning Collective. This newsletter uses a unique, community-based approach, where a group of educational developers and educators share ideas and offer resources that are relevant to the educational development community (Norell et al., 2024). Links to both of these newsletters can be found in this chapter's Workshop Toolkit.

Journals and Other Publications

Journal articles are useful for keeping up with the latest research and developments in the field and gaining insight into the work that other professionals are doing. As an educational developer, three journals that I find useful in my work are:

- *To Improve the Academy*
- *The Journal on Centers for Teaching and Learning*
- *The International Journal for Academic Development*

Additionally, there are various publications that help me stay updated on important news, emerging trends, and practical approaches being used in higher education. These include:

- *EDUCAUSE Review*
- *Faculty Focus*
- *The Scholarly Teacher*
- *The Chronicle of Higher Education*

Additional Strategies

In addition to Brookfield's (2017) four lenses, there are many other strategies we can use to reflect on our practices and hone our craft as facilitators. Let's explore some additional options next.

Self-Observation

Observing yourself facilitating workshops can be a powerful form of learning. This is particularly easy to do with virtual workshops, as platforms (such as Zoom) have built-in recording capabilities. Simply record your virtual workshop and watch the recording afterward. As you do so, reflect on what worked well, what didn't, and what you would do differently next time.

Self-observation can also be done when facilitating on-site workshops (although it will require slightly more prep). For example, you can put your phone or tablet on a tripod, place it in a corner of the room with the device facing you, and use the built-in camera app on the device to record the session. Alternatively, you can use a laptop to record the session. Or, if you're facilitating the workshop in a room that has built-in recording software (such as a HyFlex classroom), you can use the classroom system to record the workshop. If you're planning to record an on-site workshop, be sure to inform participants beforehand, just as you would with a virtual workshop.

Podcasts and Videos

Listening to podcasts has become one of my favorite forms of ongoing professional learning. Some of my favorite higher education podcasts include:

- *Teaching in Higher Ed* (hosted by Bonni Stachowiak)
- *Think UDL* (hosted by Lillian Nave)

- *Tea for Teaching* (hosted by John Kane and Rebecca Mushtare)
- *Accessagogy* (hosted by Ann Gagné)
- *Limed: Teaching with a Twist* (hosted by Matt Wittstein)
- *Intentional Teaching* (hosted by Derek Bruff)
- *Dead Ideas in Teaching and Learning* (hosted by Amanda Irvin)
- *Centering Centers* (hosted by Lindsay Doukopoulos)

I also really enjoy listening to podcasts about the art of facilitation. Most of these podcasts are hosted by and include guests from other industries, such as business, healthcare, and government. Listening to people who facilitate in other contexts has greatly enriched my understanding of the art of facilitation, and I have enjoyed learning new tips and tricks that I can adapt for my work. Some of my favorite facilitation podcasts include:

- *Facilitating on Purpose* (hosted by Beth Cougler Blom)
- *Facilitation Lab Podcast* (hosted by Douglas Ferguson)
- *First Time Facilitator* (hosted by Leanne Hughes)
- *There's a Workshop for That!* (hosted by Nathy Ravez)
- *ATD Accidental Trainer* (hosted by Alexandria Clapp)

In addition to podcasts, YouTube videos can be a great source of facilitation inspiration. There are popular facilitators (such as Jan Keck and Chad Littlefield) and companies (such as Voltage Control and AJ&Smart) who share interesting behind-the-scenes tips and tricks about their facilitation techniques. Additionally, you can search for recordings of past on-site or virtual workshops facilitated by people whom you admire to learn from their approaches.

Websites, Online Courses, and Webinars

There are many websites you can visit to learn about the science of learning, active learning techniques, facilitation strategies, and more. While some websites are geared toward instructors, many of the techniques can also be adapted for use in professional learning workshops. Below are a few recommendations:

- Teaching Tools Active Learning Library (https://teaching.tools/activities)
- Retrieval Practice (https://www.retrievalpractice.org/)
- K. Patricia Cross Academy (https://kpcrossacademy.ua.edu/)
- Liberating Structures (https://www.liberatingstructures.com/)
- SessionLab Library of Facilitation Techniques (https://www.sessionlab.com/library)

You can also take online courses to expand your knowledge and skills about teaching, technology, and facilitation. For example, OneHE offers a variety of free and paid online courses and resources, many of which were designed by notable educational developers and faculty developers in the field. While most of the courses are geared toward instructors, you could still complete the courses to build your own pedagogical toolkit and learn about important teaching and learning principles that you can incorporate into your facilitation approach. Additionally, OneHE has several courses that are specifically geared toward educational developers and faculty developers who are seeking to establish or grow a CTL on their campus.

If you're seeking to advance your technology skills, many technology companies offer free or low-cost courses and certifications. For example, the Apple Education Community has a free online learning center where you can learn new iPad and MacBook skills and earn certifications. Other companies (such as Google and Wakelet) also offer a variety of online courses and certifications.

One outcome of the COVID-19 pandemic has been the proliferation of webinars, many of which are free or low-cost/pay-what-you-can. These online events provide additional opportunities for ongoing professional learning. For example, 3Play Media offers webinars about accessibility. Alchemy offers webinars for higher education instructors and academic leaders. The Florida Instructional Designer Network (FL-IDN) offers webinars about topics relevant to instructional designers, educational technology specialists, and others. Training Magazine Network, The Bob Pike Group, and Flow Ahead offer webinars about a wide range of facilitation, training, learning, and technology topics led by facilitators from various industries. Many technology companies (such as Apple, Mentimeter, and Padlet) also offer free webinars that can help you stay updated on the latest features and applications of particular tools.

Professional Learning Networks

Professional learning networks (PLNs) are defined as "systems of interactions made up of people, spaces, and tools that support learning and professional growth" (Krutka et al., 2017, p. 247; Trust et al., 2016, p. 28; Trust et al., 2017, p. 1). An individual may engage with their PLN on-site, virtually, or both, and social media has also become a popular space for these interactions (Krutka et al., 2017; Trust et al., 2017; McPherson et al., 2015). Through their PLN, higher education professionals can collaborate with others; acquire new knowledge, skills, and resources; stay updated on the latest educational trends; and much more (Trust et al., 2017).

My PLN on social media has played a significant role in my professional growth. Currently, I am most active on two platforms (LinkedIn and Bluesky), where I follow a diverse group of people from around the world: educational developers, faculty developers, college professors, educational technology coaches, K-12 teachers, administrators, and facilitators from various industries. My PLN has generously shared helpful resources, introduced me to new ideas, and stretched my thinking about various topics. Additionally, I have been able to contribute to the conversation by sharing ideas and resources of my own (Noah, 2022).

I am also a member of the POD Network, which is a network of educational developers and faculty developers who are "devoted to improving teaching and learning in higher education" (POD Network, n.d.). The POD Network offers a variety of avenues to connect with and learn from others in the field via an annual conference, PODLive webinars, institutes, special interest groups, publications, podcast episodes, and more. They also have an active listserv where people can ask questions, exchange resources, discuss relevant topics, share information about upcoming events, seek advice, and offer/provide other types of support.

If you're an educational developer, one tool that can help you reflect on and expand your PLN is the Educational Developer Professional Development Map (EDPDM), developed by Donnell et al. (2018). The EDPDM helps educational developers identify their existing networks of support and possible avenues for expansion in terms of four key areas: "mentorship," "sharing expertise," "professional learning," and "work/life balance" (Donnell et al., 2018, p. 12). Additionally, the tool prompts educational developers to consider how they can contribute to other people's networks. You can learn more about the EDPDM via the link in this chapter's Workshop Toolkit.

Celebrate Success

As you reflect on your workshop facilitation practices and pursue ongoing learning opportunities, be sure to take the time to pause and celebrate your growth and success. Facilitating professional learning is hard work, and there will be ups and downs along the way. By pausing regularly to celebrate what is going well and the strengths you bring to your work, you can maintain the motivation to keep going even on the days when things don't go according to plan.

One celebration strategy that I've found meaningful is saving positive feedback and uplifting comments from workshop participants in an "Encouragement" folder on my computer. This folder includes powerful comments from workshop feedback surveys, screenshots of kind comments participants have shared in the chat (during virtual workshops), and emails that participants have sent me after workshops to express their gratitude. Another celebration practice I have is maintaining a gratitude calendar. Each evening, I write down one thing I'm grateful for or something that brought me joy. Oftentimes, if I facilitated a workshop earlier in the day, my gratitude note is about that, whether it is gratitude for the connection I felt with participants or gratitude for the positive feedback I received. These moments of micro-celebration remind me of the strengths I bring to this work and the impact I'm having, especially on the not-so-sunny days when self-doubt and imposter phenomenon rear their ugly heads.

Set Goals for the Future

Finally, it's important to set professional learning goals for yourself. What do you want to learn more about? What new skills do you want to develop? How do you wish to expand your capabilities as a professional learning facilitator? Select 1–2 areas of focus, and turn them into professional learning goals. Be sure to include a plan for how you will make those goals a reality, focusing on small but meaningful actions you can take. Here is one possible structure you could use to craft your professional learning goals:

I want to _____ so that _____, which will _____. To do so, I will _____.

Example: I want to learn more about digital accessibility so that I can make my workshop materials more accessible, which will reduce barriers to learning. To do so, I will start by attending a webinar about how to write alt text.

You may also wish to set aside time at the end of each month, quarter, or semester to engage in more holistic reflection on your facilitation practices and what you want to do differently in the future. A helpful structure for this is the popular Start, Stop, Continue strategy (Gray et al., 2010). Ask yourself:

- What should I start doing to create more meaningful and impactful professional learning experiences?
- What should I stop doing?
- What should I continue doing?

If you're an educational developer, the New Learning Compact (NLC) framework can also serve as a helpful goal-setting tool (Bass et al., 2019). The framework document includes practical activities you can use to reflect on professional learning at all levels (i.e., individual, community, institutional, and ecosystem) and identify specific areas of strength and growth. For example, one community-level professional learning principle that I personally recognize as an area for growth is "Learn from and with students," which entails partnering with students as part of the professional learning process. With this principle in mind, I can set goals and create an action plan for the future.

Another helpful goal-setting resource for facilitators who work in CTLs is the "Center for Teaching and Learning Matrix" developed by the American Council on Education and the POD Network. This matrix helps CTLs identify their current status in relation to 17 key areas, such as the scope, content, and reach of their programs and services (Collins-Brown et al., 2018). By taking the time to assess where your CTL currently stands for each category in the matrix, you can identify your center's strengths and areas for growth and use this information to craft appropriate goals for the future.

Recap

- Use Brookfield's (2017) four lenses to reflect on and refine your workshop facilitation practices.
- Explore resources and seek opportunities that can help you to continue honing your craft.
- Celebrate your success.
- Set goals for the future.

Sticky Note Reflection

Your Choice: Respond to one of the following questions:

A) Which of Brookfield's (2017) four lenses do you most frequently use to reflect on your workshop facilitation practices? Why? What is one new lens you would like to be more intentional about using in the future?

B) What are 1–3 resources from this chapter that you would like to explore further?

Workshop Toolkit

Scan the QR code or visit the URL to access additional resources related to this chapter.

www.tolunoah.com/workshop-toolkits

Design Time

Set 1–2 professional learning goals that you would like to focus on within the next month. Craft an action plan for each goal, and block off time on your calendar to work toward your goals.

Facilitators' Lounge

Join the Facilitators' Lounge to connect with other readers and share your takeaways, strategies, and next steps!

www.tolunoah.com/facilitators-lounge/

References

Adams, M., Bell, L.A., Goodman, D.J., & Shlasko, D. (with R.R. Briggs & R. Pacheco) (Eds.). (2023). *Teaching for diversity and social justice* (4th ed.). Routledge.

Addy, T. M., Younas, H., Cetin, P., Rizk, M., Cham, F., Nwankpa, C., & Borzone, M. (2023). The development of the Protocol for Advancing Inclusive Teaching Efforts (PAITE). *Journal of Educational Research and Practice, 12*(0), 65–93. https://doi.org/10.5590/JERAP.2022.12.0.05

Bass, R., Eynon, B., & Gambino, L.M. (2019). *The New Learning Compact: A framework for professional learning and educational change*. Every Learner Everywhere. www.everylearnereverywhere.org/resources/the-new-learning-compact/

Brookfield, S.D. (2017). *Becoming a critically reflective teacher* (2nd ed.). Jossey-Bass.

Center for Research on Learning and Teaching. (2024). *Workshop pre-facilitation questionnaire for "Workshop on Workshops."* University of Michigan. https://docs.google.com/document/d/1gwHoZR6SEavHqcobqiJEZ-Os513GCEMgPgCN0XapYLw/edit?usp=sharing

Collins-Brown, E., Haras, C., Hurney, C., Iuzzini, J., Magruder, E., Sorcinelli, M.D., Taylor, S.C., & Wright, M. (2018). *A center for teaching and learning matrix*. American Council on Education & POD Network. https://podnetwork.org/resources/center-for-teaching-and-learning-matrix/

Donnell, A.M., Fulmer, S.M., Smith, T.W., Bostwick Flaming, A.L., & Kowalik, A. (2018). Educational Developer Professional Development Map (EDPDM): A tool for educational developers to articulate their mentoring network. *Journal on Centers for Teaching and Learning, 10*, 3–23. https://openjournal.lib.miamioh.edu/index.php/jctl/article/view/195

Gray, D., Brown, S., & Macanufo, J. (2010). *Gamestorming: A playbook for innovators, rulebreakers, and changemakers*. O'Reilly.

Howles, D.L. (2022). *Next level virtual training: Advance your facilitation*. ATD Press.

Krutka, D.G., Carpenter, J.P., & Trust, T. (2017). Enriching professional learning networks: A framework for identification, reflection, and intention. *TechTrends, 61*, 246–252. https://doi.org/10.1007/s11528-016-0141-5

McPherson, M., Budge, K., & Lemon, N. (2015). New practices in doing academic development: Twitter as an informal learning space. *International Journal for Academic Development, 20*(2), 126–136. https://doi.org/10.1080/1360144X.2015.1029485

Noah, T. (2022, June 13). *Taking ownership of your professional learning with Twitter*. Faculty Focus. www.facultyfocus.com/articles/academic-leadership/taking-ownership-of-your-professional-learning-with-twitter/

Norell, L., Woldman, J., Atias, D., Southard, K., Creighton, C., Donnell, A., Smith, A., & Pokorski, R. (2024, October 22). *Introducing the Engaged Learning Collective*. https://engagedlearningcollective.substack.com/p/introducing-the-engaged-learning

POD Network. (n.d.). *About*. https://podnetwork.org/about/

Silverman, S. (n.d.). *Beyond the scope*. https://beyondthescope.substack.com/

Trust, T., Carpenter, J.P., & Krutka, D.G. (2017). Moving beyond silos: Professional learning networks in higher education. *The Internet and Higher Education, 35*, 1–11. https://doi.org/10.1016/j.iheduc.2017.06.001

Trust, T., Krutka, D.G., & Carpenter, J.P. (2016). "Together we are better": Professional learning networks for teachers. *Computers & Education, 102*, 15–34. https://doi.org/10.1016/j.compedu.2016.06.007

CONCLUSION

This book began with an invitation to dream about your ideal professional learning situation. I encourage you to revisit that dream and consider how the ideas we've explored throughout this book might support you in making that dream a reality.

I would also like to take a moment to share my personal hopes for you, the reader. I hope that as a result of reading this book and applying the strategies within it, you feel:

- Equipped with the knowledge, skills, and tools to design and facilitate meaningful workshops
- Capable of creating engaging, enriching, and effective professional learning experiences with lasting impact
- Inspired to try out some new ideas and make them your own
- Confident in who you are as a facilitator and the unique skills and approaches you bring to this role
- Challenged to consider how you can continue fostering more inclusive and equitable professional learning experiences
- Empowered to generate new ideas and share your unique insights and approaches with others
- Curious to continue learning about the art and science of facilitation
- Joy as you partner with participants in their learning

As you design and facilitate professional learning workshops, remember to keep the Workshop Wheel (Figure C.1) in mind by considering how you can create learning experiences that are relevant, purposeful, structured, inclusive, connective, active, reflective, ongoing, responsive, and distinctive. If it's helpful, you may even want to write or type these principles on a sheet of paper to keep nearby on your desk as a physical reminder.

Additionally, as we discussed in Chapters 11 and 12, I encourage you to consider how you can refine your workshop workflow and engage in ongoing reflection and learning so that you can continue to hone your craft as a facilitator over time.

As we wrap, please take a moment to pause and reflect on what you've read by answering these questions:

- What was your biggest takeaway for each of the principles in the Workshop Wheel?
- Which piece of the Workshop Wheel is your greatest area of strength?
- Which piece of the Workshop Wheel would you like to prioritize as an area for growth?
- How has your understanding of how to design and facilitate meaningful workshops shifted as a result of reading this book?
- What have you learned about yourself as a workshop designer and facilitator?
- What is one small change you will make in your workshop design and/or facilitation practices moving forward?

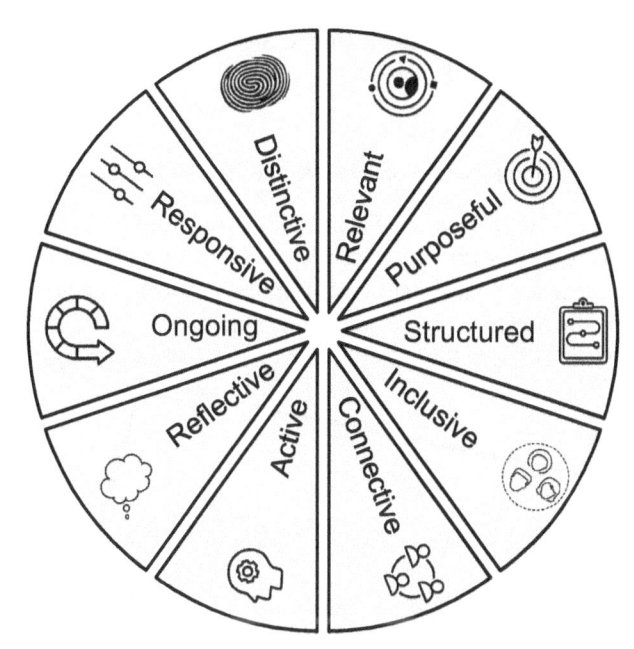

FIGURE C.1 The Workshop Wheel

- How could you apply the Workshop Wheel principles to your design and facilitation of *other* types of professional learning experiences (such as institutes and courses)?

I would love to hear your reflections! Please feel free to reach out and share your thoughts with me. You can scan the QR code or visit the link to connect with me on social media or to get in touch with me via my website.

www.tolunoah.com/connect

Finally, I would like to leave you, the reader, with the last word. I invite you to share a key message, insight, or takeaway from this book on LinkedIn or Bluesky using the hashtag, #TheWorkshopWheel. For example, you can:

- Write your thoughts on the sticky note (or another sheet of paper) and take a picture of it
- Type your thoughts in an online document
- Record a video
- Create an audio recording
- Draw a sketchnote and take a picture or screenshot of it

However you choose to share, please remember to keep accessibility in mind (e.g., by including alt text for your photo, captions for your video, etc.). Check out the hashtag as well to connect with other readers and expand your professional learning network. The art of facilitation is ever-evolving, and we can continue to learn and grow in community.

APPENDIX

Alphabetical List of All Digital Tools Mentioned in the Book

- **Adobe Connect**: www.adobe.com/products/adobeconnect.html
- **Adobe Express**: www.adobe.com/express/
- **Adobe Firefly**: www.adobe.com/products/firefly.html
- **Adobe Podcast**: https://podcast.adobe.com/
- **Bitly**: https://bitly.com/
- **Blackboard**: https://www.anthology.com/products/teaching-and-learning/learning-effectiveness/blackboard
- **Brightspace**: www.d2l.com/brightspace/
- **Bulb**: https://my.bulbapp.com/
- **Butter & Butter Scenes**: www.butter.us/
- **Canva & Canva Whiteboard:** : www.canva.com/
- **Canvas**: www.instructure.com/canvas
- **ChatGPT**: https://chat.openai.com/
- **Claude**: https://claude.ai/
- **Clips**: https://support.apple.com/guide/clips/welcome/ios
- **DALL-E**: https://openai.com/index/dall-e-3/
- **Discord**: https://discord.com/
- **Dropbox:** www.dropbox.com/
- **Edpuzzle**: https://edpuzzle.com/
- **Engageli**: www.engageli.com/
- **FigJam**: www.figma.com/figjam/
- **Flippity**: www.flippity.net/
- **Freeform**: https://support.apple.com/guide/freeform/welcome/mac
- **GarageBand**: https://support.apple.com/garageband
- **Genially**: https://genial.ly/
- **Goblin Tools' Magic ToDo**: https://goblin.tools/
- **Google Chrome**: www.google.com/chrome/
- **Google Docs**: https://docs.google.com/
- **Google Drawings**: https://docs.google.com/drawings/

- **Google Drive**: www.google.com/drive/
- **Google Forms**: www.google.com/forms/about/
- **Google Gemini**: https://gemini.google.com/
- **Google Meet**: https://workspace.google.com/products/meet/
- **Google Sheets**: www.google.com/sheets/about/
- **Google Sites**: https://sites.google.com/
- **Google Slides**: www.google.com/slides/about/
- **Goosechase**: www.goosechase.com/
- **GoReact**: https://get.goreact.com/
- **Headliner**: www.headliner.app/
- **Hypothesis**: https://web.hypothes.is/
- **iMovie**: https://support.apple.com/imovie
- **Kahoot**: https://kahoot.com/
- **Kami**: www.kamiapp.com/
- **Keynote**: www.apple.com/keynote/
- **Loom**: www.loom.com/
- **Mentimeter**: www.mentimeter.com/
- **Microsoft Copilot**: https://copilot.microsoft.com/
- **Microsoft Excel**: https://www.microsoft.com/en-us/microsoft-365/excel
- **Microsoft Planner**: https://tasks.office.com/
- **Microsoft PowerPoint**: www.microsoft.com/en-us/microsoft-365/powerpoint
- **Microsoft Teams**: www.microsoft.com/en-us/microsoft-teams/group-chat-software
- **Microsoft Word**: www.microsoft.com/en-us/microsoft-365/word
- **Midjourney**: www.midjourney.com/home
- **Mighty Networks**: www.mightynetworks.com/
- **Miro**: https://miro.com/
- **Moodle**: https://moodle.org/
- **Mote**: www.mote.com/
- **Mural**: https://mural.co/
- **Nearpod**: https://nearpod.com/
- **Notes**: https://support.apple.com/guide/notes/welcome/mac
- **Numbers**: www.apple.com/numbers/
- **Padlet & Padlet Sandbox**: https://padlet.com/
- **Padlet TA**: https://ta.padlet.com/
- **Pages**: www.apple.com/pages/
- **Pear Deck**: www.peardeck.com/
- **Perplexity**: www.perplexity.ai/
- **Perusall**: www.perusall.com/
- **PlayPosit**: https://go.playposit.com/
- **Plickers**: https://help.plickers.com/hc/en-us
- **Poll Everywhere**: www.polleverywhere.com/
- **Qualtrics**: www.qualtrics.com/
- **Quizizz**: https://quizizz.com/
- **Screencastify**: www.screencastify.com/
- **ScreenPal**: https://screenpal.com/
- **Scribe**: https://scribehow.com/
- **SessionLab Session Planner**: www.sessionlab.com/

- **Shortcuts**: https://support.apple.com/guide/shortcuts-mac/welcome/mac
- **Slack**: https://slack.com/
- **Slido**: https://slido.com/
- **SurveyMonkey**: www.surveymonkey.com/
- **ThingLink**: www.thinglink.com/
- **Todoist**: https://todoist.com/
- **Trello**: https://trello.com/
- **Voice Memos**: https://support.apple.com/guide/voice-memos/welcome/mac
- **VoiceThread**: https://voicethread.com/
- **Wakelet**: https://wakelet.com/
- **Webex**: www.webex.com/
- **Zoom**: https://zoom.us/
- **Zoom Whiteboard**: www.zoom.com/en/products/online-whiteboard/

ABOUT THE AUTHOR

Tolulope Noah, EdD, is an educational developer with a deep passion for teaching, learning, and technology. She works as the instructional learning spaces coordinator at California State University, Long Beach, where she designs and facilitates professional learning programs for instructors. Previously, Tolu worked for Apple as a senior professional learning specialist, helping educators nationwide explore how they could use technology to enhance teaching and learning. She also has 16 years of teaching experience in higher education and K-12, and she facilitated professional learning programs for other professors and teachers throughout this time. She was an associate professor in the undergraduate teacher education program at Azusa Pacific University, where she received the university-wide Teaching Excellence Faculty Award in 2019. Prior to becoming a professor, Tolu was an award-winning teacher in Los Angeles.

Tolu believes in the transformative power of professional learning, and she enjoys designing and facilitating engaging workshops and keynotes about a variety of teaching, learning, and technology topics. She also writes about teaching and facilitation, and her work has been featured in *EDUCAUSE Review*, *Faculty Focus*, and *Edutopia*. You can learn more about Tolu on her website, www.tolunoah.com, and connect with her on social media here:

- LinkedIn: www.linkedin.com/in/tolu-noah
- Bluesky: @drtolunoah.bsky.social

INDEX

Note: Figures are indicated by *italics*. Tables are indicated by **bold**. Endnotes are indicated by the page number followed by 'n' and the endnote number (e.g., 33n2 refers to endnote 2 on page 33).

accessibility: access friction 80; access needs 80; definition 66; digital 66–8, 149, 152, 191; in grouping techniques 106; of materials 66–8, 191; modality considerations 8–10; in physical and virtual spaces 80–2, 204
active learning 112–14; activate prior knowledge 114–17; apply learning 121–4, *124*, 137–42, 180–1; choice-based 63, 124–8, *126–7*; chunking and scaffolding 53–5, 123, 156, 202; closing 56, 58–9, **60**; discussion 100–4; interactive 66, 69, 82, 99–100, 104–5, 118–21; metacognitive 115–16, 118, 120; opening activities 53, 97–9, 114; process new information 117–21; reflection 135–7; structure provided for 107–8
active listening 20, 22, 98–9, 155–6
Angelo, T. A. 163
annotation 51, 101, 103, 119, 204
anticipation guide *117*
Artificial Intelligence (AI) 122, 136, 151, 197
The Art of Gathering (Parker) 29, 36, 88, 135
assessments: formative 43, **44**, 45–6, 119, 135–6, 163; self-assessment 124, 164
attention-deficit/hyperactivity disorder (ADHD) 175, 183
authenticity 11, 21, 30, 113, 122, 182, 184
autonomy: choice-based activities 63, 124–8, *126–7*, 144, 203; learners' need for 28, 30

backward design 37, 179, 182
Bali, Maha, 184–5
Becoming a Critically Reflective Teacher (Brookfield) 137, 207–13
Behling, K. T., 79–80
Bell, L. A., 3, 56, 62, 77, 88, 211

belonging *see* connection
breakout rooms 85–6, 100–2, 107, 125, 202–3
Briggs, R. R. 70, 82, 89, 211
Brookfield, S. D. 104, 137, 168, 207–13
Bruff, Derek 114, 156

Cafeteria Learning 63
card sort 2, 104, 192
carousel 104–5, 165
Cavanagh, S. R. 95–6, 164
Center for Leadership & Educational Equity (CLEE) 87–8, 103, 164–5
Center for Teaching and Learning Matrix 21, 217
Centers for Teaching and Learning (CTLs): faculty participation in professional learning 28–9; identifying needs 22–3, 25, 143–4, 179; modality considerations 7–10; resources 212; types of programs offered by 5–7
chat: engagement 9, 84, 87, 115, 175, 180–1; leveraging power of 201–2; logs, 151, 167; preparing Chat Comments document 195, *196*
choice-based activities 63, 124–8, *126–7*
chunking 53–5, 123
Citizen, Leticia 138, *139*
Classroom Assessment Techniques (Angelo and Zakrajsek) 163
closing activities 56, 58–9, **60**
co-facilitation 31, 208–9
Cohn, Jenae 85–6
communication: Open the Front Door (OTFD) framework 89; options for 125, 127–8, 144; post-workshop 153, *154*; pre-workshop 82–3, 180, 199–202
competence 28, 30, 121–2, 182

connection: belonging and relatedness 28, 30, 93–4; facilitator-to-learner 97–9; learner-to-facilitator 94–7; learner-to-learner activities 99–100, 164–5; learner-to-learner discussion 99–105; learner-to-learner grouping techniques 105–7; professional learning connections stool *94*; structure provided for 61, 107–8, 176
consultations, pedagogical, 155–156, *157*, 158
context 24–5, 68–9
Costa, Karen 4, 84–5, 174–6
The Courage to Teach (Palmer) 172
COVID-19 7–8, 113, 175, 180, 215
Creating Significant Learning Experiences (Fink) 1, 37–8
curated collections *151–2*
curiosity 11, 55, 102–3, 163, 204
currie, sarah 66

data collection *see* evaluation
design, inclusive *see* inclusive design
design thinking 22–3, 25, 26
digital facilitation *see* virtual facilitation
discussion: discussion diamond *100–1*; discussion partners card *106–7*; protocols 102–4
distinctive style 172–4
duration considerations 6–7, 26–8, 31–2, 77

emotion 11, 43, 87, 96, 142, 144, 182
Eng, Norman 61, 68, 100, 176–8
engagement 12, 79, 84–6, 185, 203
entrance tickets 114
evaluation: to shape future programming 167; types of data 45–6, 59
exit ticket 59, 138–40, *141*, 142
Eyler, Joshua R. 11; *see also* How Humans Learn (Eyler)

facilitation: co-facilitation 31, 208–9; facilitator and participant zone *65*, 100, 113; practices, 31; preparation (*see* workflow optimization); resources 212, 214
facilitation, inclusive *see* inclusive facilitation
facilitation, on-site *see* on-site facilitation
facilitation, virtual *see* virtual facilitation
facilitation tips *see* workflow optimization
facilitator: distinctive style 172–4; Facilitator Map *173*; goal-setting 216–17; intersectionality 172–4; interviews to showcase distinctive styles 174–85; personal presence 96–7; *see also* resources for facilitators
faculty development: components of effective 29–30, 93–4, 112, 164; factors impacting participation in 28–9, 93–4; Faculty Development Matrix *5*; modality considerations 7–10; protect participant time 31–2, 50, 68, 77; respect educators' knowledge 31, 98; types of professional learning activities 4–6
failure 11, 121–2, 183–4
feedback: provided to participants 27, 122, 164–5; soliciting of 59, 165–9, 180, 208–9

Fenning, C. 158–9
Fenwick, Stephanie, 120
Fink, L. Dee 1, 37–43, *38*, *40*, **42**, 142, 165
flexibility 56, 64–5, 163
flipped learning 41, 62–3
4A Learning Sequence *60–1*

Gagné, Ann 66
gallery walk 121, 143
gamified tasks 104
geometric forms reflection 138, 140, *141*
goals and objectives for a workshop: participant goal setting for transfer 137–8, 140, 155–6; purposeful 37–9, *40*, 41–6, *42*; relevant to learners' 21–6, 29–30, 122; responsiveness to learners' 83–4, 98, 124; structure to achieve 53–5, 58–9, 63, 67, 70
Goodman, D. J. 3, 56, 62, 77, 88, 211
group agreements 87–8
grouping techniques 106–7
growth mindset 183–4

Hamilton, Lindsey 144
handouts 66–7
Hitting Pause (Rice) 128, 211
Hogan, K.A. 76, 86–7
How Humans Learn (Eyler) 11; authenticity 21, 30, 113, 122; curiosity 102–3; emotion 96, 144; failure 121–2; sociality 93–4, 113, 142
Howles, D. L. 7, 9, 27, 153, 199, 203, 207
how-to guides 149, *150*
Hughes, Leanne 83, 204
humor 96

identity 172–4
implicit bias 85
inclusive design: barrier mitigation 78–80; materials and methods 77–8; movement options 82; pre-workshop communication 82–3, 180, 199–202; scheduling and modality 77; spaces 80–2
inclusive facilitation: engagement options 84–6, 203; group agreements 87–8; manage difficult dynamics 88–9, 176; observation protocol for evaluation of 208–9; provide breaks 89; use participants' names 84, 86–7
inclusive teaching mindset 76
integrated course design 38–9
interactive *see* active learning
interleaving 6, 123
intersectionality 172–4
introductory activities 53, 97–9, 114

jigsaw *105–6*

Kirby, Cait S. 66, 80, 140, 149
Kirkpatrick, J. D. 44–6, 59, 167
Kirkpatrick, W. K. 44–6, 59, 167
knowledge and skills ratings *115–16*
K. Patricia Cross Academy 128

learners: incorporating goals of 42–3; learning edge 88; understanding needs and context of 22–5, *143–4*, 179
Leon, Rudy 168
Lesoski, Carly 80
Liberating Structures 103–4, 122, 138, 143, 165
Littlefield, Chad 99, 204, 214

Macro Workshop Plan: activities 44; assessments 43; circumstances 39–41; examples **41–6**; goals 41–3; impact 44–6; relevance 39; template *40*
Make It Stick (Brown et al.) 153
Marzano's Five Avenues to Understanding **51**, *52*, 53–6, *55*
Masland, Lindsay 101, 181–3
materials: handouts 66–7; inclusivity of 77–8; slides 67–8
McCreary, Michael 80, 140
McTighe, J. 37, 164
metacognitive exercises 115–16, 118, 120–1
microaggressions 86–89, 178
Micro Workshop Plan: beginning of workshop 51–3, **54**; middle of workshop 53–6, **57–8**; end of workshop 56–9, **60**; template *52*
Minute Paper 135–6
modality considerations 7–10, 77
multidirectional learning 98, 201–2; *see also* connection
multimedia design principles 67–8

needs assessment 22–3, 33n2, 179
Neuhaus, Jessamyn 12
New Learning Compact (NLC) 12, 216–17
NLC community level: break boundaries 31; create supportive professional communities 87, 93–4, 100; involve all sectors of the professoriate 22; learn from and with students 14, 217
NLC individual level: connect with practice 21, 30, 113–14; engage inquiry and reflection 135, 153; protect participant time 31–2, 50, 68, 77; respect educators' knowledge 31, 98
New World Kirkpatrick Model *40*, 44–6, 59, 197
Nist, Shawna Lafreniere 120
Norell, Liz 80
norms 87–8

Oettingen, Gabriele 140, 142
ongoing learning opportunities: personalized support 153, 155–8; post-workshop communication 153, *154*; resources 148–52
on-site facilitation: accessibility needs 80–2; activities (*see* active learning); benefits and limitations of 7–9, 77; optimize workflow 192, *193*, 195, 202; pacing and monitoring 56; self-observation 213
opening activities 53, 97–9, 114
organization 189, *190*, 192, *193–6*, 198–9
Ouellett, M. L. 70, 82, 89

Pacansky-Brock, Michelle 176
pacing 56, *64–5*, 189, *191*
Parker, Priya 29, 36, 88, 135, 181, 185
pedagogical consultations 155–6, *157*, 158
Penney, Mandy 66, 80
persistence 53, 88, 93, 164
planning *see* Macro Workshop Plan; Micro Workshop Plan
Plotts, Courtney 179–81
plus-one approach 79–80, 151–2
POD Network 21, 215, 217
preparation *see* workflow optimization
PRESENTING (Eng) 61, 68
priming 82–3, 202
professional learning networks 215
Protocol for Advancing Inclusive Teaching Efforts (Addy et al.) 208–9
purpose 36–7; backward design 37; incorporating learners' goals 42–3; integrated course design 38–9; Macro Workshop Plan 39, *40*, **41–6**; taxonomy of significant learning 37–43, *38*, *40*, **42**

QR Codes: QR Code Tic-Tac-Toe 125, *127*; uses of 158, 191

Reach Everyone, Teach Everyone (Tobin and Behling) 79–80
reflection: action planning 137–43; goal-setting 216–17; individual and corporate 142–3; on learning 59, 135–7; lenses facilitators can use for 207–13; multimodal 144; post-workshop 153–5; pre-reflection activities 143–4; questions for facilitators 1, 210–11, 221
relatedness *see* connection
relevance: applied in Macro Workshop Plan 39; context 24–5; focus 25–6; format 26–8; fulfillment 28–32; learners 22–3; Relevance Map *21*; of topic and content 29–30
representation 12, 77–9, *151–2*, 204
resources for facilitators *see also* facilitator: books 67–8, 103–4, 128, 158, 163, 211–12; journals and other publications 213; newsletters 212–13; online resources 103, 128–30, 214–15; podcasts and videos 213–15; professional learning networks 215
resources for participants 148–52
responsiveness: before workshops 83, 162; during workshops 163–6; after workshops 166–9
retrieval practice 100, 119–20, 153
Rice, G. T. 128
Rivera, Echo 68
roadmap 53, 94–5, 199–201

Sanchez, Michael 82, 94
Sathy, V. 76, 86–7
scaffolding 53–5, 156, 202
scheduling considerations 6–7, 31–2, 77

self-determination theory (SDT) 28–30, 121–2, 142, 165, 181–2
self-disclosure 95
Shafar, Brooke 80
Silverman, S. 76, 82, 112, 212
slides 67–8
social annotation *see* annotation
sociality 11, 93–4, 113, 142
Souza, Tasha 58, 89, 95, 122, 178–9
spacing 6, 119–20
Sparkshops 61–2
strategies, facilitation *see* workflow optimization
structure (Micro Workshop Plan): beginning 51–3, **54**; middle 53–6, **57–8**; end 56–59, **60**; template *52*
structure, additional options 60–4, *61*
support menus 156–8, *157*
The Surprising Power of Liberating Structures (Lipmanowicz and McCandless) 103–4
surveys 22–3, 45–6, 59, 166–9

taxonomy of significant learning (Fink) 37–43, *38*, *40*, **42**
Teaching for Diversity and Social Justice (Adams, et al.) 62, 77, 211–12
Technological Pedagogical Content Knowledge (TPACK) *68–9*
technology: digital tools library **71**; facilitating participant comfort with 70–1, 201; selecting and using 69–70
templates: discussion diamond *101*; Macro Workshop Plan *40*; Micro Workshop Plan *52*; planning and application *124*; workshop to-do list *193–4*
39 Ways to Make Training Stick (Fenning) 158–9
time management and pacing 56, *64–5*, 188, 189, *191–2*
Tobin, T. J. 79–80
Tolu's Typical Workshop Structure *see* Micro Workshop Plan
total-participation mindset (Himmele and Himmele) 114
TQE method (Thompson) *118*
Training from the BACK of the Room! (Bowman) 61, 128
transfer of learning 26–7, 29, 79, 119–20, 122, 137–42, 148–56
Transparency in Learning and Teaching (TILT) 108

turn-and-talk 100
Turner, Kia 138, *139*

Universal Design for Learning (UDL) 12, *13*
UDL principle, multiple means of action and expression 12, 79; expression and communication 125, 127–8, 144; interaction 66, 69, 82; strategy development, 43, 66, 80, 135, 137, 142, 164
UDL principle, multiple means of engagement 12, 79, 84–6, 185, 203; emotional capacity 43, 87, 142; sustaining effort and persistence 53, 88, 93, 164; welcoming interests and identities 21, 53, 88–9, 96, 104, 122, 124, 144
UDL principle, multiple means of representation 12, 77–9, *151–2*, 204; building knowledge 66, 77, 79, 113, 114, 122, 148; language and symbols 67, 77, 79; perception 77, 79, 107
unofficial start 51, 84

values 38, 172–3, 175, 179–83, 185
virtual facilitation: accessibility 66–8, 81–2, 149, 152, 191; activities (*see* active learning); benefits and limitations of 8–10; camera usage 80, 81, 84–6, 185; collaboration 100–2, 158–9; Costa's approach to 175–6; optimize workflow for 192, *194*, 195, *196*, 197–204; scheduling 31–2; self-observation 213; tools 68–71, **71**, 150–1

welcoming environment for learning 21, 53, 88–9, 96, 104, 122, 124, 144
What? So What? Now What? 62, 138
Wiggins, G. 37, 164
WOOP 140, 142
workflow optimization: access to materials 191; organization 189, *190*, *192*, *193–6*, 198–9; tech check 195–7; time management 188, 189, *191–2*; use of AI 197; virtual 198–204
workshop facilitation *see* facilitation
workshops: length and format 6–7, 31–2; modality 7–10; overview 26–8; purposeful planning of 36–7; working definition 26–7
workshop structure *see* structure (Micro Workshop Plan)
Workshop Wheel model *14*, *220–1*
Wow/How/Now 138, *139*

Zakrajsek, Todd 45–6, 59, 163, 183–4

For Product Safety Concerns and Information,
please contact our EU representative GPSR@taylorandfrancis.com
Taylor & Francis Verlag GmbH, Kaufingerstraße 24,
80331 München, Germany

Printed by Integrated Books International,
United States of America